Every time a Catholic mother ~~uld read, I
have a ready answer: Lisa He~~ ~~on the saints, pro-
vides a rich pattern of learning, reflection, prayer, and practical Cath-
olic-living suggestions, based on the lives of fifty-two great heroes and
heroines of our faith. It is a book that every mother (and father, son,
and daughter too) will find accessible, inviting, and above all, useful.

James Martin, S.J.
Author of *My Life with the Saints*

As Catholics we have just begun to tap into the incredible treasure
trove of the communion of saints. That's why I am so grateful for Lisa
Hendey's new book. Whether you're a spiritual mom like me or a mom
with children who keep you on the move, *A Book of Saints for Catholic
Moms* will provide much joy, guidance, and companionship on your
journey.

Teresa Tomeo
Host of *Catholic Connection*
Motivation Speaker/Bestselling Catholic Author

Joy-filled and easy to read, this book focuses on simple spiritual goals
to which women of all ages and life stages can aspire. Lisa Hendey
knows exactly what inspires and encourages so many Catholic moms,
and in this book, she absolutely delivers it.

Danielle Bean
Editorial Director, *Faith & Family*

God bless Lisa Hendey for bolstering Catholic mothers by sharing her
intimate companionship with fifty-two of her favorite saints. She provides a brand new look at them, complete with their well-worn wisdom, reminding us that we are never alone.

Donna-Marie Cooper O'Boyle
Author of *A Catholic Woman's Book of Prayers*
Host of EWTN's *Everyday Blessings for Catholic Moms*

Lisa Hendey once again demonstrates that Catholicism is a treasure map—it may be old, but it still leads to treasure. The challenges of motherhood have increased exponentially over the past several decades, but the heroes and heroines of Christianity still have the answers.

Matthew Kelly
Author of *Rediscover Catholicism*

Lisa Hendey's Catholicism is as pure and joyful as the saints she writes about. *A Book of Saints for Catholic Moms* is a gracefully written introduction to the holy exemplars who can teach, sustain, and bless mothers.

Paula Huston
Author of *The Holy Way*

Inspiring, informative, and engaging, Lisa Hendey's newest book should be on every Catholic mom's nightstand. Page after page, the saints come alive through Lisa's personal stories, powerful prose, and practical advice. We all need companions on the spiritual journey. With Lisa's book in hand, you'll never be alone.

Mary DeTurris Poust
Author of *Walking Together*

Lisa Hendey brings us an opportunity to learn more about the saints in a way that's uniquely suited for the nitty-gritty of everyday life. You'll experience the saints as real people even as you grow in your faith journey.

Sarah Reinhard
Author of *Welcome Baby Jesus*
Host of SnoringScholar.com

A Book of Saints for Catholic Moms

52 Companions for Your
Heart, Mind, Body, and Soul

Lisa M. Hendey

ave maria press AMP notre dame, indiana

Founded in 1865, Ave Maria Press is a ministry of the United States Province of Holy Cross.

www.avemariapress.com

ISBN-10 1-59471-273-5 ISBN-13 978-1-59471-273-9

Cover image © Peter Barritt / SuperStock.

Cover and text design by Katherine Robinson Coleman.

Printed and bound in the United States of America.

Library of Congress Cataloging-in-Publication Data

Hendey, Lisa M.
    A book of saints for Catholic moms : 52 companions for your heart, mind, body, and soul / Lisa M. Hendey.
        p. cm.
    ISBN-13: 978-1-59471-273-9 (pbk.)
    ISBN-10: 1-59471-273-5 (pbk.)
    1. Mothers--Prayers and devotions. 2. Christian saints--Prayers and devotions. 3. Catholic Church--Prayers and devotions. I. Title.
    BX2170.M65H46 2011
    248.8'431--dc23
    2011025284

To Anne and Pat

with love and thanksgiving

for a lifetime of

faith, family, and fun

Heart

Mind

Body

Soul

CONTENTS

Each morning in my quiet devotional time, I read a page from a well-worn illustrated book on the lives of the saints. Before I dive into the day's biographical entry, I glance with a smile at the inscription on the inside cover. In my mother's loopy handwriting are inscribed the words,

> To my darling Pat with love.
> Merry Christmas!
> Anne
> 1975—One of the best years of our lives

The sight of this love letter from my mother to my dad never ceases to make me smile. Who would think that a book on the saints could be so romantic? And yet for my parents, who've made a lifetime of growing and enjoying their domestic church, it feels perfectly natural. I can't remember exactly when I "borrowed" the book from my father, but having the companionship of the saints on my daily walk toward heaven has been a part of my morning for as long as I can remember.

Being a mom is a journey filled with great joys but also marked by great challenges. Blessedly, it is never a path we walk alone. We travel in the companionship of family, friends, our communities, and a Church that lovingly supports us through time-honored traditions, powerful teachings, and life-sustaining sacraments. We are loved unconditionally by a Triune God and nurtured by a Blessed Mother, who wants nothing more than to carry us to her beloved son.

And yet at times we need extra support and encouragement for those days when the trials feel greater than our emotional, intellectual, and physical reserves. For those moments when we think we simply can't measure up or when the path expected of us feels too ominous, it helps to have companions.

Many of us find this companionship under our own roofs, with spouses who share our trials and triumphs and children who make it all somehow worth the tremendous effort. We have extended families who give us a moral compass and a sense of identity, and friends who are there for us in good times and in bad. If we're fortunate, we have a secondary faith family within our parish communities where our spiritual needs are lovingly tended.

In its wisdom, our Catholic Church has provided for us an additional set of companions—the Communion of Saints who have gone before us along the path to life's greatest goal. For as much as we hope to build solid marriages, to educate emotionally secure and successful children, and to leave behind our own personal legacies, our ultimate challenge in this world will never be an easy one. What we all truly desire, that "pearl of greatest price," is an eternity spent in heaven with the Trinity, our Blessed Mother, and that Communion of Saints, including our loved ones, after our work here on earth is finished.

So often, the highway to heaven feels like we're walking five steps forward and ten steps back. For moments like that, we can turn to those holy souls who have modeled the way for us. They have led ordinary lives and yet accomplished extraordinary things, often overcoming seemingly impossible obstacles.

The Communion of Saints contains a host of names we know, and many we hold dear in our own hearts but who remain unknown to most of the rest of the world. I love to contemplate that alongside my favorite patron saints sit my grandparents who—along with my parents—taught me what faith-filled parenthood should truly be. The Church may never formally canonize Patty, Wayne, Leroy, and Bessie, and yet for me they are the friends I often beseech for spiritual aid and sanity when life is at its craziest.

My life today is filled with "saints" who bless me each day with their friendship, their support, and their prayers. For each of you who have been such an important part of this project in any way, I thank you for your continual love and encouragement.

I wish to publicly thank three amazing individuals who were a frequent sounding board and reference team for me during the writing of this book. To Terry Jones (saints.sqpn.com), Dr. Paul Camarata (saintcast.org) and my soul sister Pat Gohn (amongwomenpodcast.com), I appreciate your constant sharing of your knowledge with me and the many ways in which you lead so many of us to build friendships with the saints through your work.

To the many talented writers who are at the heart of CatholicMom.com, thank you for the gifts you share so freely with me and with families and parishes around the globe. To my friends and colleagues at the Star

Quest Production Network and at Faith & Family Live, you continue to amaze, to educate and to fuel me with the work you do each day to teach and to express our faith in new and creative ways.

To my personal faith family at St. Anthony of Padua, including my pastor Monsignor Robert D. Wenzinger, my dear friend Martha, and my fellow staff members and parishioners, thank you for being a spiritual home for our family.

To each of my friends, whether we've met in person or whether we connect each day on Facebook, Twitter, and around the web, thank you for guiding me along the path to sainthood and for being such a large part of my work—your quick responses to my queries so frequently guide me to amazing new insights and information. And to my Fresno girlfriends, there will never be sufficient words to tell you how much you mean to me each and every day.

To Thomas Grady and my family at Ave Maria Press, who continue to support my work and to open the door wide to new opportunities, I thank you from the bottom of my heart for enabling so many of my dreams to come true. A special note of thanks to my editor and dear friend Eileen Ponder, who always knows the right words and has taught me so many important lessons in our work together.

To my family, the world's best parents, my siblings by birth and through marriage, and my adorable and highly talented nephews, you are simply the most special, generous, fun and loving group of people I know.

And to the three saints who share my heart and my home, it is a daily joy to walk along life's path to heaven with you. To Adam, who put up with so many crazy days during all the writing and travel and who is my world's most giving spirit, you are a shining star. To Eric, who even from thousands of miles away shares his love with us, you make our world better each day. To Greg, the love of my life and the man of my dreams, thank you for your neverending encouragement and for blessing me each day in so many ways.

To God—Father, Son and Holy Spirit—Our Blessed Mother, and the Communion of Saints, for your constant love and intercession, please accept this small work as a sign of my unending thanks, praise and love.

Introduction

In this book, I hope to point you to saintly companions for your own life as a Catholic mom. In my first book, *The Handbook for Catholic Moms*, I shared the importance of nurturing ourselves as moms in four components of our lives: heart, mind, body, and soul. In this resource, I share with you the saintly friends who have supported me emotionally in my relationships, in my intellectual pursuits, in the physical care of my body, and most importantly in my spiritual development.

As you read this book, I invite you to walk hand in hand with these women and men, emulating the lessons they have laid out for us. I encourage you to turn to them in earnest prayer in those moments when you need intercession. This book is meant to be a resource to you in whatever way best supports you in your vocation. I have shared here my reflections on fifty-two members of the Communion of Saints, with a weekly focus for each one. You may find it most useful to simply follow the weeks for a year's worth of saintly company. Or, you may find it more useful to tend to your heart, mind, body, and soul by focusing on a particular saint whose example seems to match your need. Each saint is tagged with a simple graphic, depicting which of the four essential aspects of my life he or she has most directly touched: Heart, Mind, Body, and Soul.

We will come to discover the lives of these wonderful spiritual mentors by looking at the following topics for each of them:

- *Stories:* a brief biographical sketch

- *Lessons:* reflections on what I have learned from the saint

- *Traditions:* popular devotions and practices associated with him or her

- *Wisdom:* a quote from or about the saint

- *Scripture:* daily verses for you to pray with, inspired by the saint

- *Activities:* a weeklong project or idea for you to enjoy privately and another to share with your child or children

- *A Prayer for Our Family:* an invocation for our saintly companion's intercession to be shared with your family every day of the week

- *Something to Ponder:* simple questions on which to reflect throughout the week

Please know that as you journey your way through this book, you remain in my prayer. Although we may never meet in person, we share many goals in common, the greatest of which is our own personal quest for sainthood and the leading of our families to heaven. Enjoy your travels, marvel along the roads paved for us by these saintly friends, and know that you too are destined to be a saintly companion in your own unique way.

Blessed Virgin Mary

A Spiritual Mother for Us All

First Century
Patronage: Mothers
Memorials: January 1 (Mary, Mother of God), March 25 (Annunciation), August 15 (Assumption), December 8 (Immaculate Conception)

THE BLESSED VIRGIN MARY'S STORY

The ancient tradition of the Church tells us that Mary was the daughter of Anne and Joachim. She first appears in the Bible in the first chapter of Matthew's gospel with the story of the angel's appearance to Joseph, when the angel instructed him not to divorce his betrothed wife as he intended, because the child she bore was from God. In the first chapter of Luke's gospel, we find the more detailed story of Mary's early life. She was living in Nazareth and betrothed to Joseph when the archangel Gabriel announced to her that she was to be the Mother of

God. She visited and helped care for her elderly cousin Elizabeth during her pregnancy and traveled with Joseph to Bethlehem, where she gave birth to Jesus. After the Holy Family took refuge in Egypt to protect Jesus from King Herod, Mary returned to Nazareth with Joseph and raised Jesus according to the customs and beliefs of her Jewish faith. She was present with Jesus as he began his public ministry at the wedding feast of Cana and at his crucifixion, where he gave her to the care of Saint John. After Jesus' Ascension, she was among the first members of the Christian community. The Church regards the Blessed Mother so highly that in 1950 Pope Pius XII promulgated the dogma of the assumption, declaring that after Mary's earthly life was complete she was taken to the glory of heaven, body and soul.

LESSONS FROM MARY

How does one write a book about the saints and not include the Blessed Virgin Mary, the mother of our Savior and the world's first and best Christian? There is so much to say, and yet no words can adequately capture the role of Mary, our "New Eve," Mother to the Church and Mother of the Word Incarnate. I love to look at depictions of Mary in art from around the world—portrayed in every age, skin color, and garb—and realize that she is indeed mother to each of us, regardless of the constraints of time and location. Her goal has always been to lead us into more perfect communion with her son. And yet at the same time, she is for so many of us a spiritual support—a true mom, a spiritual sister, a best friend.

Mary's *fiat*, her "yes" to what surely must have been a moment of terror and anxiety looking at a future full of the unknown, makes her the perfect disciple. In those moments when following Christ feels too difficult, while I am aiming to open my life fully to God's plan instead of my own and making sacrifices to do the right thing, Mary's simple statement, "May it be done to me according to your word," is the only guidebook I need.

My good friend Martha and I have talked many times about how we'd love to sit down to coffee with Mary and ask her to tell us *her* version of the story—the realities of a life marked by great joys and the most piercing of sorrows. What trust and faith enabled her to face being pregnant and unwed in a society that clearly would have rejected her? How proud was she at the moment she saw Jesus teaching in the synagogue or performing his first miracle at Cana? Did she feel sad as he grew into his own and left her behind to spread his Gospel of love? How could she bear the grief of seeing her son be put to death?

Martha and I may never get our dreamed-of coffee date, but the good news is that Mary is fully present to me at every moment of every day, waiting to take my hand and carry me to her son. From those painful mothering moments with sick and sleepless babies to my current emotional roller coaster as I watch my sons mature and prepare to leave me for lives of their own, she is at my side as a confidante and friend, a mother. Fearless and yet tenderhearted, human and yet untouched by sin, Mary was, is, and always will be the first and best Catholic mom.

TRADITIONS

The Rosary, one of the Church's greatest devotional prayers, encourages the faithful to meditate upon the mysteries of Christ's life and key moments in the life of his mother, Mary. Around the world, Catholics venerate Mary with prayer, processions, and religious imagery. She is known by hundreds of titles and is the focus of dozens of devotions, great works of art, and numerous hymns. Many miracles have been attributed to her intercession, particularly in places of her apparitions like Lourdes, Guadalupe, and Fatima.

MARY'S WISDOM

My soul proclaims the greatness of the Lord; my spirit rejoices in God my savior. For he has looked upon his handmaid's lowliness; behold, from now on will all ages call me blessed.

—Luke 1:46–47

THIS WEEK WITH SCRIPTURE

Sunday: Luke 1:38

Behold, I am the handmaid of the Lord. May it be done to me according to your word.

> *I am your handmaid, Father. Help me to hear and to answer your will for my life.*

Monday: Acts 1:14

All these devoted themselves with one accord to prayer, together with some women, and Mary the mother of Jesus, and his brothers.

> *Mary, help me to follow your perfect example of prayer and lead me to your son, Jesus.*

Tuesday: Luke 2:34–35

Behold, this child is destined for the fall and rise of many in Israel, and to be a sign that will be contradicted (and you yourself a sword will pierce) so that the thoughts of many hearts may be revealed.

> *In my sorrow, Lord, help me to find consolation in your unending love.*

Wednesday: Luke 2:19

And Mary kept all these things, reflecting on them in her heart.

> *My God, you alone know the inner workings of my heart. In your goodness, hear and answer me.*

Thursday: Luke 1:45

Blessed are you who believed that what was spoken to you by the Lord would be fulfilled.

> *Jesus, equip me to believe more fully the truth of your promises.*

Friday: Luke 1:46–47

My soul proclaims the greatness of the Lord;
my spirit rejoices in God my savior.

> *My spirit rejoices in you, Lord.*

Saturday: John 2:5

Do whatever he tells you.

> *Emmanuel, I want to do your Father's will as Mary did. I will follow her and hold her hand as she draws me to you.*

SAINT-INSPIRED ACTIVITIES

For Mom

In your prayer corner or other quiet place, create a small altar for Mary with a holy card, medal, statue, or other image of her. Speak to the Blessed Mother in prayer, focusing on the Church's Marian traditions including the Rosary, Hail Mary, and Hail Holy Queen.

With Children

Plant a "Mary Garden" with flowers named for Our Lady, or display a rose in your home and pray a decade of the Rosary as a family.

A PRAYER FOR OUR FAMILY

Pray as a family each day this week:

Blessed Mother Mary,
you said "yes" to God and in doing so became mother to our Savior Jesus Christ.
Help us to follow your example of discipleship
by following and loving Jesus as you did.

We ask your intercession on behalf of the poor and the suffering,
and for peace in our world.
Be with us in our celebrations
and those moments when life is painful and difficult.
Help us to accept God's perfect plan for our lives.
Take our hands and lead us to your son, Jesus.
Amen.

SOMETHING TO PONDER

In what ways is Mary a spiritual mother to you? How does she draw
you closer to her son, Jesus Christ, and mentor you in your own life
as a mom?

2

Saint Zita of Lucca

Diligence in Domestic Tasks

1218–April 27, 1272
Patronage: Homemakers, Domestic Workers, Servers
Memorial: April 27

ZITA OF LUCCA'S STORY

Zita of Lucca was born in 1218 at Monsagrati, a town in Tuscany of central Italy, to a poor but devout Catholic family. Always obedient, Zita left her family home at the age of twelve to begin a lifetime of service in the home of the wealthy Fatinelli family in nearby Lucca. Zita's pious nature, her prayerful habits, her daily Mass attendance, and her cheerful attitude were a constant source of annoyance to the weaver and his family, as well as to her fellow servants. But she persisted in her devotion to her duties and her employer, and she eventually

won over the household and was appointed head of the domestic servants. With equal care, she dedicated herself to service of the poor—
she was known for her charity, often going without food to give her
own portion to the needy. Zita faithfully served the Fatinelli family
and her God until her death, and she was immediately acclaimed a
saint by those who knew and loved her.

LESSONS FROM ZITA

Domestic responsibilities are on every mom's "to do" list, no matter
how much time she spends at home. For the most part, I tend to dread
seeing items such as "clean boys' toilets" or "go to the market" on my
list of chores. I'm not one of those women who is by nature a gifted
domestic. My husband has put up for years with a wife who'd rather
blog than bake and who's better at coding than cooking.

But learning about the life of Zita of Lucca has given me a new take
on my attitude about household duties. The Reverend Alban Butler
wrote of Zita that she fully embraced her domestic position as a gift
from God. Zita saw all work as a form of penance for sin, and she
was therefore happy to be in a position to serve the God she loved so
greatly. She saw her constant obedience to her employers as a sign of
her obedience to the will of God. For her, work and prayer were inter-
changeable, and a constant rhythm of devotions accompanied her day.
Learning about Zita's attitude hasn't exactly made me joyous to see
overflowing mounds of dirty laundry, but it has reminded me that my
station in life is a blessing. With my work around the house, I serve not
only my husband and sons but also the God who has gifted me with
shelter, with comfort, with sustenance, and with the love of my family.

Zita was known in her community for her constant commitment
to charity. She took food from her own plate to feed the poor, gave her
bed to beggars, and was known for ministering to the sick. One famous
legend about Zita tells of her attendance at Mass one cold winter night.
Wearing a great fur coat she had borrowed from her master, she spot-
ted a poor man lying near the door to the church in the freezing cold.
She took the coat from her back and offered it to him. Of course, by the
end of Mass the man and her boss's coat were nowhere to be found.
When she returned home, she faced the wrath of Mr. Fatinelli. But
the next morning, the coat was mysteriously returned to her door, as

though by angels. For this reason, and in commemoration of Zita's benevolent soul, the door to the basilica in Lucca where her remains are kept is referred to as "The Angel Portal."

This and other stories of Zita's life remind us that even if we do not have abundant means, there are always people in greater need who rely on our compassionate assistance. When Zita was given oversight of her master's household, she took it upon herself to run the family's affairs with even greater economization and attention to detail than they had run them. This enabled the family to prosper but also to use their means to support others in their community. As the keeper of my family budgets, I have the same opportunity to run my home with an eye toward efficiency and charity. When I am careful to be a good steward of our family's income, when I use my time efficiently in carrying out my daily chores, and when I work with a positive and loving attitude, I follow in the footsteps of Zita, who has taught me so much about the dignity of being a domestic engineer.

TRADITIONS

In Lucca, families celebrate Saint Zita's feast day each year with a fresh-flower market and a special blessing of both bread and flowers. She is also celebrated in England, where she is known and loved as Saint Sitha.

ZITA'S WISDOM

A servant is not pious if she is not industrious; work-shy piety in people of our position is sham piety.

THIS WEEK WITH SCRIPTURE

Sunday: Luke 21:1–4

When he looked up he saw some wealthy people putting their offerings into the treasury and he noticed a poor widow putting in two small coins. He said, "I tell you truly, this poor widow put in more than all the rest; for those others have all made offerings from their surplus wealth, but she, from her poverty, has offered her whole livelihood."

> *Jesus, Faithful Witness, help me to always remember that there are those whose needs exceed my own, and let me respond in love and compassion.*

Monday: Proverbs 31:27

She watches the conduct of her household,
and eats not her food in idleness.

> *God, Governor of my days, may I work without idleness to serve my family and to show my love for you.*

Tuesday: Tobit 4:8

Son, give alms in proportion to what you own. If you have great wealth, give alms out of your abundance; if you have but little, distribute even some of that.

> *We are so blessed, Lord. Help us to bless others with our abundance, giving without selfishness and expecting nothing in return.*

Wednesday: Psalm 51:9

Cleanse me with hyssop, that I may be pure;
wash me, make me whiter than snow.

> *Jesus, Living Water, you have cleansed me with your love.*

Thursday: Proverbs 31:20

She reaches out her hands to the poor,
and extends her arms to the needy.

> *Today, Lord, may I extend my arms to all those in need, including my family in need of my love and attention.*

Friday: Tobit 12:8

Prayer and fasting are good, but better than either is almsgiving accompanied by righteousness. A little with righteousness is better than abundance with wickedness.

> *Father of infinite understanding, you give so much to me. Help me to give in return and to love as you do, with righteousness and abundance.*

Saturday: Proverbs 31:25

She is clothed with strength and dignity,
and she laughs at the days to come.

> *Clothe me, Lord, with your strength and your dignity, and help me face whatever waits for our family with no anxiety and with great hope in you.*

SAINT-INSPIRED ACTIVITIES

For Mom

Saint Zita once gathered crusts and scraps of uneaten bread in her apron to carry them to the poor. When challenged by her employer who thought she was stealing from him, she opened her apron, and lovely flowers tumbled to the ground. Treat your family to fresh flowers on the dinner table, and carry out your domestic work with a positive attitude.

With Children

Saint Zita returned home from Mass late one day, and she hurried in fear that she was late for her job of baking bread for the Fatinelli family. She arrived to find a perfect loaf prepared, as if by angels. Bake two loaves of fresh bread in honor of Zita. Enjoy one together at home, and share one with friends or neighbors.

A PRAYER FOR OUR FAMILY

Pray as a family each day this week:

Charitable Saint Zita of Lucca,
you spent your life working for others and serving the poor.
Please help us to carry out our chores with love,
with care, and with a positive attitude.
May we look for opportunities to consume less
and ways to share what we have with those who are in need.
Intercede for our loved ones who are struggling with illness, debt,
or anxiety.
Help them, and all in our family, to know the constant love and
compassion of God,
our Father in heaven.
Amen.

SOMETHING TO PONDER

Do you have a positive or a negative attitude about cooking, cleaning,
yard work, and other household chores? How can you better unite
your household work with your prayer life?

3.

Saint Gerard Majella

Good Health in Pregnancy and Childbirth

April, 1726–October 16, 1755
Patronage: Pregnant Women, Childbirth, Mothers
Memorial: October 16

GERARD MAJELLA'S STORY

G erard Majella was weak and in poor health from his birth into a poor tailor's family in Muro, Italy. When he was twelve his father died, and Gerard took over his father's trade so that he could support his mother and siblings. This pious young man, a daily communicant, desired greatly to pursue a priestly vocation but was repeatedly denied admission. At the age of twenty-three, he was able to fulfill his calling as a professed lay brother of the Redemptorist Order. Brother Gerard was hard-working, prayerful, and always generous. In addition to his work as a gardener, porter, and health-care aid, he traveled extensively with missionary priests. Over time, his wise counsel was increasingly sought out, and numerous miracles were attributed to him. Gerard died from complications of tuberculosis at the age of twenty-nine after devoting his all-too-brief life to service of others and to following God's providence.

LESSONS FROM GERARD

Inquiring minds may wish to know why an eighteenth-century lay brother should evolve as one of the few undisputed patron saints of mothers, and particularly of expectant mothers. As is the case with so many patronages, there is no one particular story that can definitively explain it. But the more I learn about the life of Gerard, the more stories I hear of families who have blossomed in wonderful ways thanks to his spiritual friendship, and it grows increasingly more natural to turn to him for guidance and prayer.

Accounts of Gerard's life point to an instance of his being falsely accused of fathering a child. Always known for his devout obedience, Gerard refused to vindicate himself by breaking his religious order's rule of "no excuses." Instead, he suffered his penance of being denied Communion for months until his name was eventually cleared.

Others attribute the many lives saved by Gerard's prayers for mothers in labor and their young infants to Gerard's patronage. These miraculous intercessions continued and became increasingly widespread following his death. Indeed, among my own friends, there are so many stories of babies being named after Gerard by moms who profoundly credit his prayers for the miraculous birth of their children.

The more I learn about the lives of our communion of canonized saints, the more I see God intervening through the lives of simple, humble people. Gerard Majella was indeed one of these, and the witness of his life holds great inspiration for Catholic moms. His work—like so much of what we do each day—was often behind the scenes and filled with hands-on tasks that didn't take great training or education. And yet by the time he died, people were flocking to him for his counsel. In these moments, his message was consistent—follow the will of God.

Today's modern medical solutions have greatly blessed, but can also complicate the path to motherhood. Lower childhood mortality and a focus on prenatal health care have greatly diminished the physical risks to both mother and child. But things like prenatal fetal testing and reproductive technologies also pose ethical questions for Catholic families. In these instances, the ability to follow Gerard's vow to "do that which is always most pleasing to God" can bring a great solace to us moms.

Gerard was credited with the ability to see into people's souls and to know their hearts and intentions. In many ways, we moms often have this gift with our children. I can see one of my sons walk to the car after school with a certain slouch and know that he's had a difficult day. I can glance at his brother and tell by the turn of his lips if he's stressed or upset. Just as Gerard shared his charism of relying on God's providence with those who trusted him for spiritual development, I have the gift but also the great responsibility of forming the consciences of my family.

Whether God has blessed your family with one child or ten, or if you're still praying for the miracle of a baby in your life, the gift of motherhood is an endless joy marked by moments of great grace and also great sorrows. Some of us will know multiple births; some will experience the loss of miscarriage or the searing pain of infertility. For the times when our hearts are filled with happiness, with gratitude, with grief, or with longing and sorrow, it's good to know that we can turn to Gerard Majella and seek his intercession for ourselves and our children, always trusting that God's plan of love for us will see us through.

TRADITIONS

Many pregnant women wear a medal bearing Saint Gerard's likeness and prayerfully ask his protection. The nine-day Saint Gerard novena remains popular in many places. Saint Joseph's Church in Dundalk, Ireland, a Redemptorist parish, holds an annual novena each year culminating on the saint's feast day. This major faith festival is attended by tens of thousands of visitors each year.

GERARD'S WISDOM

Here the will of God is done, as God wills, and as long as God wills.

This Week with Scripture

Sunday: Genesis 22:17

I will bless you abundantly and make your descendants as countless as the stars of the sky and the sands of the seashore.

> *Thank you, Lord, for the gift of life and for the precious blessing of each of my children.*

Monday: Proverbs 31:28–29

Her children rise up and praise her;
her husband, too, extols her:
"Many are the women of proven worth,
but you have excelled them all."

> *Father, help me to be a worthy wife and mother. Fill me with your strength and your energy to carry out all of the callings of my vocation.*

Tuesday: Isaiah 40:11

Like a shepherd he feeds his flock;
in his arms he gathers the lambs,
Carrying them in his bosom,
and leading the ewes with care.

> *You gather us into your arms; your care is so apparent. Help me to rest in those arms, to rest in your love.*

Wednesday: Matthew 18:4–5

Whoever humbles himself like this child is the greatest in the kingdom of heaven. And whoever receives one child such as this in my name receives me.

> *Today, Jesus, help me to humble myself like my children, to receive them, and to see to their needs with patience and with joy.*

Thursday: Isaiah 66:13

As a mother comforts her son,
so will I comfort you;
in Jerusalem you shall find your comfort.

> *I find my comfort in you, Lord. Please comfort my friends who desperately seek to be mothers. Bless them with the peace of trusting in your perfect plan.*

Friday: Psalm 40:6

How numerous, O LORD, my God,
you have made your wondrous deeds!
And in your plans for us
there is none to equal you.

> *May I use the blessing of this day to declare your goodness, to testify to your love, and to shine your light to everyone I meet.*

Saturday: Psalm 127:3

Children too are a gift from the LORD,
the fruit of the womb, a reward.

> *For your gifts, Lord, for each of the children you have placed in my womb, for those who will someday know the gift of life, and for those who rest in your embrace, I thank you with all my heart.*

SAINT-INSPIRED ACTIVITIES

For Mom

Pray in a special way to follow God's will for your mothering journey. Spend a few moments journaling about what the gift of being a mother has meant to you.

With Children

Share the miracle of childbirth with your children. Tell each of them about the day they were born, and show them ultrasound scans, baby pictures, and videos of their birthdays.

A PRAYER FOR OUR FAMILY

Pray as a family each day this week:

Humble and obedient Saint Gerard,
your life was filled with simple tasks and great miracles.
You always sought to follow God's will for your life,
trusting that his plan was perfect.
Please intercede for our family this week.
Bless our children as they grow in love and faith,
and guard their health and safety.
Bless our mother as she does her best to serve God and our family.
Bless our father as he leads us closer to Christ and to one another.
Help us to listen for God's plan for each of us
and to lovingly accept his will for our lives.
May we follow your example of love, of goodness, and of trust
until we one day join you in heaven.
Amen.

SOMETHING TO PONDER

How are you being called to trust in God's will as a mother?

4.

Saint Francis de Sales

Living a Devout Life

August 21, 1567–December 28, 1622
Patronage: Writers, Educators, Hearing Impaired
Memorial: January 24

Francis de Sales's Story

The eldest child of François de Boisy and Françoise de Sionnz was born in 1567 to a noble family. Francis was a brilliant student and earned doctoral degrees in both civil and canon law, but ultimately he persuaded his family to permit him to become a priest. He had an arduous but successful missionary tour in Chablais, where he ministered to the area's Calvinist families and ultimately won many converts. A noted preacher and prolific writer, Francis de Sales was appointed Bishop of

Geneva in 1602. His spiritual friendship with Saint Jane Frances de Chantal led to the founding of the Order of the Visitation. Francis de Sales is best known for his spiritual writings, including *Introduction to the Devout Life* and *Treatise on the Love of God*. This humble man, who brought an accessible spirituality to so many, died in 1622.

LESSONS FROM FRANCIS

Long before I knew the story of his life, Francis de Sales was a part of my world. An old, dog-eared paperback copy of his amazing spiritual masterpiece, *Introduction to the Devout Life*, has been in my devotional reading stack for years. Originally written for Madame de Charmoisy and subsequently adapted to meet the needs of those he spiritually directed, the definitive edition of *Introduction to the Devout Life* remains relevant for many spiritual seekers today.

Saint Francis recognized and responded to the desire of "real world" laity like you and me to live out a call to sanctity within the confines of our own vocations. About the effort to find suitable devotion according to one's station in life, Francis wrote:

> No indeed, my child, the devotion which is true hinders nothing, but on the contrary it perfects everything; and that which runs counter to the rightful vocation of any one is, you may be sure, a spurious devotion. Aristotle says that the bee sucks honey from flowers without damaging them, leaving them as whole and fresh as it found them. But true devotion does better still, for it not only hinders no manner of vocation or duty, but, contrariwise, it adorns and beautifies all. Throw precious stones into honey, and each will grow more brilliant according to its several colors—and in like manner everybody fulfills his special calling better when subject to the influence of devotion: Family duties are lighter, married love truer, service to our King more faithful, every kind of occupation more acceptable and better performed where that is the guide.
>
> —St. Francis de Sales
> *Introduction to the Devout Life*

In my world, some days my "devout life" is perfectly precise—reciting devotions on schedule according to the Liturgy of the Hours, arriving on time at Mass with an appropriately attired clan, displaying a positive and loving attitude in all tasks, and making a great recollection of conscience before I drift off to sleep. But truthfully, most days are a far cry from Francis de Sales's prescriptions. In those moments, my imitation of Christ may mean an hour in the parking lot listening to a friend who needs a shoulder to cry on, or a really good conversation with my teen who is questioning all authority, including the Church's teachings. It may mean mopping a dirty floor without complaining or cooking a meal for a sick friend. More often than not, despite my best intentions, my days don't usually go according to the perfect road map I've designed in my head. And that's okay.

Learning more about the humble, tireless, and passionate Francis de Sales has taught me the importance of spiritual friendships, like the one he shared with Saint Jane Frances de Chantal. I've also settled into the role that I am called to play as a part of the Body of Christ, right here in my own home. But when I'm tempted to compromise in my spiritual life because I'm too tired, or too busy, I try to remember Francis's exhortations to strive for spiritual perfection. I'm then jolted out of the complacency that permits me to make excuses, when I know I can and should do a better job of being more Christ-like.

It was Francis who wisely wrote, "The difference between a good person and a devout one is this: the good person keeps God's commandments, though without any great speed or fervor; the devout not only observes them but does so willingly, speedily, and with a good heart." How many times do I compromise being the "good person" and blame my shortcomings on my busyness as a wife and mom? In truth, my vocation allows me so many lovely opportunities to imitate Christ's compassion, his fervor for God's commandments, and his loving service to others. Far from being my excuse, my job as "mom" should help me strive for an even greater attempt to live out my faith each day. In those many times when I'm tempted to settle for "good enough," Francis de Sales inspires me to give God and those I love my very best in all things.

TRADITIONS

Saint Francis de Sales's role as patron saint of the hearing impaired stems from his years of catechesis of Martin, a hearing-impaired young man the bishop met when he came to the bishop seeking alms. Saint Francis de Sales devised a system of sign language to educate and provide sacramental preparation for Martin, who went on to be confirmed and to serve Francis for many years.

FRANCIS'S WISDOM

Retire at various times into the solitude of your own heart, even while outwardly engaged in discussions or transactions with others, and talk to God.

THIS WEEK WITH SCRIPTURE

Sunday: 2 Corinthians 7:1

Since we have these promises, beloved, let us cleanse ourselves from every defilement of flesh and spirit, making holiness perfect in the fear of God.

> *Gracious and Loving One, I seek to find perfect holiness in you.*

Monday: James 1:25

But the one who peers into the perfect law of freedom and perseveres, and is not a hearer who forgets but a doer who acts, such a one shall be blessed in what he does.

> *Today, I will be a doer and will hope to bless others with my actions.*

Tuesday: 1 John 4:12

No one has ever seen God. Yet, if we love one another, God remains in us, and his love is brought to perfection in us.

God, you are present in the faces of my family. Help me to seek perfection in you by better loving them with all my heart.

Wednesday: 2 Corinthians 13:11

Finally, brothers, rejoice. Mend your ways, encourage one another, agree with one another, live in peace, and the God of love and peace will be with you.

Help me to seek your peace and to be an instrument of it for those I encounter throughout my week.

Thursday: 1 Peter 5:8–9

Be sober and vigilant. Your opponent the devil is prowling around like a roaring lion looking for [someone] to devour. Resist him, steadfast in faith, knowing that your fellow believers throughout the world undergo the same sufferings.

In my moments of doubt and weakness, enable me to resist that which draws me away from your perfect love, Lord.

Friday: James 3:17–18

But the wisdom from above is first of all pure, then peaceable, gentle, compliant, full of mercy and good fruits, without inconstancy or insincerity. And the fruit of righteousness is sown in peace for those who cultivate peace.

All wisdom, peace, and happiness come from you, Lifter of my heart.

Saturday: Matthew 5:48

So be perfect, just as your heavenly Father is perfect.

Father, despite my imperfections, help me to strive to be perfect in loving you.

SAINT-INSPIRED ACTIVITIES

For Mom

Commit to slowly and thoughtfully reading Saint Francis de Sales's book *Introduction to the Devout Life*. The book is available free of charge on the Internet in print (www.catholicity.com/devoutlife/) or audio (www.archive.org/details/IntroDevout) versions.

With Children

Saint Francis de Sales said, "You will catch more flies with a spoonful of honey than with a hundred barrels of vinegar." Invite your family to be extra kind to one another. When your children are tempted to fight with a sibling or friend, encourage them to try being kind and loving instead and to see what happens.

A PRAYER FOR OUR FAMILY

Pray as a family each day this week:

Humble and devout Saint Francis de Sales,
you always answered God's call in your life,
even when it took you into situations that were filled with challenges.
Help us to make regular prayer and Christ-like service of others a
priority in our family.
When we are tempted to take spiritual shortcuts
or to compromise on doing the right thing,
help us to remain committed to God's teachings
and to look for every opportunity to follow the example of Jesus.

May we recognize the many opportunities we have each day to love
as Christ did
and to strive for life forever with him in heaven.
Amen.

SOMETHING TO PONDER

In what ways does your role as a mother help you to live a devout life?
What aspects of your vocation hinder you? How can you take small
steps to overcome these challenges toward living a more Christ-like
life?

5.

Saint Monica

Mothering with Prayer

ca. 333–387
Patronage: Mothers, Married Women
Memorial: August 27

MONICA'S STORY

Monica was born in North Africa and raised in a devout Christian family. At an early age, she was given in marriage to Patricius of Tagaste, and she found herself living with this ill-tempered man and his unkind mother, neither of whom shared her faith. Monica's sweet disposition and pious example ultimately led to her spouse's conversion shortly before his death. Widowed, Monica was left to care for the couple's children. Monica prayed incessantly for her eldest, Augustine, to leave his worldly ways and find true faith. After seventeen years, Monica's prayers were answered when her spiritual director (who was later canonized as Saint Ambrose) baptized her son. Augustine consecrated himself to celibacy and later was made a saint and Doctor of the Church. Monica, who never stopped praying for her family, died peacefully only a few months after Augustine's baptism, content in her son's salvation.

Lessons from Monica

Perhaps of any saint, I have spent the most time talking with Monica, the patroness of mothers and wives. Long before I was Eric's mom and Adam's mom, I was Greg's wife. He is a loving, amazing man who for our first several years together did not share my Catholic faith. In so many ways, ours was the perfect marriage, and yet my heart carried a burden of sorrow that grew even heavier with the births and baptisms of our sons. As our family grew and my own personal commitment to my faith life flourished, I became more acutely aware of missing my husband at the eucharistic table. In every way, this wonderful man supported and encouraged the boys and me in our Catholic home, yet his personal path to Christ truly present in the Eucharist unfolded quietly over several years.

As I watched Greg's quiet devotion, and knowing the goodness of his heart, I let Monica became a prayer companion for me in a unique and special way. I asked her intercession to help me have the grace to accept my husband's faith journey and to respect the ways in which it differed from my own. For so many years, I prayed and prayed, calling on Monica's intercession to know the grace and perseverance that had enabled her to endure years of worry and waiting as she prayed for her husband and son. When Greg joined the Church through the Rite of Christian Initiation of Adults, my heart knew a joy I never thought it could contain. And every Sunday, when I see my husband and sons receive the Eucharist, that happiness often prompts quiet tears. It's a sensation I hope I never begin to take for granted.

My family's unity in the Eucharist has brought me immeasurable joy that is still playing out as I watch my sons grow into young men. But this is a blessing that not every mom will know. Many families live lovingly together while practicing different faith traditions, respecting and even cherishing the distinctions in belief and practice. Some of us will also confront children or other loved ones making a conscious decision to leave the Church. This can be particularly painful to those of us who have fully devoted ourselves to forming our children in the faith or who have kept Christ at the center of our marriages. It's easy to blame ourselves and our own shortcomings for other people's choices. Sadly, many of us lose hope in these situations. Yet hope is one of God's greatest gifts for his children—hope in him, hope in salvation, hope for what lies beyond the joys and sorrows of our days here on earth. Like Monica, we must strive to cling to that hope and trust that the Holy Spirit continues to work in our lives and the lives of our loved ones.

What we know of Monica's often-unhappy path through life comes to us, ironically, through the words of her once-wayward son, Saint Augustine of Hippo, who would later recognize the power of his mother's prayers as he wrote her life story in his own *Confessions*. His mother had gone to her grave peacefully, resting in the knowledge that the one thing she most wanted in life had been accomplished. Most Catholic moms share a common goal at the top of our "to do" list: to help our families be faithful disciples and so earn eternal rest in heaven. That Monica was able to see the conversion of both her husband and son, that she raised two other children who committed themselves to religious life, and that she herself was a devout woman who prayed and studied constantly makes her an amazing intercessor for any mother.

One common denominator for any Catholic mom, regardless of family size or age, is prayer. From the moment we set eyes upon our children, in fact even before they depart our wombs, we are praying for them. We pray for the big things like their health, lifelong goals, and vocations and for the little things like bumps and bruises, a turn on the pitcher's mound, and chemistry quizzes. We pray while we nurse them, when we drop them off at school, and as they drive out of our garages. Long after they grow up and move away, we will still pray for them, quieting ourselves into a consulting role in their lives. But we never—ever—stop our prayers for them.

Monica's constancy of devotion, the fact that she never gave up on her husband or her son, is a touchstone for me when I wonder if my pleas to God are futile. I hope always for joy in my family, but it's likely that our path to heaven may be littered with speed bumps, twists, turns, and even dead ends. Monica reminds me that prayer is the fuel that keeps me moving forward and that heaven is life's greatest destination.

TRADITIONS

Members of Saint Monica's Sodality pray novenas through the intercession of Saint Monica for the return of loved ones to the Church and for those who experience pain and duress due to a loved one's loss of faith.

MONICA'S WISDOM

Nothing is far from God.

THIS WEEK WITH SCRIPTURE

Sunday: Proverbs 31:10–12

When one finds a worthy wife,
her value is far beyond pearls.
Her husband, entrusting his heart to her,
has an unfailing prize.
She brings him good, and not evil,
all the days of her life.

> *Thank you for the perfect gift of my husband. Help me to be a good partner to him, to remember to pray for him, and to treasure the gift of our family together.*

Monday: 1 Corinthians 13:4–7

Love is patient, love is kind. It is not jealous, [love] is not pompous, it is not inflated, it is not rude, it does not seek its own interests, it is not quick-tempered, it does not brood over injury, it does not rejoice over wrongdoing but rejoices with the truth. It bears all things, believes all things, hopes all things, endures all things.

Give me patience, Lord, kindness, and gentleness, too. Help me to endure all the challenges of my day, to be patient, kind, and loving with my children, and to see your face in theirs today.

Tuesday: 1 Peter 4:8

Above all, let your love for one another be intense, because love covers a multitude of sins.

Prince of Peace, let my love for my family be intense, and let it spur me to prayer for each of them and service to them, even when I am weary.

Wednesday: Ephesians 6:1–3

Children, obey your parents [in the Lord], for this is right. "Honor your father and mother." This is the first commandment with a promise, "that it may go well with you and that you may have a long life on earth."

Today, Father, I pray for my parents. Whether they are here on earth or with you in heaven, they gave their lives and their faith to me. Bless them with good health, but most of all with great contentment and rest in you.

Thursday: Psalm 5:2–4

Hear my words, O LORD;
listen to my sighing.
Hear my cry for help,
my king, my God!
To you I pray, O LORD;
at dawn you will hear my cry;
at dawn I will plead before you and wait.

Hear my words, God, especially my prayers on behalf of my beloved children and spouse. Let them know with certainty the constancy of your love.

Friday: Mark 11:24

Therefore I tell you, all that you ask for in prayer, believe that you will receive it and it shall be yours.

> *Remind me in my moments of unbelief that your plan is perfect and that your grace is complete.*

Saturday: Philippians 4:8–9

Finally, brothers, whatever is true, whatever is honorable, whatever is just, whatever is pure, whatever is lovely, whatever is gracious, if there is any excellence and if there is anything worthy of praise, think about these things. Keep on doing what you have learned and received and heard and seen in me. Then the God of peace will be with you.

> *I want you, Lord, for myself and also for my husband and children. Help us to know your peace in our home.*

SAINT-INSPIRED ACTIVITIES

For Mom

Pray in a special way with and for your children. Find time to have a quiet conversation with each of them, assuring them of your love and prayers especially for them.

With Children

What we know of Saint Monica's life comes to us from her son Saint Augustine. Invite your children to draw a picture of you or write about you, explaining what they would want someone to know about their mother.

A PRAYER FOR OUR FAMILY

Pray as a family each day this week:

Saint Monica, wife, mother, and child of God,
you never stopped praying for the ones you loved.
Help us to pray for every person in our family,
especially for those who may be facing challenges or difficulties.
Help us to be patient with one another,
to calm our tempers, and to be kind and loving to each other.
May we follow your example of perfect faith in God,
knowing that his love gives us great hope to face even the biggest
challenges in our lives.
Amen.

SOMETHING TO PONDER

How do you share your faith with your children and support them
through prayer? How do you show your love for your children?

6

Saint Joseph

Answering God's Will in Our Daily Work

First Century
Patronage: Workers, Fathers, Universal Church
Memorials: March 19 (Saint Joseph), May 1 (Saint Joseph the Worker)

JOSEPH'S STORY

In the first chapter of Matthew's gospel, we find the genealogy of Jesus. Through the lineage of Joseph, Matthew carefully chronicles Jesus' descent from the house of David, as was prophesied of the Messiah in the ancient traditions of Judaism. Upon learning of Mary's pregnancy following their betrothal, Joseph considered quietly divorcing her, but he instead followed the angel's instructions to marry her and to raise the child she carried as his own. A woodworker, Joseph was known to have been of modest means, but he always remained sincerely devoted to the practice of his faith, taking his family each year to Jerusalem for Passover. On two occasions, he was the recipient of divine messages. Both times, he followed God's will immediately by sheltering the Holy Family. Tradition holds that Joseph died of natural causes prior to the beginning of Jesus' adult ministry.

LESSONS FROM JOSEPH

Although he is one of our most popular saints, little biographical data exists on the life of Joseph. What we do know comes from the early chapters of the gospels of Matthew and Luke. Church teaching and popular devotions to Joseph have lifted him from the humble beginnings described in the gospels to a devoted intercessor, popular across the globe.

We often recognize great saints for their ability to proclaim the faith or for the extraordinary sufferings they endured during their earthly lives. And yet in Saint Joseph we find a man who was perhaps best known for being simple, humble, and always rock-solid in his faith. On two occasions when Joseph's gut told him one thing, he followed God's will and did the polar opposite. Intending to divorce his betrothed wife quietly so as to save her from shame, he instead followed the angel's instruction to commit to a life of supporting and protecting Mary and the infant she bore. Later in Matthew's gospel, Joseph again listened to God's messenger and led his family to safety in Egypt during Herod's massacre of the infants in and around Bethlehem (Mt 2:13–18).

We find these stories about Joseph in the Bible, and yet no words are directly attributed to him there. For me, Joseph's silent consistency is perhaps the greatest mark of his character, and the most important trait I hope to emulate. In an age when an overabundance of communication technologies makes silence an endangered commodity, I have great respect for a man who simply followed God's will, took care of his family, and stayed out of the spotlight. In my home, we often say to one another, "Put your head down and do your work." I don't know how this saying started, but I love to contemplate Joseph as a man who knew how to keep his head down and work hard. His greatest responsibility in life was to provide for Mary and Jesus. And as it is for so many of us parents who work long hours to feed and shelter our families, Joseph's diligence was his greatest path to heaven.

Joseph's traits of industry, humility, and loyalty provide a daily role model for me in my work as a mother. When much of my day is filled with mundane tasks in the service of my family, I can look to the patron saint of workers to help me go about my business with the proper attitude. Also from this wonderful saint, I learn to listen always for God's messages about his true desire for my life. When tempted to divorce myself quietly from work or developments that don't fit *my* agenda, I look to the man who twice experienced the grace of hearing—and more importantly following—exactly what God wanted him to do.

TRADITIONS

One of the most popular traditions associated with Saint Joseph is the burying of a statue in the yard of a home that is being sold. The roots of this tradition date back to Saint Teresa of Avila, whose devotion to the saint led her to consecrate a plot of land her religious order desired to purchase by burying medals of Saint Joseph. Later, Saint André Bessette, who shared a similar devotion to Joseph, also repeated this practice. Once a homeless husband seeking shelter for his wife who was ready to give birth, Saint Joseph has long been a favorite intercessor for those struggling with housing concerns.

JOSEPH'S WISDOM

Behold, the virgin shall be with child and bear a son, and they shall name him Emmanuel, which means "God is with us." When Joseph awoke, he did as the angel of the Lord had commanded him and took his wife into his home.

—Matthew 1:23–24

THIS WEEK WITH SCRIPTURE

Sunday: Ephesians 2:8–9

For by grace you have been saved through faith, and this is not from you; it is the gift of God; it is not from works, so no one may boast.

> *God in heaven, help me to put my head down and do my work this week for your glory. Help me complete any tasks I have been avoiding.*

Monday: Proverbs 12:11

He who tills his own land has food in plenty,
but he who follows idle pursuits is a fool.

> *Just for today, Father, help me to take a bit of my idle time and spend it in quiet prayer.*

Tuesday: Colossians 3:23–24

Whatever you do, do from the heart, as for the Lord and not for others, knowing that you will receive from the Lord the due payment of the inheritance; be slaves of the Lord Christ.

> *Jesus, help me to avoid the spotlight, and keep me from becoming bitter or resentful when I feel my work is being taken for granted.*

Wednesday: 2 Timothy 2:15

Be eager to present yourself as acceptable to God, a workman who causes no disgrace, imparting the word of truth without deviation.

> *In my workplace, let me serve as a light to others, Lord, a quiet witness to the majesty of your grace and goodness.*

Thursday: Luke 6:38

Give and gifts will be given to you; a good measure, packed together, shaken down, and overflowing, will be poured into your lap. For the measure with which you measure will in return be measured out to you.

> *Good and Gracious God, enable me to always be fair and just in the disposition of my work by seeking justice for those treated inhumanely or unfairly.*

Friday: Ecclesiastes 9:10

Anything you can turn your hand to, do with what power you have; for there will be no work, nor reason, nor knowledge, nor wisdom in the nether world where you are going.

> *As I go about my work, Lord, aid me in performing each task to the best of my abilities, giving my best as a sign of my love for you.*

Saturday: Proverbs 31:30–31

Charm is deceptive and beauty fleeting;
the woman who fears the LORD is to be praised.
Give her a reward for her labors,
and let her works praise her at the city gates.

> *Today and always, let my service to my family be my best, most important, and most beloved form of work, for in loving and serving them, I better love and serve you.*

SAINT-INSPIRED ACTIVITIES

For Mom

Focus on quietly and lovingly doing your household tasks with a servant's heart. Emulate Saint Joseph's example by praying to hear God's will for your life, and by saying, "Yes, Lord," when you sense his direction may not line up with your personal desires.

With Children

On or near the feast of Saint Joseph, plan to celebrate with a "Saint Joseph's Altar." Prepare a simple feast and welcome friends or family into your home. Consider tying this meal in with an act of service or almsgiving to aid a charitable organization in your community.

A PRAYER FOR OUR FAMILY

Pray as a family each day this week:

Good Saint Joseph,
even though you were quiet and humble, your life changed the course of our world.
Be with us as we work to follow your example.
We want to hear and heed God's plan for our lives.
May we quietly and yet intently listen for that small, still voice that leads us along the path that God has planned for each of us.
Help us to say "yes" even when we'd rather not.
Help us to serve lovingly and without expectation of reward.
Help us to treasure Mary and Jesus as you did.
Amen.

SOMETHING TO PONDER

How do you attempt to discern God's plan for your work? What steps do you take when God's agenda and yours don't intersect?

7

Saint Sebastian

Caring for Our Bodies through Physical Fitness

Third Century
Patronage: Athletes, Soldiers
Memorial: January 20

SEBASTIAN'S STORY

Legend teaches us that Sebastian was born of a wealthy family in Milan, that he was educated, and that he eventually rose through the military ranks to become a captain of the Roman guard and a favorite of Emperor Diocletian. Despite great risk to his own safety, Sebastian went out of his way to care for imprisoned Christians and to evangelize his fellow soldiers and the prison guards. Upon discovering that Sebastian was a Christian, Diocletian had the young soldier tied to a tree and shot with arrows. Sebastian survived the persecution and was nursed to health by Saint Irene. Refusing to give up his beliefs, Sebastian raised the ire of Diocletian again by preaching his beliefs and was ultimately martyred for his faith.

LESSONS FROM SEBASTIAN

When my boys were in elementary school, Sebastian was often a favorite pick for annual "lives of the saints" reports because of his status as the patron saint of athletes. Few of the boys looked into the true reasons behind this patronage, claiming him instead because they loved sports and archery. I remember a second-grader, dressed in a soccer uniform and gripping a bow and arrow, extolling the virtues of this third-century hero.

So what can the life of Sebastian teach a modern-day mom? Precious few of us will ever face overt persecution for our beliefs, but it's likely that, at some point in our lives, we will each know social challenges, belittling, or blatant hostility when we live out our Christian values. Recently, I had one of these moments in a physician's office when I tried to explain to my doctor why I would not accept her prescription for a form of artificial birth control. Laughing at me, this doctor (who is no longer my doctor!) inferred that my convictions were primitive, ignorant, and unnecessary. As I walked out of her office, I felt the sting of being attacked on the basis of my religion. Granted, no one was shooting arrows at me, but her treatment of me in that situation required that I rely on what I knew to be right and stung my heart like barbs hitting me physically.

It takes a great deal of physical and emotional strength to carry out our vocation to motherhood. From giving birth to learning to do everything with one hand while we juggle twenty pounds of baby on our hip, there are nonstop physical demands in a mother's workday. We run short on sleep, we rarely give ourselves sick days, and the care and feeding of our broods often requires every ounce of physical reserve that we can muster.

Sebastian must have taken great care of his physical body to live up to the demands of his military career. His survival of a brutal physical attack points to the fact that he was likely in very good shape. But more important than his physique was the state of his soul. He was an unapologetic Christian, going outside himself to minister to others, to spread the faith by teaching, and ultimately to pay the highest price for his beliefs. Most of the prime athletes I know have more than just physical prowess. It is the combination of their body and their mental and emotional focus that fashions them into winners.

To run the race of Catholic motherhood, we need to strengthen ourselves emotionally, mentally, physically, and spiritually. Part of this means building our stamina through fitness, exercise, good nutrition, and proper sleep. But if you're like me, you can find many excuses every day for not taking that walk around the block or for sitting on the grass while the kids play tag nearby rather than joining in the running.

Physical fitness doesn't have to be all about marathons or hitting the gym. It can be a lovely bike ride with the kids on an autumn afternoon, watching the leaves change colors as you feel the warmth of the sun on your skin. It can be playing a dance video game with your preteens, taking a walk with your husband, or doing exercises with your newborn. Next time you feel like making excuses for not taking care of yourself physically, think of Sebastian and the strength he summoned to continue preaching the Good News up until the hour of his death. And then, *just do it.*

When I glorify God by using the physical body he has given me, I tell him, my family, and myself that I am worth caring for. Just as the Bible states that the famous "Proverbs 31 Woman" was "girt about with strength," I need to be ready, willing, and able for the plans God has for me.

TRADITIONS

Many places around the world enjoy major celebrations on Saint Sebastian's feast day. From Puerto Rico to Connecticut, from Nicaragua to Sicily, January 20 marks a time of liturgical celebrations, street processions, and good food all in the name of the patron saint of athletes.

SEBASTIAN'S WISDOM

The devil strains every nerve to secure the souls that belong to Christ. We should not grudge our toil in wresting them from Satan and giving them back to God.

THIS WEEK WITH SCRIPTURE

Sunday: Hebrews 12:11

At the time, all discipline seems a cause not for joy but for pain, yet later it brings the peaceful fruit for righteousness to those who are trained by it.

> *Help me to remember, Lord, that physical and spiritual disciplines may cause temporary pain, but they will lead to eternal happiness.*

Monday: 1 Corinthians 6:19–20

Do you not know that your body is a temple of the holy Spirit within you, whom you have from God, and that you are not you own? For you have been purchased at a price. Therefore, glorify God in your body.

> *For those times when I do not glorify you with my body but rather look at my own shortcomings, I am sorry, Lord.*

Tuesday: 2 Timothy 2:1

So you, my child, be strong in the grace that is in Christ Jesus.

> *Strengthen me, Jesus, for all that lies ahead—the ups and downs, the obstacles and the opportunities. Thank you for the gift of this day.*

Wednesday: Philippians 4:13

I have strength for everything through him who empowers me.

> *Father, any strength I have comes from you. In those moments when I feel weak and overcome, embolden me to share your love.*

Thursday: 1 Corinthians 9:24

Do you not know that the runners in the stadium all run in the race, but only one wins the prize? Run so as to win.

> *I want to win, Lord. I want the prize for myself and for my family. Help me to keep my eyes on you, to keep running the good race, and to never give up.*

Friday: Psalm 37:23–24

Those whose steps are guided by the LORD,
whose way God approves,
May stumble but they will never fall,
for the LORD holds their hand.

> *Guide my steps today, God; hold my hand and carry me.*

Saturday: Isaiah 40:31

They that hope in the LORD will renew their strength,
they will soar as with eagles' wings;
They will run and not grow weary,
walk and not grow faint.

> *My hope is in you, Father. Renew my strength, and let me be a light to my family that they may know your strength and your love through my service to them.*

SAINT-INSPIRED ACTIVITIES

For Mom

Try a new exercise routine. Experiment with a class at your local park, check out a DVD at the library, or sign up for a local 5K walk with a friend.

With Children

Hold a "field day" at your house. Come up with a list of possible sports you can play together: backyard soccer, touch football, running races, or even a game of hide-and-go-seek. Spend the day outside, enjoy a picnic lunch, and discuss with your kids the gift of a physically healthy body.

A PRAYER FOR OUR FAMILY

Pray as a family each day this week:

Saint Sebastian,
you were strong and brave and true.
Help us to follow your example by caring for our bodies
and for those around us.
May we be compassionate to those who need our help.
May we care for our bodies, since they are a gift from God.
May we be unafraid when our beliefs are challenged
or threatened by others.
Please carry our intentions to God as we try to love all those in need
with the same grace you showed in your time.
Amen.

SOMETHING TO PONDER

What obstacles prevent you from being more physically active? How can you incorporate more fitness activities into your life?

8

Saint Francis of Assisi

Renewal of Faith

1181–October 3, 1226
Patronage: Families, Catholic Action, Environmentalism
Memorial: October 4

FRANCIS OF ASSISI'S STORY

Born in 1181 at Assisi in Umbria, central Italy, Francesco Bernardone was christened "Giovanni" after John the Baptist and raised in a wealthy merchant's family. His youth was spent in frivolous pursuits before his military tour as a knight, but then he was captured and spent a year in imprisonment. His captivity, a subsequent prolonged illness, and instances of divine intervention spurred a profound conversion experience that led Francis to renounce his wealth and inheritance. He instead pursued a life of radical poverty and total commitment to the Gospel. He spent time in solitude, in prayer, and in manual labor repairing churches, and he began to attract followers who committed themselves to his spiritual precepts. This informal band soon blossomed into the Friars Minor, and later a group of cloistered women formed whom he called the Order of Poor Ladies (later known as the Poor Clares after Saint Clare of Assisi, who had a great influence on the order). Later still, Francis founded the Third Order of Brothers and Sisters of Penance, a fraternity of laity devoted to Franciscan spirituality and works of charity.

Out of humility, Francis was never ordained a priest, but he traveled extensively while preaching prior to withdrawing into his final years of private prayer. After having received the marks of the stigmata, Francis suffered debilitating illness and great pain. He paid a final visit to Saint Clare and her sisters and composed perhaps his most famous writing, the "Canticle of the Sun," prior to his death in 1226.

LESSONS FROM FRANCIS

My earliest formal religious-education experiences were marked by a deep connection with Francis and his profound love for the Eucharist and for the life of Christ. From kindergarten through fifth grade, the Poor Clare Sisters who taught me at Saint Barbara's elementary school laid that groundwork, following in the footsteps of women formed for centuries under the safe shadow of Clare's wing. I recall their frequent invitations to involve us in their work in the missions. As I entered my sixth-grade year, a change at our school brought new Franciscan sisters from New York, and this band of vibrant young women set my soul on fire with their passion for the Gospel.

In retrospect, I owe a great debt of gratitude to both of these communities of women religious with each sister flavored by her unique charisms, and to the embodiment of Franciscan spirituality they instilled in their spiritual children. Habited and veiled Sister Esther, more comfortable in her native Spanish, taught me to look outside the comfort of my suburban home and to see the very real needs of children just like me living in destitute poverty only a few hours away in Mexico. She helped me to prepare for my First Communion by instilling in me a perfect reverence for the Eucharist and a respect for the grace of the Sacrament of Penance. In preparing me for Confirmation in eighth grade, Franciscan Sister Jean Marie helped me to see that being Catholic meant something more than simply showing up for Mass on Sunday, and she taught me that I too had a calling to serve our Church with my gifts.

In looking at the life of Francis, it's easy sometimes to focus on the statuesque version of him out in my garden, preaching to the birds and standing watch with Brother Sun and Sister Moon. But that "touchy feely" saint likely has little to do with the real man who literally gave the clothes off his back to change his world and serve the poor. I find myself drawn most to his passion for Christ. His care for lepers and the impoverished, his absolute disavowal of owning things, and his deep attachment to the beauty of creation are all directly born of an all-consuming love for Christ and a profound desire to follow as nearly as possible the Gospel message of peace.

Francis lived in a world not unlike mine—a world that knew a Church that seemed to be in great peril of collapse. He taught his brothers and sisters to rise above the politics, the temptations to take spiritual shortcuts, and the desire to take the easy way out. The Church I know and love today faces similar dangers. Technological advances, societal pressures, and even material comforts make it easy to begin compromising my values. I can't imagine being one of Francis's followers, asked to leave everything behind and to commit myself to a life linked as closely as possible to Christ's. "I fall too short," I'd be tempted to tell the one who devoted himself to perfect poverty, simplicity, and humility.

But Francis, Sister Esther, and Sister Jean Marie won't let me off that easily. I may not have the means, the talents, or the holiness to reform and renew the whole Church. But along with my husband Greg, I have the opportunity and the responsibility to commit myself to radical, ongoing transformation of my own domestic church, starting with myself. Francis teaches me to watch for the little opportunities that arise daily to be more Christ-like—for a more perfect love of my spouse and boys, a more compassionate heart that looks to give instead of to receive, a more careful stewardship of God's creation, and a more profound desire to know and be fueled by Christ ever-present in the Eucharist. God called Francis saying, "Go and repair my house, which as you see is falling into ruin." Francis invites me, a simple Catholic mom, to go and do the same.

TRADITIONS

Our present-day nativity sets were handed down as a tradition from Saint Francis, who as legend tells it built the first one in Greccio one Christmas, just a few years before his death. Francis desired to celebrate Mass and to pay homage to Christ's birth in a way that was as close as possible to what the child of Bethlehem knew when he entered our world. Saint Francis's first crèche included hay, livestock, and Mass celebrated around the manger.

FRANCIS'S WISDOM

Sanctify yourself and you will sanctify society.

THIS WEEK WITH SCRIPTURE

Sunday: Psalm 142:6

I cry out to you, LORD,
I say, You are my refuge,
my portion in the land of the living.

> *You, Lord, are my refuge and my portion.*

Monday: Matthew 10:8

Cure the sick, raise the dead, cleanse lepers, drive out demons. Without cost you have received; without cost you are to give.

> *Father, you give with no cost. Help me to serve you without regard to price.*

Tuesday: Ephesians 1:18–19

May the eyes of [your] hearts be enlightened, that you may know what is the hope that belongs to his call, what are the riches of glory in his inheritance among the holy ones, and what is the surpassing greatness of his power for us who believe.

Enlighten my heart to your call. I want to answer you with my life.

Wednesday: Colossians 1:18

He is the head of the body, the church.
He is the beginning, the firstborn from the dead,
that in all things he himself might be preeminent.

> *Jesus, help me to love and to serve you in the Church and to know that, in you, all things are possible.*

Thursday: Psalm 16:5

LORD, my allotted portion and my cup,
you have made my destiny secure.

> *Thank you, Father, for a destiny that is secure and perfect in your love.*

Friday: Matthew 16:24

Then Jesus said to his disciples, "Whoever wishes to come after me must deny himself, take up his cross, and follow me."

> *Help me, Jesus, to make the sacrifices necessary to follow you with a willing heart and a loving attitude.*

Saturday: Matthew 5:3

Blessed are the poor in spirit,
for theirs is the kingdom of heaven.

> *Strength to the poor, allow me the blessings of poverty, simplicity, and humility today and always.*

SAINT-INSPIRED ACTIVITIES

For Mom

Spend time with Christ in eucharistic adoration or read chapter 10 of Matthew's gospel, which inspired Saint Francis to reform his life.

With Children

Hold a family discussion on God's presence in the natural world around us and how your family might become stewards of creation by better caring for pets or the environment. Print out and pray the "Canticle of the Sun" together.

A PRAYER FOR OUR FAMILY

Pray as a family each day this week:

Humble Saint Francis,
you desired to live as much like Jesus as possible.
Help us to learn more about the Gospel and to share it
with those we meet.
May we look for chances to support the poor,
to be caretakers of the world around us,
and to live Jesus' teachings as you did.
We ask your intercession for our Church;
may it lead us to a radical love of God
and more perfect service to one another.
Amen.

SOMETHING TO PONDER

How are you being called to repair the domestic church in your home? How can you respond to Francis's call to sanctify society by sanctifying yourself?

9

Saint Elizabeth of Portugal

A Loving Marriage and Peaceful Family Relationships

1271–July 4, 1336
Patronage: Brides, Peace, Against Jealousy
Memorial: July 4

ELIZABETH OF PORTUGAL'S STORY

Elizabeth was born to a royal family in Sargossa, named after a relative who later became Saint Elizabeth of Hungary, and married to King Denis of Portugal, by family arrangement, before her thirteenth birthday. Known for her piety and charitable nature, Elizabeth had to endure years of her husband's infidelities prior to his conversion to Christianity. Multiple times in her life, she played the role of peacemaker between warring factions of her own family. Upon the death of her husband, she retired to a life of prayer as a Third Order Franciscan in a Poor Clare convent she had founded.

LESSONS FROM ELIZABETH

We moms are often the peacemakers in our families. How many times have you uttered the words, "Can't we all just get along?" or something similar when refereeing squabbles between siblings? Elizabeth was born into a family divided by political battles. She went on to watch the same problems erupt between her husband Denis and her own son, Alfonso IV. She was able to barter a truce between a man who had repeatedly cheated on her and fathered illegitimate children, and the son who felt his father was playing favorites with his undeserving half brothers. Her role as matriarch and peacemaker continued through her life until the months preceding her death, when she again intervened to mediate, this time between her son and grandson.

Living in a home with three men, I've observed a few fights in my day. They typically revolve around less sensitive turf battles than those that Elizabeth had to broker. But they leave hurt feelings and chasms nonetheless. When these moments arise, turning to Elizabeth of Portugal for her wisdom, patience, and intercession helps me immensely. For those moments when I want to throw up my hands and give up, Elizabeth's model of courage and conviction provides a path to follow.

I have grown to love and respect Elizabeth's tremendous commitment to the practice of her faith. She managed to balance her duties and responsibilities as queen while caring for her family, attending daily Mass, and praying the Divine Office. Venturing beyond these devotions, she put her faith into practice by advocating for the poor, the sick, and the needy in her community. So many times in my own life, I think that I am too busy caring for my family to pay adequate attention to the prayer disciplines I would like to make habitual. Elizabeth maintained her faith life in the face of a husband who belittled it with his actions. It seems that her intense belief in God enabled her to live with the unhappiness she faced in her marriage. Rather than blaming God for moments when I feel my marriage falls short of all I've dreamed about it being, Elizabeth reminds me to keep serving my husband as he does me and to pray for our relationship with one another.

Perhaps the greatest lessons I've learned from Elizabeth come from watching the devotion she had to her marriage and her husband Denis. Although King Denis was said to have encouraged and respected Elizabeth's commitment to daily Mass, the Divine Office, and her charitable efforts, he led a lifestyle that was in direct opposition to her values. And yet she rose above the embarrassment and pain she surely felt and cared for all of his children—even those who weren't her own—respected his rule, and ultimately cared for him in his final illness. His ultimate conversion prior to his death is a tribute to the perseverance with which Elizabeth prayed for Denis.

Census bureau studies and surveys within the Catholic Church show an ever-increasing prevalence of blended families in today's society, as well as families dealing with the repercussions of divorce or separation. For those moms who face the unique challenges of pulling together new family traditions, working with other adults in cooperative parenting situations, and dealing with the stress of scheduling and interpersonal issues, Saint Elizabeth can be a special intercessor when everyday life feels complicated or overwhelming. Women facing marriage difficulties, separation or divorce have shared with me their devotion to this matriarch whose faith saw her through domestic trials and helped her sustain her loving family life.

As the patron saint of brides, against jealousy, and of peace Elizabeth of Portugal is a regular intercessor for me in my marriage, in the bad times and the good, and in my efforts to be an instrument of peace within the four walls of my home and beyond.

TRADITIONS

Nearly every city or town in Portugal has a church named after the beloved Isabel, as Saint Elizabeth is known there. The city of Coimbra, the place of her death and the home of the major shrine Santa Clara-a-Nova, is the site of a biannual *festa* devoted to the queen. Portuguese families around the world maintain a strong devotion to the queen who played such an integral role in their history.

ELIZABETH'S WISDOM

If you love peace, all will be well.

THIS WEEK WITH SCRIPTURE

Sunday: 1 John 4:7

Beloved, let us love one another, because love is of God; everyone who loves is begotten by God and knows God.

Lord, help us to keep your love at the center of our marriage and to see you in one another.

Monday: Galatians 6:2

Bear one another's burdens, and so you will fulfill the law of Christ.

God, for those times when my husband is struggling or frustrated or feeling pressured by the responsibilities he bears, help me to be a support to him and to bear the load with him as a sign of my love.

Tuesday: Matthew 5:9

Blessed are the peacemakers,
for they will be called children of God.

Heavenly Father, sometimes it can get very crazy around my home. Help me to keep your peace when the children of God who live in my home declare war on one another.

Wednesday: Ephesians 5:24–25

As the church is subordinate to Christ, so wives should be subordinate to their husbands in everything. Husbands, love your wives, even as Christ loved the church and handed himself over for her.

Help me to appreciate that being subordinate to my husband means loving him completely, being your love to him in all I do, and freely accepting his love and self-giving in return.

Thursday: Proverbs 12:4

A worthy wife is the crown of her husband.

> *Saint Elizabeth, I ask your intercession to be a worthy wife and mother. May I know your goodness, your faithfulness, and your compassion as I aim to draw myself, my husband, and my children closer to Jesus.*

Friday: Hebrews 12:14

Strive for peace with everyone, and for that holiness without which no one will see the Lord.

> *For those moments when peace feels far removed, help me to cling to your word, to strive for what you promise, and to model holiness for my family.*

Saturday: Genesis 2:18

The LORD God said: "It is not good for the man to be alone. I will make a suitable partner for him."

> *Thank you, God, for the gift of my husband, my partner. Let me treasure him as a gift from you.*

SAINT-INSPIRED ACTIVITIES

For Mom

Devote yourself to loving service of your husband. Try to devise a way each week to do something extra special for the man you married. These efforts don't need to be big, fancy, or expensive; an extra smile, a fresh cup of coffee, or a decade of the Rosary prayed on his behalf are simple ways to show your love and devotion.

With Children

Talk with your children about what it means to be a peacemaker, using examples of times when they may have argued with one another or a friend. Ask them to talk about, draw a picture, or write a short story about how they made peace.

A PRAYER FOR OUR FAMILY

Pray as a family each day this week:

Saint Elizabeth,
you were the peacemaker of your family.
You loved God so much that you spent time with him every day
in prayer and in the Eucharist.
But you also loved him so greatly that you wanted to share his love
with others
by caring for the sick, the poor, and the lonely.
When your family was torn apart by fighting,
your strong belief helped bring peace and love to those separated by
hatred and jealousy.
Be with us in those times when our differences separate us from one
another.
Help us to be the peacemakers in our home and neighborhood,
and to be the heart, hands, and feet of Jesus for everyone we meet.
Amen.

SOMETHING TO PONDER

What are some ways in which you lovingly care for your husband? What else might you do? What disrupts peaceful relationships in your home?

10.

Saint John Bosco

Total Dedication to the Education of Our Children

August 16, 1815–January 31, 1888
Patronage: Students, Editors, Apprentices
Memorial: January 31

JOHN BOSCO'S STORY

Giovanni Melchior Bosco was raised by his mother, after his father, a poor farmer, died when Giovanni was only two. As soon as he was old enough, he went to work supporting his family with odd jobs and as a shepherd. He valued education, walking four miles to attend school. As a young man, he answered his calling to the priesthood, arriving the first day of seminary in clothes donated by a charity. Don Bosco dedicated his adult life to the education of the poor boys of

Turin, a rapidly industrializing city where many young men were destined to a life of illiteracy and crime. His first boardinghouse for boys eventually became a series of institutions of learning that would refine John's "preventative system" of education. The Oratory of Saint Francis de Sales, established by Don Bosco, also ignited many vocations, and his Society of Saint Francis de Sales (the Salesians) received papal approval in 1869. Don Bosco worked tirelessly as an advocate for the marginalized, providing catechesis, education, cultural formation, and apprenticeship in the trades for his students. Along with Saint Mary Mazzarello, he founded the Daughters of Mary, Help of Christians, to work with girls in the Salesian tradition. Shortly before his death, Don Bosco advised his followers: "Do not ever forget these three things: devotion to the Blessed Sacrament, devotion to Mary, Help of Christians, and devotion to the Holy Father!"

LESSONS FROM JOHN

Part of what draws me to the life of John Bosco is admittedly his relationship with his mother. As a "boy mom" of two sons, I've become acquainted over the years with the facts of raising young men. God dealt me a motherly vocation littered with Legos, superhero toys, and action movies. So a part of me smiles when I read the words Venerable Margaret Bosco (venerated in 2006 by Pope Benedict XVI) shared with her son as he prepared to depart for the seminary:

> To see you dressed in this manner fills my heart with joy. But remember that it is not the dress that gives honor to the state, but the practice of virtue. If at any time you come to doubt your vocation, I beseech you, lay it aside at once. I would rather have a poor peasant for my son than a negligent priest.

"Mamma Margaret" had a front-row seat for her son's work after he called on her to help him found his first boardinghouse for boys. I can only imagine the joy she felt at being invited to share John's work with boys for the last ten years of her life. We moms hope that the faith foundations we build for our children will stick. It must have been amazing for Margaret to witness her son's passion for not only his own faith but for the army of young souls they together served.

John Bosco lived out a lifelong commitment to "heart, mind, body, and soul" with his "preventative system" of education. His precepts remind me of a prescription given to me by my sons' first pediatrician. "Create an environment where you have to say 'no' as infrequently as possible," our doctor advised. John Bosco did this for his boys, placing them in surroundings that were most likely to decrease their opportunities for sin. His catechesis was all encompassing, taking into account not only a boy's soul, but also his mind and body. At the oratory there were Masses, sermons, and lectures, but also games, picnics, nature study, and music.

John Bosco's "total dedication" philosophy reinforces my decision as a mom to give the very best of myself to the raising of my family. This doesn't mean I don't work outside the home or find time for friends. Rather it means that I've committed myself fully to forming my boys. The love I feel for them makes it easier to sacrifice my own goals and needs at times as I help them grow into faith-filled citizens who will make our world a better place. John Bosco was a spiritual father for his boys, exemplifying my most important goal—guiding my boys to heaven. Along the way, he helped boys build skills for careers that would keep them out of trouble and that would help turn around society. I don't have an army of boys as he did, only two, but my commitment to the challenge of forming their whole persons keeps me praying for strength, wisdom, and grace every day.

John Bosco traded a tour in the foreign missions for a life of service in the slums of his own backyard. When I'm tempted to think that I'm not doing enough to help make change and improve our world, Don Bosco reminds me that my total dedication to helping the ones I love become the best they can be is the best possible use of my gifts. For those moments when I feel like I'll never have a moment of time to myself, his motto, *"Da mihi animas, cetera tolle,"* or "Give me souls, take away everything else!" helps me to keep my greatest priorities in perspective.

TRADITIONS

Saint John Bosco trained young men in many occupations, including printing and bookbinding. He is the first saint to grant a press interview, and he is invoked as the patron saint of editors and the Catholic press.

JOHN'S WISDOM

I promised God that until my last breath I shall have lived for my poor young people. I study for you, I work for you, I am also ready to give my life for you. Take note that whatever I am, I have been so entirely for you, day and night, morning and evening, at every moment.

THIS WEEK WITH SCRIPTURE

Sunday: Psalm 31:17

Let your face shine on your servant;
save me in your kindness.

> *In your kindness, Father, save me.*

Monday: 1 Thessalonians 4:17

Then we who are alive, who are left, will be caught up together with them in the clouds to meet the Lord in the air. Thus we shall always be with the Lord.

> *Help me, Lord, to give my entire self to you and to lead my family to a life with you always.*

Tuesday: John 13:35

This is how all will know that you are my disciples, if you have love for one another.

> *Jesus, help me today give my love to my family in a way that is worthy of being your disciple.*

Wednesday: Hebrews 11:40

God had foreseen something better for us, so that without us they should not be made perfect.

> *You have a perfect plan, God. Bring it to fruition in me.*

Thursday: 1 Corinthians 15:58

Therefore, my beloved brothers, be firm, steadfast, always fully devoted to the work of the Lord, knowing that in the Lord your labor is not in vain.

> *Rock of Ages, firm and steadfast in all things, help me to find my strength and devotion in your love.*

Friday: 1 Thessalonians 5:24

The one who calls you is faithful, and he will also accomplish it.

> *Faithful Giver, accomplish your will in me.*

Saturday: Mark 9:36–37

Taking a child he placed it in their midst, and putting his arms around it he said to them, "Whoever receives one child such as this in my name, receives me; and whoever receives me, receives not me but the One who sent me."

> *Help me to have the faith of a child and to shine a path for my children that they may receive you, Lord.*

SAINT-INSPIRED ACTIVITIES

For Mom

Take a special outing with your sons or spend one-on-one time with them in your home. If you don't have sons, pray this week for the future husbands of your daughters or special young men in your life.

With Children

John Bosco taught his young friends using unique techniques such as juggling and magic shows. Choose a Bible story or parable and plan a quick family skit or puppet show for Dad, neighbors, or younger children.

A PRAYER FOR OUR FAMILY

Pray as a family each day this week:

Good Saint John Bosco,
you gave yourself fully to the boys in your care,
seeing to the education of their hearts, minds, bodies, and souls.
Help us to strive for complete wisdom,
but more importantly for the salvation of our souls.
Remind us to serve the poor as you did,
sharing with them our gifts but also our prayers.
Encourage us in our efforts to learn and to share our lessons
with our friends and family.
We turn with you to the intercession of Our Lady, Help of Christians,
for her constant love and support.
Amen.

SOMETHING TO PONDER

In what ways do you struggle with a total commitment to your motherly vocation?

11.

$\mathcal{B}$lessed $\mathcal{J}$ohn $\mathcal{P}$aul II

Reverencing the Gift of Our Sexuality

May 18, 1920–April 2, 2005
Memorial: October 22

JOHN PAUL II'S STORY

K arol Józef Wojtyla was born in Wadowice, Poland, in 1920, the youngest of three children. By his twentieth birthday, every member of his immediate family had died, shaping his lifelong commitment to the promotion of marriage and family issues. Ordained in 1946, Karol's writings, pastoral sensibilities, and leadership eventually led him to the papacy in 1978. This first-ever Slavic pope and first non-Italian pope in almost 500 years visited 129 countries. His beatification of 1,340 souls and his canonization of 483 souls served as a sign to many of his profound belief in the universal call to holiness. His long reign as pope, charismatic personality, and extensive travel made him popular all over the world. His prolific writings, his role in the fall of communism, his dignified survival of assassination attempts and declining health, and his outreach to leading figures of other religions made him one of our most beloved of popes. At the time of his death in April 2005, many called immediately for his canonization, and he was beatified in May of 2011.

LESSONS FROM JOHN PAUL II

Pope John Paul II is one of my favorite intercessors when I struggle with the body issues that crop up in my vocation as a mom. His prolific writings speak so eloquently about his belief in the sanctity of all human life, but for me it is the way in which he lived out his vocation that offers the most telling life lessons.

From his childhood, Karol Wojtyla loved to glorify God with his physical body. Friends from his youth describe his love for soccer and games played between rival Catholic and Jewish community teams, and his voluntary desire to "sub in" as goalkeeper for the opposing Jewish team when they found themselves short of players. This man, once described as the "Keep Fit Pope," loved kayaking, camping, hiking, and swimming. He was said to have jogged in the Vatican gardens and to have had a regular weight-lifting regimen in his fifties. Photos of a sunglass-donning Father Wojtyla hiking in Greece or a ski–suit–clad pontiff skiing on the slopes have become iconic reminders of his true love of athleticism.

Perhaps that is why my heart hurt all the more as we watched him quietly, and with tremendous dignity, accept the crosses of physical pain, aging, and disability. For his entire papacy, John Paul II wrote and spoke about the dignity of all human life. The grace with which he accepted his physical decline in his final years gave us an eloquent lesson that encouraged me to look at the elderly and physically infirmed in my own life with new, more loving eyes.

But as a wife and mom perhaps the greatest lessons I have learned from John Paul II have come from his teachings known as the "Theology of the Body." Honestly, after so many years of hearing the pontiff vilified by a society that bemoaned his commitment to thousands of years of Church teachings on the dignity of all human life, a light turned on in my heart when I read his writings and teachings for myself. I'll be the first to admit that I still struggle with fully understanding the complexity of many of the documents. But coming to understand my relationship with my own body, with my spouse in the act of marital love, and with the larger world around me in light of this teaching has given me a vast appreciation for this man's true commitment to the place of marriage, of family, and of the role of women in the future of our civilization.

Knowing that my love for my husband and children is a reflection of Christ's love for his Church helps me to see the true value of self-giving love. In loving my husband, my children, and the world around me to the fullest of my abilities, in treasuring my sexuality and in teaching my children to view theirs as a gift from God, and in trying to treat every person in my path with the greatest dignity possible, I continue to learn daily lessons from the man who will presumably be canonized Saint John Paul II one day.

TRADITIONS

Since their inception in 1985, annual celebrations of World Youth Day in Catholic dioceses—and international celebrations of the event every two or three years—have energized and inspired young Catholics with a growing commitment to their faith. Pope John Paul II's initiation of these popular events and his visual commitment to vocations has prompted an influx of "JPII priests" with a deep fervor for the life and teachings of the Church.

JOHN PAUL II's WISDOM

All human life, from the moments of conception and through all subsequent stages, is sacred.

Therefore the Church gives thanks for each and every woman: for mothers, for sisters, for wives; for women consecrated to God in virginity; for women dedicated to the many human beings who await the gratuitous love of another person; for women who watch over the human persons in the family, which is the fundamental sign of the human community; for women who work professionally, and who at times are burdened by a great social responsibility; for "perfect" women and for "weak" women—for all women as they have come forth from the heart of God in all the beauty and richness of their femininity; as they have been embraced by his eternal love; as, together with men, they are pilgrims on this earth, which is the temporal "homeland" of all people and is transformed sometimes into a "valley of tears"; as they assume, together with men, a common responsibility for the destiny of humanity according to daily necessities and according to that definitive destiny which the human family has in God himself, in the bosom of the ineffable Trinity.

—Mulieris Dignitatem, #31

This Week with Scripture

Sunday: Genesis 1:27–28

God created man in his image;
in the divine image he created him;
male and female he created them.
God blessed them, saying to them: "Be fertile and multiply; fill the earth and subdue it. Have dominion over the fish of the sea, the birds of the air, and all the living things that move on the earth."

> *God, thank you for creating me in your image. Please help my husband and me to lovingly treasure the gift of our fertility and to embrace your divine will for our family.*

Monday: Matthew 19:4–6

[Jesus] said in reply, "Have you not read that from the beginning the Creator 'made them male and female' and said, 'For this reason a man shall leave his father and mother and be joined to his wife, and the two shall become one flesh'? So they are no longer two, but one flesh. Therefore, what God has joined together, no human being must separate."

> *Loving Father, I want to love you more and better through my love for my husband. Let me see opportunities to become one with you by serving him.*

Tuesday: Genesis 2:23–24

The man said:
"This one, at last, is bone of my bones
and flesh of my flesh;
This one shall be called 'woman,'
for out of 'her man' this one has been taken."
That is why a man leaves his father and mother and clings to his wife, and the two of them become one body.

> *In those times when I feel distant from my partner, help me to cling to him. May our love be united even when we feel the challenges of the world pulling us apart physically and emotionally.*

Wednesday: Matthew 5:27–28

You have heard that it was said, "You shall not commit adultery." But I say to you, everyone who looks at a woman with lust has already committed adultery with her in his heart.

> *Bless me with the virtue of chastity. Let me model a purity of heart and body for my children.*

Thursday: Romans 8:5

For those who live according to the flesh are concerned with the things of the flesh, but those who live according to the spirit with the things of the spirit.

> *God, we face so many evil influences in our world today. Help us to live according to your spirit in all things.*

Friday: Ephesians 5:21

Be subordinate to one another out of reverence for Christ.

> *As I serve my husband, help me to see each act of love as a sign of reverence, as a gift to you who gave us the original gift.*

Saturday: Ephesians 5:29–30

For no one hates his own flesh but rather nourishes and cherishes it, even as Christ does the church, because we are members of his body.

> *Lord, I desire to love and treasure my body as you designed it. I want to see my part in the larger Body of Christ. Help me to use this flesh, weak as it is, to give glory to you and to draw others nearer to the light of your love.*

SAINT-INSPIRED ACTIVITIES

For Mom

Spend time learning about Blessed John Paul II's "Theology of the Body." For more information, visit your public library and check out *Man and Woman He Created Them: A Theology of the Body* by Dr. Michael Waldstein, or search online for other resources.

With Children

In honor of Blessed John Paul II, play a family soccer game. Head to your backyard or a local park, run around outside for an hour, and then enjoy a picnic and discuss the ways in which we glorify God through our bodies.

A Prayer for Our Family

Pray as a family each day this week:

Blessed John Paul II,
our beloved friend and intercessor,
journey with our family as we seek to discover the true genius of our
physical bodies.
Let us treat our bodies as gifts from you,
loving and serving you through the simple things we do to take care
of one another.
Protect our hearts from any worldly temptations that might separate
us from you or from each other.
Thank you for your example of vitality, of purity, and of courage.
May we follow your model of treating everyone with dignity and
respect, especially those too weak to defend themselves.
Amen.

Something to Ponder

How can you more fully embrace and express your marital relationship as a gift from God?

12

Saint Jerome

A Love for and Devotion to Sacred Scripture

ca. 342–September 30, 420
Patronage: Scripture Scholars, Librarians
Memorial: September 30

JEROME'S STORY

Jerome was born to a wealthy pagan family in Stridonius, Dalmatia, in 342. He spent much of his life preparing for the work that would ultimately be his legacy. His youthful studies, travels, and affinity for languages led him to eventually find his life's work translating the scriptures. He was a gifted linguist and scholar, a man whose abilities and intellect could certainly have been applied toward more worldly pursuits. But following his personal acceptance of Christ, he became absolutely single-minded. His translations of the scriptures were rendered not only with scholarly attention to detail, but more importantly with a heart intent on knowing the life of Christ intimately and on sharing it with others. Jerome's translation of sacred scripture, known as the Vulgate, formed the basis for the commonly accepted Latin translation of the Bible. This in turn became the text from which many of our current English translations were prepared. Jerome lived out his final years founding monasteries and religious orders in Bethlehem, aiding needy refugees in the Holy Land, and writing and living in a cave close to the birthplace of Jesus Christ.

LESSONS FROM JEROME

Jerome's fierce temper is a recurring theme in stories about his life. He didn't pull many punches, especially in his dealings with those whose lives, writings, or words were contrary to the true teachings of the Church. In reading his work, I find myself wanting to emulate his hunger for scripture. He led a painfully ascetic existence, eschewing personal comfort for spiritual diligence and as a means of exorcising his personal temptations. While I'm not prepared to leave my family and take up solitary residence in the desert or a cave, I would love to have Jerome's fiery hunger for sacred scripture, as well as his courage in defending what he knew to be the truths of our Church. As a mom, I've tried to take God's word in the Bible and to teach it to my children in words and images they can understand, instilling in them a love for scripture and a confidence in God's wisdom as they face challenges and decisions.

Recently, my friend Alli shared with me her experience of a minor "mom miracle" that she is convinced occurred in her home through the intercession of Jerome. Alli's first-grade son was struggling with such severe behavioral issues that they sought professional counseling. His temper and flare-ups made homework sessions a daily nightmare, so when his teacher assigned a saint report, Alli feared the worst. The young boy was assigned to write on the life of Jerome, to do an oral presentation, and to don a Saint Jerome costume for the annual All Saints' Day parade. In their research, mother and son learned of Jerome's horrific temper problems and of the saint's conviction that his faith in God had been the only "cure" for this disorder. Alli immediately began praying through the intercession of Jerome for her son. Beginning exactly on the day of the parade, this young saint-in-the-making suddenly was able to overcome his behavioral and anger issues and soon thereafter discontinued his therapeutic sessions. To this day, Alli maintains a tremendous devotion to the saint well-known for his cranky disposition, believing that it was Jerome's intercession which helped her son live up to his full potential.

TRADITIONS

Saint Jerome is often pictured in art with a lion seated nearby. Varying legends relate a story of the lion's devotion to Saint Jerome following his removal of a thorn from the beast's paw. These legends provide a look at the "softer side" of a saint often known for his difficult temperament.

JEROME'S WISDOM

I interpret as I should, following the command of Christ: "Search the Scriptures," and "Seek and you shall find." For if, as Paul says, Christ is the power of God and the wisdom of God, and if the man who does not know Scripture does not know the power and wisdom of God, then ignorance of Scriptures is ignorance of Christ.

THIS WEEK WITH SCRIPTURE

Sunday: Romans 10:12–15

For there is no distinction between Jew and Greek; the same Lord is Lord of all, enriching all who call upon him. For "everyone who calls on the name of the Lord will be saved."

But how can they call on him in whom they have not believed? And how can they believe in him of whom they have not heard? And how can they hear without someone to preach? And how can people preach unless they are sent? As it is written, "How beautiful are the feet of those who bring [the] good news!"

Father in heaven, please help me to follow the example of Saint Jerome, who dedicated his life to deliver your Good News to the world.

Monday: 2 Peter 1:20–21

Know this first of all, that there is no prophecy of scripture that is a matter of personal interpretation, for no prophecy ever came through human will; but rather human beings moved by the Holy Spirit spoke under the influence of God.

Lord, aid me in remembering that my personal interpretation of your word matters less than following your Gospel teachings to be a light and a source of your love to others.

Tuesday: Matthew 6:19–21

Do not store up for yourselves treasures on earth, where moth and decay destroy, and thieves break in and steal. But store up treasures in heaven, where neither moth nor decay destroys, nor thieves break in and steal. For where your treasure is, there also will your heart be.

When worldly goods and ambitions tempt me, help me to remember that your word, your truth, and your love are all the treasures I need.

Wednesday: Ephesians 6:16–17

In all circumstances, hold faith as a shield, to quench all [the] flaming arrows of the evil one. And take the helmet of salvation and the sword of the Spirit, which is the word of God.

May we always cling to your word as a powerful tool in balancing against those temptations that draw us away from you and from one another.

Thursday: Psalm 119:105

Your word is a lamp for my feet,
a light for my path.

> *Help me to turn to your word when I reach forks in the road*
> *and don't know which way to turn.*

Friday: John 20:30–31

Now Jesus did many other signs in the presence of [his] disciples
that are not written in this book. But these are written that you may
[come to] believe that Jesus is the Messiah, the Son of God, and that
through this belief you may have life in his name.

> *Jesus, help me to embrace the Gospel and have life in your*
> *name by living what you taught.*

Saturday: 2 Timothy 3:16–17

All scripture is inspired by God and is useful for teaching, for refuta-
tion, for correction, and for training in righteousness, so that one
who belongs to God may be competent, equipped for every good
work.

> *God, knowing and living your word equips me. May I*
> *remember always to use what Saint Jerome has shared with*
> *me to do your good work in my world.*

SAINT-INSPIRED ACTIVITIES

For Mom

Follow Saint Jerome's lead and begin making sacred scripture a part of
your spiritual life by reading and studying the Sunday gospel for the
week. Find the Liturgy of the Word online at usccb.org/nab and spend
a few moments each day letting Sunday's gospel shape your week and
inspire a few minutes of quiet devotional prayer.

With Children

Enjoy reading some classic Bible stories with your children, using either a translation specifically for them or your family Bible. Have children draw a picture from their favorite story and send these to a friend or relative as a tribute to Saint Jerome's correspondence.

A PRAYER FOR OUR FAMILY

Pray as a family each day this week:

Saint Jerome,
you used your wisdom, your talents, and your heart
to bring God's word to the people of your day,
helping them to know the Gospel in a way they could understand
and come to love.
Strengthen us as students of the sacred scriptures
so that we may take Jesus' message and share it with our family,
our friends, and our community.
We want to live by the Gospel truths,
to love God with our whole hearts, and to love our neighbors, too.
Thank you for the gift of your writing.
May we embrace God's word in the Bible
and grow closer to him each day of our lives.
Amen.

SOMETHING TO PONDER

What are some of your favorite Bible verses or stories? Why are these passages special to you?

13.

Saint Margaret of Scotland

Paving a Way to Heaven for Our Families

ca. 1045–November 16, 1093
Patronage: Parents of Large Families, Against Death of Children
Memorial: November 16

MARGARET OF SCOTLAND'S STORY

Margaret was born into a royal family living in exile in Hungary. Her father, King Edward, an uncrowned and exiled king of England, and her mother, Agatha, a Hungarian princess, eventually moved the family to England. An educated, pious young girl, Margaret desired a religious vocation, but at the age of twenty-four she was married to the Scottish king, Malcolm III. The king, forty years old at the time of this second marriage, was illiterate and ill mannered, but he grew incredibly devoted to his queen. He often deferred to her advice and was supportive of her religious devotion. Together, they raised a family of eight children. Queen Margaret was responsible for great reform in Scotland, both culturally and spiritually. Her efforts to better align the Church in her new homeland with Rome led to rigorous spiritual revival among her people. Along with personally seeing to the education of her children, Queen Margaret cared for the poor, built churches and hostels for pilgrims, and promoted laws that better protected all Scottish citizens. She died only days after learning of the battlefield deaths of her husband and eldest son.

LESSONS FROM MARGARET

I have a dear friend who reminds me a lot of Margaret. This working mom of eight often gets more done before breakfast than I accomplish in an entire day. Her ticket to success? An active prayer life, coupled with a joyous attitude about her vocation as a Catholic mom. When we read about the life of Margaret, we find that a common theme running through her life is her devotion to strict prayer rituals and to the faith education of her children.

One parish named after the "Pearl of Scotland," as Margaret is known, recounts in its biographical account of its patroness that, "It is an interesting fact that of all the saints canonized by the Church of Rome, Margaret stands alone as the happy mother of a large family." This Catholic mother of eight who homeschooled, worked, was devoted to charity, and still found time to pray is the perfect spiritual companion for moms today who struggle to "do it all."

Margaret's confessor and biographer spelled out King Malcolm's reliance on his wife, particularly that he saw that "Christ truly dwelt in her heart." King Malcolm and Margaret often served the poor in person. They rose together to pray in the middle of the night not only during Lent, which was not uncommon, but also during a second penitential season the queen observed before Christmas. Together they instituted laws that reinstated observance of Sunday as a day of rest, by closing businesses and prioritizing a day of respite and prayer. This was a royal family who didn't just pay lip service to their faith, but rather grew in personal holiness while inspiring an entire nation to greater faith. Margaret's example reminds me to be a more loving spiritual companion to my husband—to dwell less frequently on his shortcomings and to focus more readily on helping him along his own path to sainthood through my prayer and loving personal service to him.

Most of us Catholic moms are not royalty. But in our homes, along with our husbands, we rule the roost—we are the queens of our domain. Along with all of our other domestic and professional duties, we often set the tone for the spiritual devotion of our families. Whether we are blessed with one child or with ten, whether our children are adopted or come to us through the blending of families, when we seek baptism for our children we promise to make their faith formation a top priority in our lives. This can often be a struggle, but in our moments of difficulty we can remember to turn in prayerful intercession to Margaret of Scotland, a busy mom who seemed to make it all work.

Margaret knew her fair share of hardship, raising one son who eventually disappointed his family and losing another along with her beloved husband to an early death in battle. But ultimately, her faith in Christ and her love for her family were her greatest legacies. She died surrounded by the children who loved her, anxious to seek her eternal reward.

On those days when I feel that the constant needs of my family or my professional work are draining me, when I lack time for personal prayer and can't seem to find the energy to help my friends in need, I remember the example of a Scottish queen who was able to live out the mandates of the Gospel, paving a way to heaven not only for herself but also for her husband, her children, and her people. Like Margaret, within my own home I have the opportunity to create a more loving, charitable, and prayerful culture, changing my little corner of our world.

TRADITIONS

Today, a relic of this remarkable woman rests in Saint Margaret's Roman Catholic Memorial Church in Dunfermline, where the Catholic schoolchildren celebrate a Mass in honor of their patroness each year on her feast day.

MARGARET'S WISDOM

I have two favors to ask of you: the first is, that you will remember my poor soul in your prayers and in the Holy Sacrifice, as long as God leaves you here below; the second is, that you will look to my children, and teach them to fear and love God.

THIS WEEK WITH SCRIPTURE

Sunday: Exodus 20:8–10

Remember to keep holy the sabbath day. Six days you may labor and do all your work, but the seventh day is the sabbath of the LORD, your God.

> *Today is your day, Lord. Help me to set work and worries aside and to make time with you and family on this Sabbath.*

Monday: Luke 18:22

There is still one thing left for you: sell all that you have and distribute it to the poor, and you will have a treasure in heaven. Then come, follow me.

> *Jesus, Light of the World, help me to treasure you over all else and to share my blessings freely with those in need.*

Tuesday: Psalm 51:14

Restore my joy in your salvation;
sustain in me a willing spirit.

> *You, Everlasting Strength, sustain me. Restore my joy in you.*

Wednesday: Proverbs 22:6

Train a boy in the way he should go;
even when he is old, he will not swerve from it.

Guide of our family, help my husband and me to train our children as they should go so that their path may lead to happiness with you forever.

Thursday: 1 Corinthians 3:9

For we are God's co-workers; you are God's field, God's building.

You are the builder, Lord. Help me to work in cooperation with your divine plan in order to build the faith of the family I love so dearly.

Friday: Mark 10:14–15

Let the children come to me; do not prevent them, for the kingdom of God belongs to such as these. Amen, I say to you, whoever does not accept the kingdom of God like a child will not enter it.

Father, help me to come to you as simply as my children do, with a heart of faith and trust. Draw us each nearer to your kingdom.

Saturday: 1 Peter 3:8–9

Finally, all of you, be of one mind, sympathetic, loving toward one another, compassionate, humble. Do not return evil for evil, or insult for insult; but, on the contrary, a blessing, because to this you were called, that you might inherit a blessing.

Shepherd of our family, may we always be a blessing to each other, compassionate, humble, and loving.

Saint-Inspired Activities

For Mom

Saint Margaret was an accomplished needleworker and used her skill at this hobby to create lovely altar cloths and vestments for her church.

Inquire about how you might help out with the liturgical environment or physical plant of your parish.

With Children

Saint Margaret reinstituted prayerful observance of Sunday as a day of rest in Scotland. Plan a special family day for this Sunday. Attend Mass together, enjoy a family meal, and consider playing a faith-related game, praying the Rosary, or reading Bible stories together in front of a cozy fire.

A PRAYER FOR OUR FAMILY

Pray as a family each day this week:

Good Saint Margaret of Scotland,
you were queen of your country and also queen of your home.
By example, you taught your children to love Jesus,
care for the poor, and work for justice as he taught us.
Open our eyes to those around us who are in need of our help and
our love.
Remind us to make prayer a priority in our lives
and to share God's love with all whom we meet.
Remember us to God as we work our way toward life with him
forever in heaven.
Amen.

SOMETHING TO PONDER

How are you paving a pathway to heaven for your family?

14.

Saint Benedict of Nursia

Writing Our Rule of Life

ca. 480–547
Patronage: Students, Against Temptations
Memorial: July 11

BENEDICT OF NURSIA'S STORY

Following his childhood in a noble Italian home with his twin sister Scholastica, Benedict began his academic career in Rome, but he discontinued his studies after becoming frustrated by the worldly and immoral character of the environment there. He retreated to Subiaco to live as a hermit. Others came requesting his leadership, and over time he established twelve monastic "deaneries"; but he ultimately left Subiaco due to a rift caused by jealousies and power struggles. Next

Benedict took a small group of companions and established a monastery at Monte Cassino, where he completed his life's work. His "Rule" governed not only his own brotherhood of monks but would go on to become the foundation for monastic life in Western Europe, with a consequent significant influence in the development of Western civilization.

LESSONS FROM BENEDICT

Although he lived over fifteen centuries ago, much of what life dealt to Benedict is very relevant to my life today as a modern Catholic mom. Perhaps this is why his Rule, written centuries ago and half a world away, continues to guide and edify not only monastic communities, but also lay individuals hoping to systematize the way in which we live out our daily lives and our commitment to spiritual disciplines.

Benedict's Rule was noted for being flexible, moderate, and yet spiritually adamant. He laid the groundwork for the administrative details and authoritarian roles that would facilitate a group of people living together in community. Two anchoring themes for his Rule were *pax* (peace) and *ora et labora* (pray and work). For those following Benedict's Rule, their primary duty of the day was participation in the Divine Office, perhaps more commonly known today as the Liturgy of the Hours. The twofold purpose of praying the Hours is to offer God praise and thanksgiving and to intercede for the needs of the world. So, while living apart from the world, Benedict's communities were deeply engaged with it through study, prayer, and the significant commerce that grew up around the monasteries. Priority was also given in the monastic day to private prayer, sacred reading, study, and manual labor.

Although it was established for those living the monastic life, there is much about Benedict's Rule that works perfectly for today's Catholic home. How many of us are looking for a little peace in the midst of our often ridiculously busy schedules? And for most Catholic moms, the concept of *ora et labora* is a melding that so beautifully helps us see the small prayers that accompany our daily work as a path to heaven. A decade of the Rosary recited while folding laundry or on a lunch break, a pause before eating lunch to share the Angelus, and small impromptu prayers throughout the course of our day create a rhythm of prayer for moms similar to the Divine Office (Liturgy of the Hours).

Benedict began his monastic life by withdrawing from a society he viewed as illicit and corrupt. He wasn't afraid to give up his inheritance, turn away from the sinfulness around him, and move to someplace with few creature comforts but great spiritual benefits. Most of us would never pull up stakes and move our families to live in a cave in the mountains. But every day, we are called, like Benedict, to be in the world but not of the world. We make small choices that are countercultural: opting not to see the latest movie hit with morally objectionable content; teaching our children to critique popular culture through the lens of faith and to reject its destructive elements, or refraining from overly materialistic lifestyles. To the outside world, we may look weird or different. Our neighbors may think we have too many kids, are too restrictive with them, or that we go to church too frequently. But if we're blessed enough to be living right, they may also wonder what the secret ingredient is that keeps us close, bonded, and happy in a world where families so often splinter and fail.

Your rule of life—the patterns by which your family works, plays, and prays together—will look different than mine. Moms with young children will often find themselves praying in fits and starts, enjoying precious moments with little learners by sharing Bible stories and teaching small prayers and traditions. Other moms may find time for blessings like communal Bible study or Rosary groups, while also balancing a return to a career with home organization duties and prayer time.

For most of us, a key common denominator of being a mom is too much to do and not enough time. And this is precisely where the blessing of having Benedict point the way comes in. In my own efforts to follow the spirit of his Rule, I endeavor to create peace in my home through loving relationships, well-established authority, and fostering respect for one another. I endeavor to be active in the world while trying not to be too worldly. I endeavor to mix work and prayer, prioritizing above all else a daily walk toward a closer relationship with God born out of structured devotions and the offering of each task I perform as an act of love.

TRADITIONS

One of the most popular traditions related to Benedict is the Saint
Benedict Medal, a two-sided circular medal that bears a cross and his
likeness, accompanied by symbols and initials that relate his charisms.
One wears the medal as a reminder of and constant prayer for God's
protection upon the one who bears it and to remind the wearer of his
or her dignity as a follower of Christ.

BENEDICT'S WISDOM

He who labors as he prays lifts his heart to God with his hands.

THIS WEEK WITH SCRIPTURE

Sunday: Matthew 6:33

But seek first the kingdom [of God] and his righteousness, and all
these things will be given you besides.

> *God, help me to seek you first, to order my day around time
> spent in company with you.*

Monday: Ecclesiastes 3:1

There is an appointed time for everything,
and a time for every affair under the heavens.

> *All time is yours, Lord. May I use the gift of this day in ways
> that are pleasing to you, which serve my family, and which
> draw me closer to the beauty of your love.*

Tuesday: Matthew 13:16–17

But blessed are your eyes, because they see, and your ears, because
they hear. Amen, I say to you, many prophets and righteous people
longed to see what you see but did not see it, and to hear what you
hear but did not hear it.

Jesus, bless me with your words, your truths, your love.

Wednesday: Ecclesiastes 3:12–13

I recognized that there is nothing better than to be glad and to do well during life. For every man, moreover, to eat and drink and enjoy the fruit of all his labor is a gift of God.

> *Loving God, today is a gift from you. Help me to be glad in my work, to see the fruits of the labor you have given me, and to praise you with my efforts.*

Thursday: Proverbs 13:4

The soul of the sluggard craves in vain,
but the diligent soul is amply satisfied.

> *When I am tired, God, feeling lazy and worn out, strengthen me. Lord, may my diligent work be a prayer and a sign of my love for you.*

Friday: John 14:6

Jesus said to him, "I am the way and the truth and the life. No one comes to the Father except through me."

> *Lord Jesus, you are the way, the truth, and the life. Let me follow the path you have laid before me to reach your Father by loving and studying your words.*

Saturday: Proverbs 16:3

Entrust your works to the LORD,
and your plans will succeed.

> *Lord, I entrust my plans, my works, my joys, and my struggles to you. Let any success be for your glory, and let any challenges be born with grace and perseverance.*

SAINT-INSPIRED ACTIVITIES

For Mom

Since the early centuries of the Church, many have prayed the Divine Office. Learn more about the Liturgy of the Hours and incorporate some portions of this wonderful liturgical prayer into your daily life. Prayer aids are available online or in print to begin praying this universal prayer of the Church.

With Children

Saint Benedict created a Rule for his monks, and many around the world still live according to this Rule. Hold a family meeting and begin to create a rule for your home, a systemized schedule for work and prayer that incorporates chores, school, career, and family prayer time. Start simply, but commit to living by your family's rule to create your own home's sense of *ora et labora.*

A PRAYER FOR OUR FAMILY

Pray as a family each day this week:

Dear Saint Benedict,
you committed your life to work, your brother monks, and your God,
filling each day with work and prayer.
Help our family to see the value of our work,
knowing that even the simplest chores can be done with a heart full
of love.
Aid us in finding ways each day to pray privately and to gather
together in prayer,
so that we might help one another to become holy.
May our simple sacrifices, our helping hands, and our daily prayers
be a sign of our love for the God who has blessed us beyond measure.
Amen.

SOMETHING TO PONDER

What activities, disciplines, and routines might you include in your personal rule for life?

15.

Saint Gianna Beretta Molla

Respecting the Dignity of All Human Life

October 4, 1922–April 28, 1962
Patronage: Pregnant Women, Against Abortion
Memorial: April 28

GIANNA BERETTA MOLLA'S STORY

Gianna Francesca Beretta was born in 1922 in Magenta, Italy, the tenth of thirteen children. Gianna's early years were marked with the untimely deaths of her sister Amelie and her mother Maria, as well as her own personal bout with an illness that placed her studies on hold for an extended period of time. She overcame these challenges and earned a degree in medicine, opened a clinic of her own, and later specialized in the practice of pediatrics. Gianna met and married

Pietro Molla, and the couple joyfully welcomed their children Pierlu-
igi, Maria Zita, and Laura. In the first trimester of her fourth pregnancy, Gianna began to experience symptoms that were later diagnosed
as a fibroma of the uterus. Counseled by her physician to undergo an
abortion to safeguard her own health, Gianna chose instead to have a
surgery, begging that the life of her unborn child be saved at whatever
cost to her own health. She carried her pregnancy to term, and on
April 21, 1962, Gianna Emanuela Molla was born. On April 28, 1962,
only days after giving birth, Gianna Beretta Molla died at the tender
age of thirty-nine. Her daughter Gianna Emanuela went on to follow
in her mother's footsteps as a physician and is active today in the pro-
life movement, continuing the powerful legacy her mother left for her
and mothers everywhere.

LESSONS FROM GIANNA

Gianna Beretta Molla paved the way to sainthood for modern moms.
In many ways, her life was a beautiful combination of embracing traditions of the past and delving into all the future has to offer. As a
professional woman, wife, and mother, she balanced many of the pressures I face today in my own life. She remained fully committed to her
career while at the same time safeguarding her relationships as wife
and mother. Long before dual-income families were the norm, Gianna
was teaching us about remaining faithful to one's callings both within
and outside the home.

During her years as a practicing pediatrician, Gianna Beretta Molla
balanced her practice of medicine with a devotion to her family, a tremendous piety, and a commitment to mothers, children, the elderly,
and the poor in her community. As a pediatrician, she sought to minister not only to her patients' bodies but to their souls as well. In my
everyday work, I try to emulate Gianna's example of being led first and
foremost by my Catholic perspective and values. Her life's work was
more than a job—it was her prayer, her witness, and ultimately her
path to sainthood. When I question my commitment to my career or
face an ethical dilemma in my work, Gianna's model of professional-
ism marked by social conscience helps me discern the route to choose.

Gianna made the truly valiant decision to continue a pregnancy she knew might lead to her death. For today's moms, the advances of medical technology make pregnancy much safer than it was for her, and yet these advances also create conflicts for parents of children who may be diagnosed with prenatal health anomalies. We may be advised by physicians who don't share our faith to terminate difficult pregnancies. As an older mom and in my personal battle with breast cancer, I've faced physicians who even ridiculed me for my willingness to remain open to life. In these moments, Gianna's valiant choice has been a beacon of hope and strength, and she remains a spiritual confidante for me in parenting challenges, in career transitions, and in my personal health-care journey.

TRADITIONS

Although Saint Gianna is one of our Church's newest saints, devotion to her has already spread widely. Many Catholic physicians are now seeking to embrace medical practices that employ new technologies while remaining committed to the Church's strong pro-life teachings. Additionally, physicians devoted to Saint Gianna's charism are working in her name to assist women formerly thought to be infertile to welcome the gift of life. Pregnant women now frequently turn to Saint Gianna as an intercessor in her role as their patroness.

GIANNA'S WISDOM

The secret of happiness is to live moment by moment and to thank God for all that He, in His goodness, sends to us day after day.

THIS WEEK WITH SCRIPTURE

Sunday: Psalm 139:13–14

You formed my inmost being;
you knit me in my mother's womb.
I praise you, so wonderfully you made me;
wonderful are your works!

Lord, I praise you for the gift of life in all its forms.

Monday: Jeremiah 1:5

Before I formed you in the womb I knew you,
before you were born I dedicated you,
a prophet to the nations I appointed you.

> *Good and Gracious God, you know me intimately just as you know and treasure the child in my womb. Today, I dedicate myself to loving you through my love for my children.*

Tuesday: Psalm 127:3

Children too are a gift from the LORD,
the fruit of the womb, a reward.

> *You have given me a great gift in my children, Lord. Help me to treat them as a treasured present.*

Wednesday: Genesis 3:16

To the woman he said:
"I will intensify the pangs of your childbearing;
in pain shall you bring forth children."

> *In pregnancy and childrearing, help me to bear physical and emotional challenges with strength, courage, and patience.*

Thursday: Luke 1:42

"Most blessed are you among women, and blessed is the fruit of your womb."

> *Blessed Mother Mary, be with me and all of those women who carry new life in their wombs or who experience the joy of motherhood through adoption or spiritual companionship.*

Friday: Deuteronomy 28:4

Blessed be the fruit of your womb,
the produce of your soil and the offspring of your livestock,
the issue of your herds and the young of your flocks!

> *God, your blessings come in many forms. Thank you for our family, for our livelihood, and for your care.*

Saturday: John 16:21

When a woman is in labor, she is in anguish because her hour
has arrived; but when she has given birth to a child, she no longer
remembers the pain because of her joy that a child has been born into
the world.

> *Jesus, be my companion in pregnancy and childbirth or in infertility, miscarriage, or awaiting adoption. Help me to bear the pains with patience and to savor each joy.*

SAINT-INSPIRED ACTIVITIES

For Mom

Spend time recalling your pregnancy journey or writing about a current pregnancy. Pray for pregnant women around the world and for those who have known the pain of infertility and miscarriage. Remember especially those in countries where lack of adequate medical care makes pregnancy and childbirth a life-threatening condition.

With Children

Adopt a crisis pregnancy center in your community. Clean out your closets, and invite your children to pass along their gently used infant clothing and toys to a mom in an unplanned pregnancy. Show your children their hospital photo or a picture from their ultrasound, and share with them the feelings you experienced when you learned you were pregnant with them.

A PRAYER FOR OUR FAMILY

Pray as a family each day this week:

Saint Gianna,
you loved your husband and children with the fullness of your heart,
and you gave your life for Gianna Emanuela, your newborn daughter.
Help our family to model your love for the sanctity and dignity of all human life.
Pray for our family members and friends who are joyfully awaiting the birth of a baby,
and send your protection to those faced with difficult pregnancies.
Pour out your healing on those who have lost a child or a loved one as she gave birth.
Please journey with us as we balance life's many demands
and in those moments when we face health challenges of our own.
May we always follow your courageous example
of commitment to life and ready service to those in need.
Amen.

SOMETHING TO PONDER

How has your commitment to your faith influenced your health-care decisions? How is your career part of your path to sainthood?

16.

Saint Alphonsus de Liguori

Finding Peace in Christ

September 27, 1696–August 1, 1787
Patronage: Theologians, Confessors
Memorial: August 1

ALPHONSUS DE LIGUORI'S STORY

Born to a Spanish mother and a nobleman father in Marianella near Naples, Italy, Alphonso de Liguori received a sound education and was considered a top-notch lawyer by the age of twenty. But in his heart he yearned for something more, so, despite his family's disapproval, he followed a vocation to the priesthood and was ordained in 1726. Alphonsus committed himself to a mission among the people and was renowned as a preacher, confessor, and one who made the faith accessible to the common person. He founded the Congregation of the Most Holy Redeemer in 1732, and although his order saw great upheaval during his lifetime, the Redemptorists are known today throughout the world for sharing the Gospel with those most greatly in need. Along with being a prolific writer, Alphonsus de Liguori was known for his profound love of Christ in the Eucharist and for the Blessed Mother. He served as Bishop of Saint Agatha until severe health problems caused him to retire. His twilight years were marked by severe pain, bouts of scrupulosity, ecstasies, and constant prayer. Alphonsus Maria de Liguori was proclaimed a Doctor of the Church for his work as a moral theologian.

Lessons from Alphonsus

As the primary faith-formation teacher for my children, I have often felt the burden and great responsibility of sharing my love for our Church with my boys in a way that does justice to its truths and beauties. I find it interesting that at every age, and through every stage of their development, the task of making something as intangible as faith accessible to them is a constant challenge. When they were little, they were much more likely to take things at face value. Now, having raised thinkers who tend to question just about everything, I find myself turning frequently in intercessory prayer to Alphonsus de Liguori for his wise, yet always loving, example.

Alphonsus was fueled in his ministry by a passion for taking the Gospel to those most in need of Christ's love, to the poor and spiritually abandoned souls living in the rural areas surrounding his home. Wherever they went to preach, Alphonsus and his brother priests set up a presence in the community, wanting to be as accessible as possible to their flock. Pope John Paul II recognized the gift of the Church's noted moral theologian, when he said of Alphonsus:

> What makes his writings such a success, and the secret of their charm, is the conciseness, clarity, simplicity, optimism, and kindness—almost tenderness. Alphonsus excluded nobody from his pastoral zeal. He wrote to all and for all.

We moms must be constantly ready to share the Gospel with our children, but we must also prepare ourselves for the real world challenges that can and will arise in our homes. When the "why" or "why not" questions come up in my home, I always try to remember to pause for quiet prayer before losing my composure. The amazing thing about these moments is that they give us the opportunity to grow in our own faith while we share it with those we love most. Next time one of your children questions you on a matter of Church teaching, why not invite her to join you in prayer and then enjoy doing a bit of research together? I fear sometimes that we moms think we need to have all of the answers, when sometimes the most prudent solution is to pause before jumping in with our version of "because I said so."

Alphonsus loved Christ and our Blessed Mother so greatly that his admiration literally overflowed into a treasure trove of books, hymns, and artistic works. But he also struggled throughout his lifetime with the spiritual burden of scrupulosity. Those who fall prey to scrupulosity obsess with great anxiety over every way in which they fall short of following God's laws. While we all sin and all have access to the Sacrament of Penance, the scrupulous person may become at once addicted to confession and yet unable to properly find grace in absolution. If you find yourself tending toward scrupulosity, experts recommend finding a committed confessor but also seeking spiritual direction and psychological support. For the rest of us, the life of Alphonsus, the patron saint of confessors, reminds us of the healing and the beauty that comes with making regular confession a part of our spiritual lives. Coupled with frequent reception of the Eucharist and a rich and active prayer life, we can find the fuel we need to follow our mission of bringing Christ's love to those around us.

TRADITIONS

Today, Redemptorist brothers and priests around the world continue Saint Alphonsus de Liguori's teaching legacy, working with the poor and abandoned, the alienated and un-churched, the hard to reach and the hard of hearing, with the spiritually destitute, with citizens and newcomers, and with the young and old of many languages and circumstances.

ALPHONSUS'S WISDOM

When we hear people talk of riches, honors, and amusements of the world, let us remember that all things have an end, and let us then say: "My God, I wish for You alone and nothing more."

THIS WEEK WITH SCRIPTURE

Sunday: Psalm 119:2

Happy are those who observe God's decrees,
who seek the LORD with all their heart.

> *It is you I seek, God, and it is your happiness alone that will help me to feel complete.*

Monday: 1 Timothy 2:3–4

This is good and pleasing to God our savior, who wills everyone to be saved and to come to knowledge of the truth.

> *Help me, Savior, to come to the knowledge of you and to lead my children to that same saving truth.*

Tuesday: Psalm 51:3–5

Have mercy on me, God, in your goodness;
in your abundant compassion blot out my offense.
Wash away all my guilt;
from my sin cleanse me.
For I know my offense;
my sin is always before me.

> *Cleanse me, Merciful Lord. My offenses are great, but your love is greater.*

Wednesday: Matthew 5:16

Just so, your light must shine before others, that they may see your good deeds and glorify your heavenly Father.

> *May my little light shine today, Father, and bring glory to your incredible goodness.*

Thursday: Romans 8:1–2

Hence, now there is no condemnation for those who are in Christ Jesus. For the law of the spirit of life in Christ Jesus has freed you from the law of sin and death.

> *Forgive me, Lord, for the times when I have fallen short or condemned others.*

Friday: Proverbs 28:13

He who conceals his sins prospers not,
but he who confesses and forsakes them obtains mercy.

> *I seek your mercy, God. Draw me nearer to you in the Sacrament of Penance. Help me to overcome my fears, knowing with certainty that you are always near.*

Saturday: Hebrews 11:1

Faith is the realization of what is hoped for and evidence of things not seen.

> *Steadfast Lord, help me to have faith beyond my simple capacity, and to hope for all you promise with great certainty.*

SAINT-INSPIRED ACTIVITIES

For Mom

Celebrate the Sacrament of Penance. In preparation for your confession, spend quiet time in an examination of conscience. Afterward, along with your penance, pray a decade of the Rosary, asking our Blessed Mother to intercede for you and for your children.

With Children

One of Saint Alphonsus's best-loved books is *Visits to the Blessed Sacrament.* Take your children for a special midweek visit to Christ present in the reserved Eucharist.

A PRAYER FOR OUR FAMILY

Pray as a family each day this week:

Good Saint Alphonsus,
you gave your life to help others learn about our faith.
You loved Jesus Christ and our Blessed Mother with all your heart.
Help us to follow your example of holiness and charity by sharing the Gospel through our words, but especially in our actions.
We ask you to intercede on behalf of all of those who do not know the love of God.
May we be God's messengers in our world,
and may we always find peace in your unending love for us.
Amen.

SOMETHING TO PONDER

Do you struggle with finding time to go to confession, or do you have other challenges that keep you from finding the grace of this sacrament? What challenges do you face in teaching your children the precepts of our Catholic faith?

17

Saint Maria Goretti

Protection for Our Children

October 16, 1890–July 6, 1902
Patronage: Youth, Victims of Rape, Poor
Memorial: July 6

MARIA GORETTI'S STORY

Maria's short life was marked with poverty and strife, yet she had a maturity and holiness well beyond her years. At the death of her father, Maria took over the household responsibilities and care of her siblings, while her mother worked to support the family in the home they shared with another tenement farmer, Giovanni Serenelli and his grown son, Alessandro. Maria was fully committed to the practice of her faith, and her piety led to early reception of her First Communion. Before her twelfth birthday, Maria was subjected to repeated sexual advances by Alessandro, which she consistently rebuffed. After a final rejection, Alessandro stabbed Maria fourteen times, leaving her at death's door. In the hours before her death, Maria forgave Alessandro for his offense. Her murderer served a prison sentence but ultimately credited her intercession for his conversion, dedicating the rest of his life to service at a Capuchin monastery. He was present along with her family at her canonization.

LESSONS FROM MARIA

Maria Goretti's brief life, so filled with tragedy, mirrors the hardship and pain that many of the world's children face. Many of our world's kids can relate to the life of a young girl called to grow up far before the end of her childhood. Like many of these, Maria's family knew poverty, hunger, and illiteracy. They lived in squalid conditions, sharing their home with strangers. Like Maria, many thousands of children face sexual assault every day of their young lives. Indeed, thousands are bought and sold as sex slaves in every nation of the world. While no mother would wish Maria's fate on her child, we can pull a few lessons from the life of this valiant young woman.

Our children are under constant assault from a world that so often attacks the values we hold to be true and good. They face a barrage of nearly pornographic images every day, growing up in a culture where terms like "cyber bullying" and "sexting" have become a part of the common lexicon. Most won't have to battle off rapists, but are confronted every day by temptations that lure them to turn their backs on what we are trying to instill in them in our homes and churches.

That Maria had the heart, the strength, and the courage to stand up against a horrific personal assault against her body and her beliefs at the age of eleven is compelling. That she had the spiritual maturity to forgive and even show compassion for her attacker seems almost incomprehensible.

Maria's legacy for me is not only the virtue with which she lived her life, but perhaps even more importantly the message of forgiveness and reconciliation she shared at the hour of her death. Her dying act of grace reminds me that I can, through the merit of my efforts, have an impact upon the world around me. In those frequent moments of debate with my children about the common excuse that "everyone else is doing it," I can turn to the boldness of Maria Goretti and invoke her intercession for my children. I can encourage them to be the ones who are *in* the world, but not *of* it, shining a light and holding fast to the belief that they can and will make a difference, one small choice at a time.

TRADITIONS

Saint Maria Goretti is recognized as a patron saint and intercessor for youth, rape victims, and the poor. She is a patron for the World Youth Day movement and a role model for modesty and purity in relationships.

MARIA'S WISDOM

Through love of Jesus, I forgive him with all my heart.

THIS WEEK WITH SCRIPTURE

Sunday: Psalm 51:12

A clean heart create for me, God;
renew in me a steadfast spirit.

> *Heavenly Father, renew my efforts to be pure, loving, and filled with your grace.*

Monday: Romans 12:2

Do not conform yourselves to this age but be transformed by the renewal of your mind, that you may discern what is the will of God, what is good and pleasing and perfect.

> *God, help me rise above all worldly pressures today as I try to listen and discern your will.*

Tuesday: Isaiah 1:16–17

Wash yourselves clean!
Put away your misdeeds from before my eyes;
cease doing evil; learn to do good.
Make justice your aim: redress the wronged,
hear the orphan's plea, defend the widow.

> *Help me, Lord, to hear the world's pleas and answer them.*
> *Cleanse me, heart and soul, to do your work.*

Wednesday: Galatians 5:25

If we live in the Spirit, let us also follow the Spirit.

> *Point me in the direction you would have me go, and fill me*
> *with the Spirit to be your hands in a world that so desperately*
> *needs your grace.*

Thursday: 1 John 2:10

Whoever loves his brother remains in the light, and there is nothing
in him to cause a fall.

> *For the many times when I have fallen, Father, I beg your*
> *forgiveness.*

Friday: 2 Timothy 2:21–22

If anyone cleanses himself of these things, he will be a vessel for lofty
use, dedicated, beneficial to the master of the house, ready for every
good work. So turn from youthful desires and pursue righteousness,
faith, love, and peace, along with those who call on the Lord with
purity of heart.

> *In my pursuit of faith, love, peace, and purity, cleanse me to*
> *be your vessel today.*

Saturday: Proverbs 6:20–23

Observe, my son, your father's bidding,
and reject not your mother's teaching;
keep them fastened over your heart always,
put them around your neck;
For the bidding is a lamp, and the teaching a light,
and a way to life are the reproofs of discipline.

> *God, I want to teach my children so many important things,*
> *to protect them, but most of all to share with them the joy*
> *of knowing your love. Equip me for the vocation you have*
> *granted me, helping me to build up my children for the path*
> *you have laid before them.*

SAINT-INSPIRED ACTIVITIES

For Mom

Saint Maria's act of forgiving her attacker left a lasting legacy. Examine a damaged relationship in your life this week and pray for reconciliation and forgiveness through the intercession of Saint Maria Goretti.

With Children

Speak with your children about the challenges of remaining pure, chaste, and committed in today's society. In an age-appropriate fashion, discuss with them how to act in instances of sexual, verbal, and other kinds of harassment. Ask them about bullying at school, and coach them about conflict resolution strategies and techniques.

A PRAYER FOR OUR FAMILY

Pray as a family each day this week:

Precious Saint Maria Goretti,
you gave your life to hold on to the faith you loved so dearly,

a faith that taught you a profound respect for your body
and your dignity.
Be with us in those moments when we do battle against the negative
pressures, degrading images, and destructive behaviors of our world.
Ask God to grant us the grace to withstand temptations
to what is wrong
and to make wise choices on behalf of what is good.
Let us follow your example of loving, forgiving,
and praying for those who have harmed us.
May we be like you were, a light for a world that is desperately in
need of hope, change, and love.
Amen.

SOMETHING TO PONDER

How can you prepare your children for the emotional and physical
challenges they will face in the future? How might you improve your
communication with your children?

18

Saint Théodore Guérin

Trusting God in Following Our Vocations

October 2, 1798–May 14, 1846
Patronage: Lafayette, Indiana
Memorial: October 3

THÉODORE GUÉRIN'S STORY

As the eldest surviving child in her family, Anne-Thérèse Guérin first realized her vocation to the religious life at the reception of her First Communion. However, the murder of her father and the inability of her mother to cope with that loss delayed her entrance into religious life until she was nearly twenty-five years old. After taking her final vows as a Sister of Providence in Ruillé-sur-Loir, France, then–Sister Théodore began to build a career in teaching. She was later called upon to travel to Indiana to begin a new mission in the Diocese of Vincennes. Despite her many misgivings and physical weaknesses, Théodore and her companions survived the treacherous journey to the New World. Théodore overcame struggles with her bishop, extreme poverty, and dangerous conditions to carry out her mission. Fueled by a fervent prayer life and love of the Eucharist, she trusted in God's divine providence and succeeded in founding schools, pharmacies, orphanages, and the nation's first Catholic institution of higher learning for women.

LESSONS FROM THÉODORE

Since I am a Hoosier by birth and the eldest daughter of two parents educated in Indiana classrooms by Sisters of Providence, a part of me claims a special kinship with the sickly French nun who overcame smallpox, perilous travel, and Church politics to say "yes" to God's will for her life. Surely any mother who has ever looked at a positive pregnancy test with shock and awe or received a middle-of-the-night call with good news from an adoption agency can know the sense of trusting in God's providence when you feel ill equipped to carry out your vocation. I'd imagine that there are many women like me who balked at the magnanimity of the responsibility of being a mom, wondering how we'd ever live up to all that is expected of us. And yet we know that God is infinitely good and that he is with us always, even when we don't feel qualified for our callings.

In a way, knowing that the word "providence" means "divine guidance or care" makes perfect sense to me when I see the religious order selected by Mother Théodore. She came to her vocation somewhat late in life. At the age of fifteen, despite her great desire to enter the convent, she became responsible for the care and support of her mother and younger sister. She'd known of her desire to serve as a nun since she was ten, and yet trusting in God's call meant waiting, enduring, and ultimately giving her life to the service of others in a way that was far different from what she had planned.

We moms often have plans for our lives. So many of us can look back at the checklists we've made that include a certain degree, a particular job, the perfect marriage, and a home full of kids, but we see circuitous paths that hold anything but the perfect one we'd sketched out.

Some of you reading this are at the beginning of that path, wondering what the future will hold for your lives. You can dream, imagine, and plot, but ultimately our vocation as Catholic moms means following Théodore's example and saying, "Yes, Lord," to the various twists and turns that fill our days.

Surviving members of Théodore's religious order write compassionately about her charism of prayer, trust in God's will, and uniting her personal sufferings to the cross and to the service of others. Théodore is quoted as having said, "With Jesus, what shall we have to fear?" In those moments when I am wracked with fear, with frustration, or with uncertainty, I always try to remember her lead in embracing the Eucharist, a life of prayer, and service to others as my personal path to sainthood.

TRADITIONS

The Sisters of Providence of Saint Mary-of-the-Woods, Indiana, continue Saint Théodore's work, serving the poor and needy in schools, parishes, health-care facilities, and social justice initiatives. Mother Théodore's legacy is also preserved with a scholarship program that recognizes the efforts of students who have "used their unique experiences, aptitudes, and abilities to make a difference in their local communities and beyond."

THÉODORE'S WISDOM

What must we do to become saints? Nothing extraordinary—only that which we do every day—only do it for the love of God.

THIS WEEK WITH SCRIPTURE

Sunday: Psalm 9:11

Those who honor your name trust in you;
you never forsake those who seek you, LORD.

Lord, help me to trust in you today, to remember that in seeking you I will find my way.

Monday: Psalm 37:5–6

Commit your way to the LORD;
trust that God will act
And make your integrity shine like the dawn.

> *Heavenly Father, so often I choose my way over yours. Let me act with integrity and with intention, carefully discerning your will when moments of choice occur.*

Tuesday: Romans 8:38–39

For I am convinced that neither death, nor life, nor angels, nor principalities, nor present things, nor future things, nor powers, nor height nor depth, nor any other creature will be able to separate us from the love of God in Christ Jesus our Lord.

> *Jesus, in those moments when I fear separation from you, remind me that your love is all I need to see me through the challenges and battles that fill my days.*

Wednesday: Psalm 25:1–2

I wait for you, O LORD;
I lift up my soul to my God.
In you I trust.

> *Lord, I commit my loved ones—my precious children and my beloved spouse—to your care and your protection. I trust in your providence, and I lift them to you.*

Thursday: Psalm 37:3

Trust in the LORD and do good
that you may dwell in the land and live secure.

> *God, I want to dwell in you—allow me to trust in the path you set before me, to do your good in my little corner of the world, and to live securely in the embrace of your love.*

Friday: Isaiah 12:2

God is indeed my savior;
I am confident and unafraid.
My strength and my courage is the LORD,
and he has been my savior.

> *I fear so often, Lord, for my children, for our finances, for the future—let me remember to turn to you in those moments when strength and courage fail me.*

Saturday: Proverbs 3:5–6

Trust in the LORD with all your heart,
on your own intelligence rely not;
In all your ways be mindful of him,
and he will make straight your paths.

> *Thank you for your providence, Lord, for the way in which you straighten my path to you. May I remember that in being mindful of you, in relying on your will, I will find the rest I seek.*

SAINT-INSPIRED ACTIVITIES

For Mom

Get outside of your comfort zone. Follow Saint Théodore's example and do something you have wanted to try but were afraid to undertake. Trust in God's providence for this project, especially if it involves being of service to others.

With Children

Find the cities of Ruillé-sur-Loir, France, and Saint Mary-of-the-Woods, Indiana, on an online mapping service, and follow the route Saint

Théodore and her sisters took to come to America. Talk about your own ancestors' path to this country and the trust they had in God's goodness to see them safely to their new home.

A PRAYER FOR OUR FAMILY

Pray as a family each day this week:

Dear Saint Théodore Guérin,
you trusted in God's plan for your life.
You overcame sickness and tragedy, strife and struggle,
to carry God's word and his love to those most in need.
Be with our family in those moments when we feel like giving up.
Remind us in our struggles to follow God's narrow path that despite the challenges and troubles we will face,
our rewards will be great.
May we rely on God's goodness when we doubt our abilities.
As we follow your example, may we always trust in the power of God's providence.
Amen.

SOMETHING TO PONDER

What obstacles keep you from fully trusting in God's plan for your life?

19.

Saint Teresa of Avila

Living Holiness in Our Humanity

March 28, 1515–October 4, 1582
Patronage: Headache Sufferers, Bodily Ills, Sick People
Memorial: October 15

TERESA OF AVILA'S STORY

Teresa Sánchez de Cepeda y Ahumada was born in Avila, Spain. When her mother died, Teresa was sent to a local Augustinian convent to be educated and protected from worldly influences. She ultimately joined the Carmelites, but she left the convent due to a prolonged and serious illness. During a period of painful medical interventions, Teresa became educated in mental prayer. Upon her eventual return to the convent, she underwent a profound conversion, completely devoting herself to Christ. This led her to found the Order of Discalced Carmelites, a reform order with stricter spiritual and physical prayer disciplines than the Carmelites. Teresa traveled extensively, founding monasteries for both men and women. She is most highly revered for her mystical writings, including her autobiographical works, *The Interior Castle* and *The Way of Perfection*. Written under obedience and showing profound divine inspiration, these were addressed to her sisters in faith but have gone on to provide spiritual nourishment for generations of Christians looking to grow in holiness.

Lessons from Teresa

Today, words like "feminist" and "reformer" often bear a political tone, conjuring divisive images rather than ones that unite and inspire. Yet both of these monikers aptly describe the woman who would go on to be canonized as Saint Teresa of Avila. Teresa of Jesus was not a great scholar. She suffered her entire life with physical ailments that would have left most of us permanently disabled or institutionalized. In her efforts to found convents and monasteries that embraced a more disciplined and Christ-centered rule and spirituality, she faced incredible opposition. Her mystical experiences were scrutinized and eventually approved as faithful, although many of her contemporaries doubted her motivations and veracity.

Despite her infirmities and the attacks on her character, Teresa of Avila is acclaimed as one of the first two female Doctors of the Church. But she never sought the spotlight. In fact, her personal "reversion" in her mid-forties left her more inclined to withdraw from society, seeking full immersion into the contemplative prayer she loved so dearly.

As a more mature mom, I find myself craving that same sense of intimacy with Christ that Teresa found in her prayer life. At times, I want to close out the world around me, hit the pause button, and go into cloister mode. Looking at Teresa's life more closely reminds me that this is not my state in life. Instead, my vocation calls me to an ever-deepening love affair with the Lord but also to openness to loving him through my actions in service of those who rely on me. Teresa's spirituality remains especially relevant for today's moms, who find ourselves deeply embedded in domestic and professional lives that seem to bear absolutely no resemblance to the life of a cloistered nun.

In her writings, she encouraged her sisters to live a balanced life—to be fueled by mental prayer and private meditation, but also to remain active in the communal practice of their faith, in the sacraments, and especially in works of charity, as is so beautifully revealed in her poem, "Christ Has No Body."

> Christ has no body but yours,
> No hands, no feet on earth but yours,
> Yours are the eyes with which he looks
> Compassion on this world,
> Yours are the feet with which he walks to do good,
> Yours are the hands, with which he blesses all the world.
> Yours are the hands, yours are the feet,
> Yours are the eyes, you are his body.
> Christ has no body now but yours,
> No hands, no feet on earth but yours,
> Yours are the eyes with which he looks
> Compassion on this world.
> Christ has no body now on earth but yours.

How can I look at these verses and not see the relevance they bear for my life? In the midst of headaches, lists that overburden, financial strains, and the simple day-to-day stresses of family life, I often feel so little energy for prayer or works of compassion. Yet Teresa of Avila teaches me that each small act of service is my love letter to Christ. She is also quick to remind me that the fuel for each task, large or small, is an active and fruitful prayer life.

When I constantly seek Christ's friendship, when I rest in the knowledge that God alone is enough, and when I give my very best to be obedient to God's will, I follow Teresa's lead. My path will not be perfect. I will know hardships. Some will come in the form of physical ailments—my own, or those of my loved ones. Others will be perhaps even more difficult to overcome—the spiritual trials I face, the lack of faith, or the "dark nights of the soul" when prayer does not come easily or at all. In these moments, I have the spiritual companionship of Teresa of Avila. Although she never gave birth, as a spiritual mother to many she faced so much of what I struggle to bear in my life. In my humanity, as I make each baby step toward Christ and each act of service for my family a prayer of thanksgiving, I give thanks to a reforming feminist who paved the way for me.

TRADITIONS

On August 27, Carmelites around the world celebrate the special feast of the Transverberation of the Heart of Saint Teresa of Avila. This event commemorates a mystical vision experienced by Teresa, a feeling of love and such profound appreciation for God's grace that it actually rendered a physical piercing of her heart. Saint Teresa of Avila is frequently portrayed in art as having her heart pierced by a spear or arrow of an angel.

TERESA'S WISDOM

Let nothing disturb you; let nothing frighten you. All things are passing. God never changes. Patience obtains all things. Nothing is wanting to him who possesses God. God alone suffices.

THIS WEEK WITH SCRIPTURE

Sunday: John 13:34

I give you a new commandment: love one another. As I have loved you, so you also should love one another.

True Vine, help me to love as you loved.

Monday: Song of Songs 7:11

I belong to my lover
and for me he yearns.

God, you are the lover of my soul. Be near to me.

Tuesday: Romans 12:21

Do not be conquered by evil but conquer evil with good.

> *Jesus, Wonderful Counselor, help me to conquer the evil I see with the good you inspire.*

Wednesday: Psalm 44:24–26

Awake! Why do you sleep,
O Lord? Rise up! Do not reject us forever!
Why do you hide your face;
why forget our pain and misery?
We are bowed down to the ground;
our bodies are pressed to the earth.

> *Father, may I remember to continually turn to you in prayer, even when I feel separated from the grace of your love.*

Thursday: Galatians 5:22–23

In contrast, the fruit of the Spirit is love, joy, peace, patience, kindness, generosity, faithfulness, gentleness, self-control. Against such there is no law.

> *Thank you, Lord, for the fruits of your Holy Spirit. Help me to embrace and to employ them.*

Friday: Proverbs 8:17

Those who love me I also love,
and those who seek me find me.

> *Lord, I seek you. Although I am unworthy, I long for your love.*

Saturday: John 14:2–3

In my Father's house there are many dwelling places. If there were not, would I have told you that I am going to prepare a place for you? And if I go and prepare a place for you, I will come back again and take you to myself, so that where I am you also may be.

*Jesus, above all else I hope to dwell with my loved ones in your
Father's house. Prepare a place for us, and help us to prepare
one another for the glory of your eternal home.*

SAINT-INSPIRED ACTIVITIES

For Mom

Saint Teresa of Avila founded the Discalced Carmelites and was known
for her spiritual reforms. Select one small penance or sacrifice. Offer
this discipline along with silent prayer for your husband and children.

With Children

Saint Teresa of Avila spread her spiritual gifts by writing about her
life. Have your children write or dictate to you a story from their own
spiritual life. Examples might include their recollections of receiving a
sacrament, how your family celebrates liturgical seasons, or even what
attending Sunday Mass means to them.

A PRAYER FOR OUR FAMILY

Pray as a family each day this week:

Saint Teresa of Avila,
you loved Jesus so greatly that you gave your whole life to him.
Be with us as we journey toward loving Christ and one another
more completely.
Remind us to follow your example of loving obedience.
Help us to bear the physical crosses and emotional burdens that make
us tired or sad.
Please intercede on behalf of our loved ones who are ill or separated
from God,
that they will know the full grace of his healing love.
Thank you for your friendship, your zeal, and your passion that help
point our way to heaven.
Amen.

SOMETHING TO PONDER

How is your mental prayer life these days? If the noise of the world is crowding out the sound of God's loving voice in your life, how can you recapture silence in your day?

20.

Saint André Bessette

Seeking Kinship with the Communion of Saints

August 9, 1845–January 6, 1937
Memorial: January 6

ANDRÉ BESSETTE'S STORY

Stemming from humble origins, André Bessette was born the eighth of twelve children and orphaned by the age of twelve. Sickly and nearly illiterate, André lived a transient life before embracing his vocation as a Holy Cross brother. His superiors doubted his capabilities, but through the intervention of the local archbishop he professed his final vows and was sent to the Collège Notre Dame of Montreal to serve as porter. André ministered to the poor and visited the sick, the homebound, and the hospitalized. A series of healings were attributed to him. Soon pilgrims from around the world began to descend upon this humble man and seek his counsel and intervention. André had an incredible devotion to his personal patron, Saint Joseph, and credited the saint with intervening on behalf of the ill, giving all glory to God for the miracles that were unfolding around him. He desired to build a great shrine in honor of Saint Joseph at the top of Mount Royal. With limited money but a passion for his work, André collected sufficient funds to honor his patron with a small structure that would later become the world's largest Josephine shrine, the Oratory of Saint Joseph. Defying all odds, André lived to the age of ninety-two and worked tirelessly until his death on behalf of the poor and those needing physical and spiritual healing. At the time of his death, over one million people came to pay tribute to the simple porter who had changed the world one prayer at a time.

LESSONS FROM ANDRÉ

In many ways, the mundane tasks that fill my life are similar to the jobs André carried out each day in his role as porter at Notre Dame. It's unlikely that many of his superiors imagined the good works that would arise through the life of this man they thought ill equipped to be a religious brother. Like André, I sit at the portal of our home, welcoming friends and tending to the needs of my family. I clean house and nurse the sick, I go to work, buy groceries, cook, and transport children—my days are filled with routine little chores that few would ever call saintly.

If left to rely on his own skills and natural abilities, it's unlikely that André would have been anything more than a humble servant. But André had a passion for his faith that enabled him to transcend his limitations and do great things. He believed so fully in the intercession of Saint Joseph that he ministered and healed in the name of the patron of laborers, devoting much of his life to the building of a fitting memorial for the earthly father of Jesus. But as strongly as he loved Saint Joseph, his love and reverence for the passion of Jesus Christ lay at the core of his life. In Jesus' name, André tended to the sick, advising them to seek medical care and to seek Christ in the Eucharist and in the Sacrament of Penance. André recognized the healing intercession of the Communion of Saints and the power of faith to bring transformation, hope, and healing.

Some days, it feels difficult to believe that the path to sainthood is paved with laundry, dishes, and dirty diapers, or with the backlog of tasks or stacks of paperwork that fill our days on the job. But like André, you and I have the chance to share life's greatest blessings with those we love most. When we wipe a feverish brow, when we match a pair of socks, when we welcome friends and neighbors lovingly into our homes, we spread our love of Christ to those who matter most. When we exercise the skills and talents God has blessed us with to care for others in our professional lives we emulate André's hospitality. André had a unique love of the poor, the needy, and those living on the margins of society. In truth, he had every reason to fail, and yet in spite of his own frailty and the lack of resources at his disposal he persevered. Looking at his life reminds me to open the doors to life's opportunities with faith, remembering to turn in confidence to the Communion of Saints who have gone before me in those moments when I feel I can't go on.

TRADITIONS

Pilgrims visiting Saint André's beautiful Saint Joseph's Oratory in Montreal often ascend a portion of its 283 stairs on their knees in penitential prayer, uniting themselves with Christ's passion and death on the cross. Students at Holy Cross College in Notre Dame, Indiana, frequently pray through the intercession of Saint André for his special favor on their behalf, placing handwritten prayers beneath a statue that resides on the campus founded by the Brothers of Holy Cross.

ANDRÉ'S WISDOM

I am nothing . . . only a tool in the hand of providence, a lowly instrument at the service of Saint Joseph.

This Week with Scripture

Sunday: Hebrews 12:1–2

Therefore, since we are surrounded by so great a cloud of witnesses, let us rid ourselves of every burden and sin that clings to us and persevere in running the race that lies before us while keeping our eyes fixed on Jesus, the leader and perfecter of faith.

> *Father God, help me to keep my eyes fixed on your Son, Jesus,*
> *as I run the race that lies before me.*

Monday: Revelation 7:17

For the Lamb who is in the center of the throne will shepherd them
and lead them to springs of life-giving water,
and God will wipe away every tear from their eyes.

> *Lamb of God, Lord Jesus, wipe the tears from my loved ones'*
> *eyes and lead us to your Father in heaven.*

Tuesday: 1 John 1:7

But if we walk in the light as he is in the light, then we have fellowship with one another, and the blood of his Son Jesus cleanses us from all sin.

> *Light my path, God, as I walk toward you.*

Wednesday: John 17:20–21

I pray not only for them, but also for those who will believe in me through their word, so that they may all be one, as you, Father, are in me and I in you, that they also may be in us, that the world may believe that you sent me.

> *Jesus, I want to be one with you. Open my heart today to fully*
> *trust, to fully embrace, and to fully love.*

Thursday: 1 Thessalonians 4:13–14

We do not want you to be unaware, brothers, about those who have fallen asleep, so that you may not grieve like the rest, who have no hope. For if we believe that Jesus died and rose, so too will God, through Jesus, bring with him those who have fallen asleep.

> *God, I pray for the Communion of Saints. For those known to the world, and for the quiet saints who have shaped my own life, may their souls and all the souls of the faithful departed rest in you.*

Friday: 2 Corinthians 4:17–18

For this momentary light affliction is producing for us an eternal weight of glory beyond all comparison, as we look not to what is seen but to what is unseen; for what is seen is transitory, but what is unseen is eternal.

> *May I bear my afflictions, my worries, and my crosses with grace, knowing that they contain the weight of your love for me.*

Saturday: Romans 8:28

We know that all things work for good for those who love God, who are called according to his purpose.

> *God, thank you for your wonderful design for my life, and for the example of the saints who teach me that your plan, your purpose, is always perfect.*

SAINT-INSPIRED ACTIVITIES

For Mom

Saint André had a passion for serving the sick, the marginalized, and the despondent. Pay a visit to a homebound parishioner, a friend, or a relative in a nursing home to deliver a warm meal or a few simple words of encouragement.

With Children

In his early childhood, André's father, a lumberman, taught his son a love for his patron, Saint Joseph. Research with your children the lives of their own patron saints. Read their stories, learn their lessons, and plan a family feast with a few meals in honor of some of your family's Communion of Saints.

A Prayer for Our Family

Pray as a family each day this week:

Saint André Bessette,
you opened the door to everyone who needed your help.
You knew that their healing and happiness could be found
in loving Jesus,
in receiving the sacraments, and in living out his Gospel promises.
Help us to look outside ourselves to those who need help.
When we are tired or feel weak and unqualified,
help us to know that we can move mountains if we but cling to
Christ's love
and the powerful intercession of the saints.
May we follow your example of passionately loving Christ and our
neighbors.
Amen.

Something to Ponder

Who are some of your personal patron saints? How have their lives of virtue provided an example for your own life?

21.

Saint Jane Frances de Chantal

Supporting Those Who Parent Alone

January 28, 1572–December 13, 1641
Patronage: Widows, Forgotten People
Memorial: August 12

JANE FRANCES DE CHANTAL'S STORY

Jeanne-Françoise Frémyot was born in Dijon, Burgundy, to a parliamentary president and his wife, who died before the child's second birthday. By the age of twenty, Jane married Christophe de Rabutin, the Baron de Chantal, and together they had six children, three of whom survived. Sadly, only eight years into the marriage Christophe perished in a terrible hunting accident, plunging his young widow into a dark depression and a period of intense prayer. Following years spent parenting her children and offering charitable acts within her community, she partnered with her spiritual director Saint Francis de Sales to found the Congregation of the Visitation of Holy Mary and devoted herself to a life of contemplative prayer and acts of charity. Jane Frances de Chantal was a renowned spiritual advisor and personally visited over sixty of her order's eighty-six houses.

LESSONS FROM JANE FRANCES

Jane Frances de Chantal found a way to turn her life's tragedies into fuel for a life committed to prayer and service. The young baroness started her married life with great joy but also knowing her share of trials. She applied her energy and focus to her husband's castle, reclaiming order in a place that had been left to fall into shambles. She bore six children with the love of her life, but sadly buried three of them. When her husband was killed in an accident and died after nine days of suffering, Jane struggled to forgive the man responsible for his death and committed herself to a vow of perpetual chastity. As a young widow, she lived with her father-in-law, but the relationship was filled with difficulties. Even the housekeeper at her new home treated her poorly.

Through all of her trials, Jane's commitment to prayer was her salvation. Rather than focusing on her own losses, she turned her attention to serving those around her, generously supporting the poor and tending to the sick. Her life was greatly changed one Lent when she heard the preaching of Francis de Sales, then a bishop, who would go on to be her lifelong spiritual director and friend. It was Francis who encouraged her to see to the care of her children before finally devoting her life to a religious vocation.

Jane Frances de Chantal is the patron saint of widows, but her life also yields lessons for moms who struggle with feelings of isolation, anxiety, or depression because of their deep desires to remain faithful to their callings. Surely, women who know the tragic loss of a spouse suffer in a way most of us can never comprehend. But many mothers face the day-in, day-out challenges of devoting our lives to the domestic needs of others and frequently being cut off from support and encouragement. Stay-at-home moms who spend most waking hours alone at home with children often face terrible loneliness and even depression.

Moms who work outside their homes often feel the tremendous pressure of having two full-time jobs and not being able to do either as well as they'd like. Women who are married to those serving in the military, who work erratic schedules or long days, or who travel frequently often face the anxiety of feeling like a single parent.

Jane found her answers to the spiritual darkness that plagued her for her entire life by focusing on something outside of herself. She built an order that was specifically for those whose lives didn't fit traditional convent settings. Her houses welcomed elderly women, widows, and others whose vocations came as a result of different paths. Always at the forefront of their work were gentleness and humility, virtues exemplified for them by their beloved Francis de Sales.

These two watchwords—gentleness and humility—have become more and more important to me in my mothering. Often, the constant demands of parenting—of giving so fully of myself to others that I have nothing left for me—can lead to my own struggles with spiritual dryness and desperation. Whether you are a widow, a single mother, or simply a mom who feels like your husband can't get home soon enough, you need to make time for prayer in your life. And in those moments when God feels distant and unhearing, I need to cling even more passionately to prayer, persevering especially in those dark nights of the soul when I begin to doubt everything. But these are also times to reach out, to seek support and companionship, and to allow friends and loved ones to journey with me as Francis de Sales and Jane de Chantal accompanied one another.

TRADITIONS

Saint Jane Frances de Chantal's Visitation Sisters continue her legacy of contemporary prayer and service in over thirty countries around the world. Whether praying, gardening, cooking, or cleaning, the sisters continue to offer their "work as a living prayer as did the Virgin Mary in her home in Nazareth."

JANE FRANCES'S WISDOM

What God, in his goodness, asks of you is not this excessive zeal which has reduced you to your present condition, but a calm, peaceful uselessness, a resting near Him with no special attention or action of the understanding or will except a few words of love, or of faithful, simple surrender, spoken softly, effortlessly, without the least desire to find consolation or satisfaction in them.

THIS WEEK WITH SCRIPTURE

Sunday: Isaiah 1:17

Learn to do good.
Make justice your aim: redress the wronged,
hear the orphan's plea, defend the widow.

> *Today, Lord, let me do good for those in my life who need my help.*

Monday: Deuteronomy 24:19

When you reap the harvest in your field and overlook a sheaf there, you shall not go back to get it; let it be for the alien, the orphan or the widow, that the LORD, your God, may bless you in all your undertakings.

> *God, help me to share my blessings and always to expect nothing in return but the joy of knowing you.*

Tuesday: Psalm 68:5–7

Sing to God, praise the divine name;
exalt the rider of the clouds.
Rejoice before this God
whose name is the LORD.
Father of the fatherless, defender of widows—
this is the God whose abode is holy,

Who gives a home to the forsaken,
who leads prisoners out to prosperity,
while rebels live in the desert.

> *Lord, come to the aid of those in my life who are poor, without shelter, and without knowledge of your saving love.*

Wednesday: Psalm 147:5

Great is our Lord, vast in power,
with wisdom beyond measure.

> *Wise and Powerful Lord, bring your loving sustenance to those who need food, shelter, strength, and courage in times of trial.*

Thursday: James 1:27

Religion that is pure and undefiled before God and the Father is this: to care for orphans and widows in their affliction and to keep oneself unstained by the world.

> *Am I stained by the world, God? Today, help me to run toward you and away from anything that separates me from your love.*

Friday: 1 Timothy 5:5

The real widow, who is all alone, has set her hope on God and continues in supplications and prayers night and day.

> *Heavenly Father, in those moments when I feel most alone, may I remember to turn to you in prayer and find my hope in you.*

Saturday: Psalm 10:13–14

Why should the wicked scorn God,
say in their hearts, "God doesn't care"?
But you do see;

you do observe this misery and sorrow;
you take the matter in hand.
To you the helpless can entrust their cause;
you are the defender of orphans.

> *Thank you, Lord, for your constant care and a love that knows*
> *no bounds.*

SAINT-INSPIRED ACTIVITIES

For Mom

Saint Jane de Chantal benefited from her spiritual direction and correspondence with Saint Francis de Sales. Consider consulting with a spiritual director on a regular basis. Seek recommendations of certified directors, priests, or religious sisters in your area who provide spiritual direction.

With Children

Saint Jane de Chantal's Visitation Sisters are known for feeding the hungry and caring for the sick. Cook together and deliver a meal to an elderly parishioner or simply a busy mom who might benefit from a night off from cooking.

A PRAYER FOR OUR FAMILY

Pray as a family each day this week:

Gentle Saint Jane de Chantal,
you found a way to help others with your prayers and service
even when your own life was filled with challenges.
We commit ourselves in a special way to praying for our friends who
are going through difficult times.
Please intercede for our friends who struggle with illness, grief, or
financial disappointment, that they may soon be happy and healthy.
Help us to remember that even when we struggle,

there are those who need our help and support.
May we follow your example of loving and caring for others.
Amen.

SOMETHING TO PONDER

Do you ever feel isolated in your role as a mom? How can you seek the support you need to lovingly carry out the demands of your vocation?

22

Saint Matthew

Serving As Good Stewards of Our Family Finances

First Century
Patronage: Accountants, Bankers, Bookkeepers
Memorial: September 21

MATTHEW'S STORY

The son of Alphaeus, Matthew, also called Levi, was a Galilean publican collecting taxes during the reign of Herod Antipas from an office in Capharnaum. When called by Jesus, Matthew left his work and immediately followed. After his calling, Matthew hosted Jesus at his home for a feast where Jesus dined with tax collectors and others who were also considered sinners by the Jewish community, bringing upon himself the disapproval of peers and religious officials. Although there is no consensus on Matthew's authorship of the gospel attributed to him, we can safely assume that he lived out the remainder of his life as an apostle of Jesus Christ and as an evangelist who fully gave himself to the spreading of the Gospel.

LESSONS FROM MATTHEW

How does the life of a first-century tax collector possibly relate to the world of today's Catholic mom? At first glance, the connection may not be apparent, but the more I learn about Matthew, the more I find myself turning to him for his intercession.

It's likely that as a publican, this Jewish tax collector whose name means "gift of the Lord" led a very comfortable life. It's also likely that his profession led him to perhaps make decisions and take actions that were contrary to his beliefs and the precepts of his Jewish faith. So when called by Jesus with the simple words, "Follow me," the gospel states that Matthew "got up and followed him." I often wonder whether this patron saint of bankers, accountants, and bookkeepers gave any second thoughts to his financial well-being or if he thought he should have given a two-week notice. Perhaps Matthew's immediate following of Jesus and welcoming Jesus into his home signaled that he was willing to completely forsake a professional environment that he felt might be leading him into sin.

As stewards of our families' finances, we may think it foolhardy and irresponsible to think about walking away from our employers. But Matthew's action does point to a few life lessons we may want to keep in mind, whether we're the family breadwinner, the budgetmaster for our homes, or simply the mom who does her best to clip coupons and compare prices at the grocery store. The truth is, regardless of how much our income is, most of us stress out over money. As wives and mothers, we're called to be responsible stewards of the gifts God gives us. But sometimes we fall prey to the sins of anxiety, envy, and materialism.

Matthew's response to Jesus' call reminds me to keep a few things in their proper perspective. My work is about more than the number on my paycheck. My husband and I have a responsibility to provide for our family, to invest ethically and responsibly, to support those less fortunate than ourselves, and to take into account God's providence. Time and time again, we hear Jesus calling us to lives of humility, of service, and of material poverty. Matthew's example does not mean that I need to drop everything, sell all of my earthly possessions, and abandon my family immediately. But it does mean that I need to embrace prayerfully and with purpose my role as keeper of my family's finances.

Matthew traded in a life of wealth for one of obscurity, uncertainty, and even pain. After Jesus' death, he made it his life's mission to spread the Gospel truths to his Jewish friends and countrymen. His greatest lesson to me comes in the verses of the sixth chapter of the gospel attributed to him: "Look at the birds in the sky; they do not sow or reap, they gather nothing into barns, yet your heavenly Father feeds them. Are not you more important than they? Can any of you by worrying add a single moment to your life-span?" As so many families struggle economically, deal with unemployment, and face other, often debilitating, financial crises, Jesus' words as delivered to us by Matthew remind me that fear and anxiety can sometimes be a true test to my faith.

The most important lesson I derive from Matthew is the reminder to remember each and every day, within the context of my own little world and regardless of the circumstances, to get up and follow Jesus.

TRADITIONS

The body of Saint Matthew lies in the crypt of the Cattedrale di San Matteo in Salerno, Italy. The residents of Salerno hold a procession in their patron's honor, carrying a statue of his likeness through the city streets and worshipping in the cathedral crypt, on his solemn feast day, September 21.

MATTHEW'S WISDOM

There is no reason for surprise that the tax collector abandoned earthly wealth as soon as the Lord commanded him. Nor should one be amazed that neglecting his wealth, he joined a band of men whose leader had, in Matthew's assessment, no riches at all. Our Lord summoned Matthew by speaking to him in words. By an invisible, interior impulse flooding his mind with the light of grace, he instructed him to walk in his footsteps. In this way Matthew could understand that Christ, who was summoning him away from earthly possessions, had incorruptible treasures of heaven in his gift.

—Saint Bede the Venerable on Saint Matthew

THIS WEEK WITH SCRIPTURE

Sunday: 1 Timothy 6:10

For the love of money is the root of all evils, and some people in their desire for it have strayed from the faith and have pierced themselves with many pains.

> *Lord, help me to be a good steward of my family's money, but to never let financial goals become more important to me than loving you and my family with all my heart.*

Monday: Acts 20:35

In every way I have shown you that by hard work of that sort we must help the weak, and keep in mind the words of the Lord Jesus who himself said, "It is more blessed to give than to receive."

> *Father, help me to use my treasures—both spiritually and financially—to be of service to others.*

Tuesday: Matthew 19:21

Jesus said to him, "If you wish to be perfect, go, sell what you have and give to [the] poor, and you will have treasure in heaven. Then come, follow me."

> *Jesus, I fall so short of being perfect. Help me to leave material concerns behind and to embrace your path with a joyful heart.*

Wednesday: Matthew 6:34

Do not worry about tomorrow; tomorrow will take care of itself. Sufficient for a day is its own evil.

> *Mother Mary, I have so many friends whose lives are filled with anxiety and concern due to financial struggles. Please help them to embrace your Son's teachings and to know his peace in their lives.*

Thursday: Psalm 37:21

The wicked borrow but do not repay;
the just are generous in giving.

> *God, we have many blessings to share. Let me always err on the side of generosity, as you did in sending your Son, Jesus.*

Friday: 2 Corinthians 9:8

Moreover, God is able to make every grace abundant for you, so that in all things, always having all you need, you may have an abundance for every good work.

> *May I count each grace, each measure of abundance, and may I recognize and praise you as their source.*

Saturday: Matthew 6:25–27

Therefore I tell you, do not worry about your life, what you will eat [or drink], or about your body, what you will wear. Is not life more than food and the body more than clothing? Look at the birds in the sky; they do not sow or reap, they gather nothing into barns, yet your heavenly Father feeds them. Are not you more important than they? Can any of you by worrying add a single moment to your life-span?

> *God, forgive me for those moments when I forget your abundant provision in my life. Let me leave all worry behind and do your will in serving as a steward for my family and in modeling compassion to my children.*

SAINT-INSPIRED ACTIVITIES

For Mom

Take stock of your family's long- and short-term financial goals. Alongside your spouse, examine your household budget, investments, insurance coverage, will, and provisions for charitable giving.

With Children

Discuss an accountability system with your children and consider adopting the "10-20-30 Go!" plan in your home. This plan combines an emphasis on prayer, reading, and participation in household chores. Find additional details at http://102030go.com.

A PRAYER FOR OUR FAMILY

Pray as a family each day this week:

Saint Matthew,
without hesitating, you left all you had to follow Jesus,
welcoming him into your home
before setting out on an unknown path
to embrace and share his teachings.
We want to follow him as you did,
caring more for the Gospel than we do for earthly treasures.
Help us to be good stewards,
to be responsible with the resources we have,
and to share our blessings with those in need.
Intercede for all those we know who are facing financial difficulties,
and help us always to be grateful in prayer and deed
for each gift in our lives.
Amen.

SOMETHING TO PONDER

How can you be a better steward of your family's financial blessings? What charitable organizations would you like to support with your time, talent, and treasures?

23.

$\mathscr{B}$lessed $\mathscr{C}$hiara "$\mathscr{L}$uce" $\mathscr{B}$adano

Finding Grace in Our Challenges

October 29, 1971–October 7, 1990
Memorial: October 29

CHIARA BADANO'S STORY

Chiara Badano was born in Sassello, Italy, to parents of modest means who had waited eleven years to welcome a child into their family. The active, lovable, and pious little Chiara grew into a busy teen who loved athletics, dancing, and being with her friends, especially fellow members of the Focolare Movement's GEN youth. At sixteen, Chiara consecrated her life to the Lord. At seventeen, a sharp pain in her shoulder while playing tennis led to her diagnosis with osteosarcoma, an aggressive form of bone cancer. Chiara continued to grow in spirituality and grace throughout her illness, ministering to the family, friends, and health-care professionals who were drawn to her deep love for Jesus Christ. Chiara "Luce" Badano died in 1990, leaving behind a lasting legacy of faith, hope, and love.

LESSONS FROM CHIARA

Some saints walk a path to virtue that extends over decades. Others live much shorter lives but leave such a lasting impact that their legacy is noted almost immediately. Chiara Badano is one of these, a teen whose love for Christ burned so brightly that she definitely earned her nickname "Luce," which means "light."

For most of her life, Chiara might have seemed like any other young, Italian, Catholic teen. Active, sporty, and filled with life, she loved hanging out with friends and was the center of her parents' universe. Through her deepening involvement in the GEN youth arm of the Focolare Movement, Chiara grew in faith and soon decided to seek a vocation to the religious life. But fate had another plan for this young lady with the infectious smile. Chiara's diagnosis with cancer sidelined her plans to become a nun or missionary, but it ultimately became her path to sainthood. The grace and courage with which she not only accepted but actually embraced her physical suffering became a testament to those around her, even the non-Christian medical personnel who cared for her.

A lot of us moms play the "what if?" game with ourselves, questioning how we would possibly handle an extended illness, or worse yet, the infirmity or disability of one of our children. For many, this improbability becomes reality, and worlds are turned inside out. Chiara's mom, Maria Teresa, knew every mother's worst nightmare on the day of Chiara's diagnosis. And yet the mom who probably thought she would need to care for her daughter became the one who was supported, when Chiara met her diagnosis with such a brave and positive attitude. Most of us would far prefer to face a health crisis ourselves than to watch one of our children suffer. Maria Teresa and Ruggero Badano had a front-row seat to a life of sanctity that ultimately would change the world as Chiara became a voice of light to the worldwide Focolare movement.

I never had the pleasure of knowing Chiara Badano, but I'm thrilled as a mom to be able to follow the example of this girl who turned deadly illness and pain into a personal *fiat*, her own "yes" to a life united with Christ's suffering. I also love that I can share Chiara's life with my teenage sons and with young people around me who so desperately need positive, faith-filled role models. Our teens are often given a bad rap as we sometimes consider them too wired and too self-serving. Yet my personal experience with teens reminds me that most of them are loving, open, and giving souls who want to make our world a better place. Chiara was like this, firmly convinced that she could make a difference, and in the end she did. Her days may have been numbered, but she went to heaven trusting that her destiny was a life united with Christ forever. So great was her anticipation for that moment that she even prepared for her own funeral Mass as she would have planned a nuptial Mass.

Chiara has become an evangelist for the youth of a world greatly in need of their contributions, spirit, gifts, and love. From her, I learn the importance of giving God my daily "yes" to all that comes along, the good and the bad. I learn not to shy away from tragedy but rather to discover in it a path to Jesus. When I'm sent reeling by a perceived calamity, I conjure in my mind the image of a smiling teen, refusing to accept morphine to alleviate her sufferings because she wished to remain "lucid" to share her hope and her joy with those seated around her. Chiara Badano witnesses for me that sometimes the things that seem like the greatest crosses to bear can become my greatest benedictions and paths to radical, life-changing love.

TRADITIONS

Founded in 1943 in the middle of World War II by Italian laywoman Chiara Lubich, Focolare aims to spread a spirituality of unity in prayer and in love. The movement continues to grow worldwide, seeking interreligious dialogue and social change.

CHIARA'S WISDOM

It's for you, Jesus; if you want it, I want it, too.

This Week with Scripture

Sunday: John 17:24

Father, they are your gift to me. I wish that where I am they also may be with me, that they may see my glory that you gave me, because you loved me before the foundation of the world.

> *Jesus, thank you for your love. Please help me to bear my small crosses, to believe more fully, and to accept more completely the blessing of your love in my life.*

Monday: 2 Samuel 22:29

You are my lamp, O LORD!
O my God, you brighten the darkness about me.

> *As I welcome the brightness of a new day, God, I thank you for the light you pour into my heart.*

Tuesday: Romans 13:11–12

For our salvation is nearer now than when we first believed; the night is advanced, the day is at hand. Let us then throw off the works of darkness [and] put on the armor of light.

> *For those moments when I have failed you, Lord, accept my sorrow.*

Wednesday: Matthew 18:20

For where two or three are gathered together in my name, there am I in the midst of them.

> *In moments of struggle and pain, Lord, strengthen me to share the gift of prayer with my children, knowing that you will be in our midst.*

Thursday: Isaiah 42:6–7

I, the LORD, have called you for the victory of justice,
I have grasped you by the hand;
I formed you, and set you
as a covenant of the people,
a light for the nations,
To open the eyes of the blind,
to bring out prisoners from confinement,
and from the dungeon, those who live in darkness.

> *You have called me, Lord. Let me walk in your light and answer your call.*

Friday: Matthew 5:14

You are the light of the world. A city set on a mountain cannot be hidden.

> *Your light shines in me, God. Let me never hide my love for you, and let my actions shine brightly for your glory.*

Saturday: Galatians 2:19–20

I have been crucified with Christ; yet I live, no longer I, but Christ lives in me; insofar as I now live in the flesh, I live by faith in the Son of God who has loved me and given himself up for me.

> *Jesus, I struggle with such small burdens compared to the immensity of your love for me. In these moments of grief, let me fully live by faith, trusting completely in you.*

SAINT-INSPIRED ACTIVITIES

For Mom

Blessed Chiara Badano was a teen who changed our world for the better. Share her story with a teen in your life or speak with your parish's youth ministry about Blessed Chiara. Further explore Focolare and consider joining the movement.

With Children

Blessed Chiara Badano believed that she could help to change the world with her message of love. Talk with your children about ways in which they can make their own little corner of the world a better, more loving place.

A PRAYER FOR OUR FAMILY

Pray as a family each day this week:

Blessed Chiara Badano,
you are a light for our family.
Jesus chose you to help spread his message of hope and of love,
and you said "yes" to his invitation,
even when you were ill and in pain.
Help us to bear the small crosses and challenges in our lives
with your courage and your grace.
Remind us to be good friends to those we know who are suffering
from illness.
Please intercede on their behalf
so that they might know healing and relief.
May we learn to say "yes" like you, to share your joy and passion for
our faith, and to always love Jesus as you did.
Amen.

SOMETHING TO PONDER

What crosses do you currently struggle with in your life? How does the certainty of God's love help you to bear these pains?

24

Saint Mary of the Cross MacKillop

Fidelity to the Church and Her Teachings

January 15, 1842–August 8, 1909
Patronage: Australia
Memorial: August 8

MARY MACKILLOP'S STORY

Born the eldest of seven children to Scottish parents who had migrated to Australia, Mary spent much of her young adulthood working to help support her family. Her path as a young teacher led her to a partnership with Father Julian Edmund Tenison Woods. Together with the young priest, Mary co-founded the Sisters of Saint Joseph of the Sacred Heart. The order worked to provide education and services to Australia's poorest of the poor, building schools across the country including in far-flung rural areas. The sisters' intent to minister wherever they saw a need eventually led to political developments within the Australian church, which ultimately resulted in Sister Mary's temporary excommunication by her bishop, who later lifted the excommunication. Sister Mary later traveled to Rome, obtaining formal approval for her order's rule, and she continued to be recognized as the spiritual force behind their good works, despite her ill health, until the time of her death in 1909. Her canonization as Saint Mary of the Cross MacKillop, Australia's first saint, on October 17, 2010, by Pope Benedict XVI is believed to have caused the largest pilgrimage of Australian citizens to the Vatican ever. Her sisters continue their good works serving and educating the poor in all corners of the world.

LESSONS FROM MARY

Living as Catholics can sometimes feel like a great challenge. As we endeavor to live our faith—in conformity with Catholic teaching, committed to justice, open to the promise of new life, and rooted in the Gospel—we may feel like odd women out. We are the ones who aren't racing to amass material wealth and ple asures but rather who are concerned with being faithful disciples of Jesus Christ and keeping our eyes set on the peace of heaven. In many ways we are called to be countercultural.

Mary MacKillop would also have been seen by many as countercultural. She founded schools and provided services for the poor all over Australia, following families wherever the need was greatest. Through economic crises, health dilemmas, and nearly constant turmoil, she persisted. Yet rather than winning acclaim for her work, she fell victim to a set of political circumstances in the Church she'd devoted her life to and was actually excommunicated by her bishop. Somehow, this amazing woman rose above the anger and heartbreak she surely felt, accepted her circumstances, and refused to denigrate the Church or blame those responsible for her fate. Surely it was her active prayer life that saw her through the pain of excommunication and that later gave her the grace to completely forgive those who had wronged her.

Some say that we now face some of the darkest hours in the history of our Church. The sexual abuse crises and a devastating shortage of priests, as well as political and ideological divisions within the Church in the United States, have driven many to abandon the faith. For those of us who remain, we often receive mixed messages and may feel confused and ill prepared to stand up for the truths we have been taught by the Church. In these moments, we can turn to the example of Mary MacKillop, a strong woman who always remained steadfastly committed to the teachings of the Church, even in her darkest hours.

Surely much of Mary's unwavering loyalty to the magisterium of the Church stemmed from a spiritual fortitude fueled by the Eucharist and by her utmost belief in the value of her mission. In those moments when I feel myself awash in negativity or tempted to go against what I know to be right and true, I turn to Mary MacKillop for her intercession and for her model of selfless devotion to others.

TRADITIONS

Today, the Mary MacKillop Memorial Chapel in North Sydney contains the tomb of Saint Mary MacKillop. The chapel, known as Mary MacKillop Place, has become a place of pilgrimage for travelers from around the world who come to seek inspiration and healing through the intercession of this amazing woman. Both Pope John Paul II and Pope Benedict XVI have prayed at the saint's tomb.

MARY'S WISDOM

Never see a need without doing something about it.

THIS WEEK WITH SCRIPTURE

Sunday: Hebrews 13:16–17

Do not neglect to do good and to share what you have; God is pleased by sacrifices of that kind.

Obey your leaders and defer to them, for they keep watch over you and will have to give an account, that they may fulfill their task with joy and not with sorrow, for that would be of no advantage to you.

Lord, enable me to look around and see opportunities to do good and to help those in need of your love.

Monday: 1 Thessalonians 5:11

Therefore, encourage one another and build one another up, as indeed you do.

May I use my words to build up those I love and to build up your kingdom here on earth.

Tuesday: 1 Peter 2:9

But you are "a chosen race, a royal priesthood, a holy nation, a people of his own, so that you may announce the praises" of him who called you out of darkness into his wonderful light.

Jesus, you call me out of darkness and into your light. I want to follow that light, to know that I am your chosen one, and to be that light to others.

Wednesday: 1 Corinthians 12:12

As a body is one though it has many parts, and all the parts of the body, though many, are one body, so also Christ.

What is my part in the body, God? As I work to discern your will for my life, I pray for the grace to see your plan for me and to know my place in the Body of Christ.

Thursday: James 5:16

Therefore, confess your sins to one another and pray for one another, that you may be healed. The fervent prayer of a righteous person is very powerful.

Please bless all of those in need of healing, Lord, especially those who have been hurt in some way by your Church. May they know your love, your grace, and your healing for their wounds.

Friday: Ephesians 2:19–20

So then you are no longer strangers and sojourners, but you are fellow citizens with the holy ones and members of the household of God, built upon the foundation of the apostles and prophets, with Christ Jesus himself as the capstone.

> *Heavenly Father, may this household you have built among us follow the path Jesus laid ahead of us.*

Saturday: Colossians 3:12–14

Put on then, as God's chosen ones, holy and beloved, heartfelt compassion, kindness, humility, gentleness, and patience, bearing with one another and forgiving one another, if one has a grievance against another; as the Lord has forgiven you, so must you also do. And over all these put on love, that is, the bond of perfection.

> *Thank you for choosing me to be your beloved, despite flaws and shortcomings. Bind me and my family always in the perfection of your love.*

SAINT-INSPIRED ACTIVITIES

For Mom

Pray for those who are struggling in our Church, including our Holy Father, priests and all those who lead us. Pay a visit or do something special for an aging priest or sister in your diocese, or make a modest financial contribution to your favorite religious order in remembrance of those who have given their lives in service to the Church.

With Children

Have your children create a poster for your home with the words, "Never see a need without doing something about it." List needs you see in your neighborhood and have the children draw pictures on the poster of simple things that they can do to help. Then make a simple plan and do it.

A Prayer for Our Family

Pray as a family each day this week:

Dear Saint Mary of the Cross MacKillop,
you never gave up your love for our Church and her people,
even when some in the Church turned their back on you.
Wherever you found a need, you also found a way to be of help.
Help us to remember those who are in need in our community.
We ask your aid in overcoming whatever obstacles we may face,
including our own doubts, weaknesses, and selfishness.
We want to follow your lead of serving the poor, the lonely, and those
who do not know the love of Christ in their lives.
Intercede for us, that we may never see a need without doing
something about it.
Amen.

Something to Ponder

What is your typical response when you see someone in need? How
can you more fully forgive those who have wronged you in some way?

25

Saint Thomas More

Finding Blessings in a Blended Family

February 7, 1478–July 6, 1535
Patronage: Stepparents, Adopted Children, Lawyers
Memorial: June 22

THOMAS MORE'S STORY

Thomas More was born and educated in London prior to serving as a page for the Archbishop of Canterbury. After time at Oxford, More studied the law, became an accomplished lawyer, and married Jane Colt, the mother of his four children. When Jane died, Thomas expeditiously married the widowed Alice Middleton and raised her daughter alongside his own children and along with an orphan girl who became his foster daughter. Thomas More had a bright legal career, rising through the political and societal ranks and ultimately being named Lord Chancellor to King Henry VIII. As tensions rose between the king and the Catholic Church, Sir Thomas More resigned his role. He ultimately refused to swear allegiance to the king following the Act of Succession, because by doing so he would have been expressing approval for the king as the rightful head of the Church of England. For this refusal, More was imprisoned in the Tower of London and his family suffered great loss and poverty. He was ultimately martyred for the crime of treason, refusing to compromise his spiritual values and belief in the primacy of the Church.

LESSONS FROM THOMAS

Thomas More is perhaps best known for his role as a statesman, an apologist, and an important figure in English political history. But when I turn to him in conversation, it's most frequently for his expertise as a loving parent. As a daddy's girl and the eldest in my family, it's easy for me to relate to the affectionate relationship Thomas cherished with his oldest daughter, Margaret. Like my own father—who calls each of us his favorite when the others aren't around—More had enough love to go around and showered it abundantly on his children.

Politics, writing, and the law aside, family life was something Thomas More treasured. He believed passionately in the faith formation of his children, encouraging them to read aloud from scriptures at the family dinner table and modeling a disciplined prayer life. He was also a firm champion of classical schooling and saw that all of his children, including his daughters, received a formal education.

When tragedy hit the More home with the death of Thomas's first wife, Jane, he was relatively quick to wed Alice Middleton. He recognized the importance of a mother for his four young children and welcomed Alice and her own daughter, also named Alice, into the home. More would also raise the orphaned Margaret "Mercy" Giggs as a foster daughter following the death of her mother, a midwife.

With more Catholics than ever living in blended families, we can look to the home of Thomas More for inspiration in meeting the challenges that stepparents, adoptive parents, and foster parents face. My good friend Heidi Hess Saxton, an adoptive mom, an author, and founder of the Extraordinary Moms Network, once described the distinctive example Thomas offers for parents facing special obstacles and blessings.

> Foster and adoptive parents need to be especially flexible and open to changes to "the plan." And yet, like Saint Thomas, we also need to be prepared to stand for truth, and to guard against the negative influences of society. As foster parents, we are often called upon to mitigate the negative effects of our children's early experiences. Loving discipline, combined with large doses of patience (of which I am naturally in short supply, but God provides!), will help to ensure that however rocky their beginnings, our children will blossom to become who God originally created them to be.

For as long as I can remember, I have pulled my sons with me into voting booths, discussed current events with them, and challenged them to be good Catholics but also good citizens. As I watch them grow into young men, I hope that these early and frequent conversations will provide them with a framework, an informed mind, but most importantly a moral perspective to guide their path through life. When the tough moments, the perilous decisions, and the forks in the road arise, I hope my boys are armed with the values, the humanity, and the decency to make right choices, even when doing so is difficult or countercultural.

Thomas More knew great success in his endeavors. His family lived in prosperity, and he counted bishops and the political elite as his friends. Yet when the time came for him to stand up for the truths he knew to be certain, he did not hesitate to turn his back on the good life and follow his soul. He went to a martyr's death with the words, "I die the King's good servant but God's first" on his lips. In the moments when I face my own tough decisions and for the times my children will have to do so in a world fraught with all kinds of craziness, I rely on Thomas More for wisdom, for intercession, and for friendship.

TRADITIONS

Saint Thomas More authored the social fantasy *Utopia* and invented the word "utopia," which is now common parlance for an ideal community or society. Originally written in Latin, the book is still widely read centuries after its original release.

THOMAS'S WISDOM

Those in the Catholic Church, whom some rebuke for praying to saints and going on pilgrimages, do not seek any saint as their savior. Instead, they seek saints as those whom their Savior loves, and whose intercession and prayer for the seeker he will be content to hear. For his own sake, he would have those he loves honored. And when they are thus honored for his sake, then the honor that is given them for his sake overflows especially to himself.

THIS WEEK WITH SCRIPTURE

Sunday: Matthew 10:39

Whoever finds his life will lose it, and whoever loses his life for my sake will find it.

> *Jesus, Lamb of God, grace me with the courage to die to self in totally loving you.*

Monday: Psalm 126:5

Those who sow in tears
will reap with cries of joy.

> *Help me, Bread of Life, to find my joy in you.*

Tuesday: 2 Corinthians 4:11–12

For we who live are constantly being given up to death for the sake of Jesus, so that the life of Jesus may be manifested in our mortal flesh.

So death is at work in us, but life in you.

> *Jesus, help me to teach my children to know that life in you is their path to eternal happiness.*

Wednesday: Psalm 34:18

When the just cry out, the LORD hears
and rescues them from all distress.

> *Father, remind me to cry out to you for help when I am lost
> and weary. Thank you for rescuing me with your love.*

Thursday: 1 Peter 4:13

But rejoice to the extent that you share in the sufferings of Christ, so
that when his glory is revealed you may also rejoice exultantly.

> *I rejoice in you, Lord.*

Friday: Hebrews 11:6

But without faith it is impossible to please him, for anyone who
approaches God must believe that he exists and that he rewards those
who seek him.

> *Perfect my faith so that I may find my reward in you.*

Saturday: James 1:12

Blessed is the man who perseveres in temptation, for when he has
been proved he will receive the crown of life that he promised to
those who love him.

> *When I am tempted, Lord, help me to seek your way and to
> show my children the path to your perfect crown—salvation.*

SAINT-INSPIRED ACTIVITIES

For Mom

Offer your prayer support to a mom living in a blended family, an adoptive mom, or a mom raising a child with special needs. Pray through
the intercession of Saint Thomas More for her and her family.

With Children

Talk with your children about their dad and the role he plays in their lives. Prepare a gift or special meal to honor him. If your children are old enough (probably middle school at least), have a family movie night and enjoy *A Man for All Seasons*. This 1966 winner of an Academy Award is based upon the life of Saint Thomas More and is rated for general audiences.

A Prayer for Our Family

Pray as a family each day this week:

Saint Thomas More, wise and brave,
you paid the ultimate price to stand up for your faith and our Church.
Be with us when we face challenges or decisions that tempt us
to go against what we know is right.
Intercede on behalf of our political leaders and judges,
that they may make good, moral decisions
in their service of our community.
We pray for those living in blended families,
for children and families awaiting adoption,
and for all those who face difficulty in their family life.
May we all know the grace of God's unconditional love
and his perfect peace in our homes.
Amen.

Something to Ponder

Are you raising your children to follow their consciences when making life decisions? When faced with choices in your own life, do you pray prior to acting?

26

Saint Margaret Clitherow

Ethical Practice of Our Occupations

ca. 1556–March 25, 1586
Patronage: Businesswomen, Converts, Martyrs
Memorial: March 26

MARGARET CLITHEROW'S STORY

Margaret Middleton was born in 1556 to Protestant English parents and married at age fifteen to John Clitherow, a wealthy, widowed businessman and civic leader. Within a few years, Margaret converted to Catholicism and began to fervently practice her faith, seeing to the catechesis of her children. At a time when the Catholic Church was persecuted in northern England, her great love for the Eucharist drew her to harbor priests illicitly in her home, where she hosted Mass and provided a haven for Catholics wishing to practice their faith. Such practices were punishable by death. Margaret's courageous activities ultimately led to her arrest. She adamantly refused to enter a plea and force a trial that would require her beloved children and servants to testify against her. As a result, Margaret Clitherow was brutally martyred for the faith she loved so dearly.

LESSONS FROM MARGARET

Margaret was just a teen when her marriage to a wealthy butcher catapulted her into running a home and the hands-on management of a bustling business. This is likely the reason that one of the few female "Martyrs of England" is noted as the patron saint of businesswomen. She was charming, full of good wit, and beloved by her neighbors and customers. In fact, even her Protestant friends and acquaintances admired her so much that they would warn her in times of danger, not wanting to see her or the Clitherow family come to harm for their illicit practice of Catholicism. In her business dealings, Margaret always fixed fair prices, never gouged her customers, and generously gave alms to those in need.

Margaret could easily have rested on her wealth, practiced the Protestantism of her husband and her society, and enjoyed a comfortable life. Instead, she steadfastly clung to her beliefs, even after she was imprisoned for not attending Protestant worship. During her time in prison, she employed her sharp intellect to learn even more about the precepts of Catholicism to teach herself Latin, and to study the gospels, the writings of the early Church Fathers, and other spiritual resources. In the end, she paid the ultimate price for standing fast in her convictions and died a martyr's death with her head held high.

As a wife, a mom, and someone with a job to do, how many times a week are you called upon to make small compromises that test your values and morals? If you're in a business setting, or even if you're simply trying to make ends meet in the management of your own home, it's easy to cut corners or to give in when ethical dilemmas arise. Whether it's a white lie at work or trying to get away with something you know to be wrong at home, when we refuse to stand up for what we know to be good, right, and true, we fail as Catholic women. When I really pay attention, I find these moral crossroads come plentifully every day, and I find myself all too often hesitating at these forks in the road and wanting to do what's expedient or what will least "rock the boat."

In these moments, I find myself turning to the example of Margaret, who never seemed to cut moral corners with her business or her personal life. In the twilight hours of her final imprisonment, Margaret mentally prepared herself for the torture she knew she would face, but she was also adamant in her protection of her spouse and children. Although John and Margaret Clitherow never reconciled their personal disparity of faith, theirs was a marriage filled with love and respect. Margaret left to her children a legacy of religious conviction, raising two sons who would go on to the priesthood and a daughter who would commit to a vocation as a religious sister.

It's inconceivable to me that I will ever be called to face in my life the choices Margaret encountered as a Catholic mom. But each day, in so many ways, I need her powerful intercession to help keep me on the straight and narrow. For the charismatic way in which she lived out her life and built her business, for the fortitude with which she pressed on in her beliefs, and for the courage and grace with which she accepted her ultimate path to sainthood, she has earned my great respect. Margaret is the type of businesswoman I strive to be—one who remembers her friends, treats her customers fairly, and doesn't back down from a challenge, regardless of the consequences.

TRADITIONS

The Shrine of Saint Margaret Clitherow in "The Shambles" area of York, England, welcomes pilgrims from around the world who visit to pray and pay their respects to this brave martyr. Visitors to the home inhabited by the Clitherow family view the "priest hole" through which priests escaped to safety if they were discovered by the authorities while celebrating Mass in Margaret's home.

MARGARET'S WISDOM

By God's grace all priests shall be more welcome to me than ever they were, and I will do what I can to set forward God's Catholic service.

This Week with Scripture

Sunday: Luke 16:10

The person who is trustworthy in very small matters is also trustworthy in great ones; and the person who is dishonest in very small matters is also dishonest in great ones.

Father, in matters small and great, let me earn your trust in me.

Monday: Proverbs 3:27–28

Refuse no one the good on which he has a claim
when it is in your power to do it for him.
Say not to your neighbor, "Go, and come again,
tomorrow I will give," when you can give at once.

Today, I will give at once to those who have need of my goods, my prayers, or my love.

Tuesday: Ephesians 4:25

Therefore, putting away falsehood, speak the truth, each one to his neighbor, for we are members one of another.

May your truth always be on my lips, Lord.

Wednesday: Ecclesiastes 11:6

In the morning sow your seed,
and at evening let not your hand be idle:
For you know not which of the two will be successful,
or whether both alike will turn out well.

Help me, God, to fill the gift of this day with industriousness: to create, to sow, to build, and to plant according to your designs for my life.

Thursday: Psalm 112:5–6

All goes well for those gracious in lending,
who conduct their affairs with justice.
They shall never be shaken;
the just shall be remembered forever.

> *Jesus, help me to follow your Gospel examples of true justice
> and to conduct all of my affairs with your perfect love.*

Friday: 1 Thessalonians 4:11–12

Aspire to live a tranquil life, to mind your own affairs, and to work
with your [own] hands, as we instructed you, that you may conduct
yourselves properly toward outsiders and not depend on anyone.

> *Father, help our family to be less concerned with keeping up
> with others and more concerned with keeping your commands.*

Saturday: Philippians 2:3–4

Do nothing out of selfishness or out of vainglory; rather, humbly
regard others as more important than yourselves, each looking out
not for his own interests, but [also] everyone for those of others.

> *I struggle with the virtue of humility, Lord. May my works be
> good and pleasing to you and helpful to others.*

SAINT-INSPIRED ACTIVITIES

For Mom

Pay close attention to ethical dilemmas that arise in your vocation.
Pray for the courage to stand up for your convictions and consider how
Saint Margaret Clitherow would respond to such situations.

With Children

Before attending Mass as a family, give your children an age-appropriate lesson on the history of the persecution some Catholics have faced in the free expression of their religious beliefs. Pray together in thanksgiving for our religious liberties and for the priests who devote their lives to sharing the Eucharist with us.

A PRAYER FOR OUR FAMILY

Pray as a family each day this week:

Brave Saint Margaret Clitherow,
you were a wife, a mom, and a businesswoman.
But the most important thing in your life was your love for Jesus
Christ and his Church.
Help us to grow in courage and wisdom when we are called to stand
up for our faith.
Lead us to right decisions when we have difficult choices to make.
Please intercede on behalf of all those in the world
who still face horrific persecutions for their love of the Lord.
May they know peace, comfort, and strength
as they journey to heaven.
Amen.

SOMETHING TO PONDER

What types of moral dilemmas and difficult choices do you face in your work? How can you seek God's will in these decisions?

27

Saint Damien of Molokai

Being the Touch of God for Others

January 3, 1840–April 15, 1889
Patronage: Lepers
Memorial: May 10

DAMIEN OF MOLOKAI'S STORY

Jozef De Veuster was born to a farming family in Tremelo, Belgium. He discerned his vocation to the priesthood early in life and joined the Congregation of the Sacred Hearts of Jesus and Mary. Having taken the name of Damien, the young man prayed daily through the intercession of Saint Francis Xavier to be a missionary. The young seminarian's greatest dreams came true when his superiors sent him to the mission field in Honolulu. Damien was ordained to the priesthood in 1864, and in 1873 he volunteered to go to the remote leper colony, Kalaupapa, on the island of Molokai to minister to those afflicted with Hansen's disease. After sixteen years living, working, and praying among them, Father Damien succumbed to the ravages of the disease and died in 1889. His renown has extended beyond his beloved Hawaii, and he is extolled by world and religious leaders as a true hero.

LESSONS FROM DAMIEN

By nature, I seem to have a weak stomach. So as a mom, one of my greatest challenges has been caring for the physical needs of my family when someone becomes ill. As a new mom, I was completely unprepared for the amount of time I'd have to spend dealing with other people's bodily functions and cleaning up the results of sick little (and then later, big) bodies. But somehow our good God provides, and I've learned to steel my stomach when confronted with things that would have knocked me out before I became a mom.

Perhaps the same was true for Damien of Molokai. I find it unlikely that when this young Flemish priest volunteered to be sent to the remote island of Molokai to care for those suffering from Hansen's disease (then known as leprosy), he could have even imagined the physical horrors he would confront—the sights, smells, and sounds of the suffering. Somehow, he was able to see beyond the sheer repugnance of their physical conditions and recognize the spiritual afflictions and virtues of his flock. The shock and disgust didn't keep Damien from ministering to every aspect of his congregation's needs. He ministered to them spiritually but also provided hands-on medical care, built their cottages and coffins, and buried their dead.

What stands out for me when I look at the life of Damien is the true dignity with which he treated his parishioners. He was able to look beyond the disease that ravaged them and see people who deserved to be treated with compassion and care. During the course of his lifetime, treatment for those suffering with Hansen's disease became far more advanced and humane as charitable donations from around the world enabled the building of medical-care facilities, orphanages, an aqueduct, and a proper church. Damien's volunteer commitment ultimately became his death sentence when he contracted and died of Hansen's disease. But before his death, he welcomed brother priests and the Sisters of Charity, who would ultimately witness the discovery of a cure for Hansen's disease and the freeing of those once held hostage physically and emotionally in Kalaupapa.

Most of us moms will never know the sheer physical, emotional, and spiritual stress faced by Father Damien, but we will find ourselves challenged quite frequently by the various illnesses and maladies that can plague any family. We will face times when our kids are bombarded with the flu, with colds, with broken bones, and even with learning disabilities and mental and stress-related illnesses. We'll need to play nursemaid not only to our children, but likely to our husbands, our neighbors, and perhaps our own parents. And many times, we will be called on to nurse others when we are sick, exhausted, and dispirited in our own right.

A few of us will find ourselves parenting children with catastrophic diagnoses, or nursing spouses with deadly diseases. We will ask God and ourselves, "Why?" and, "How?" "Why is this happening to my family? How can I possibly deal with this situation? Why me, Lord? Why this child? Why my husband?" We will plead, "I can't do this alone, Lord."

But the truth we learn from the life of Damien is that we aren't in this alone. Damien was quoted as having written to his brother, "I make myself a leper with the lepers to gain all to Jesus Christ. That is why, in preaching, I say 'we lepers'; not, 'my brethren.'" In those moments when I care for ills, big and little, Damien's example reminds me that in helping others to carry the cross of illness, and in bearing it myself, I gain the promises of Christ. I am his hands and his heart in those moments, difficult as they may be.

Let's remember to invoke Damien's aid and support when we don't feel up to the task, when we feel bitter, or when we too need nursing.

TRADITIONS

The state of Hawaii annually celebrates Father Damien Day. A statue of the saint resides on the steps of the United States Capitol building. Father Damien is often invoked as a spiritual intercessor for those suffering the physical and spiritual battles associated with HIV and AIDS.

DAMIEN'S WISDOM

Kindness to all, charity to the needy, a sympathizing hand to the sufferers and the dying, in conjunction with a solid religious instruction to my listeners, have been my constant means to introduce moral habits among the lepers. I am happy to say that, assisted by the local administration, my labors here, which seemed to be almost in vain at the beginning, have, thanks to a kind Providence, been greatly crowned with success.

THIS WEEK WITH SCRIPTURE

Sunday: Matthew 25:34–36

Come, you who are blessed by my Father. Inherit the kingdom prepared for you from the foundation of the world. For I was hungry and you gave me food, I was thirsty and you gave me drink, a stranger and you welcomed me, naked and you clothed me, ill and you cared for me, in prison and you visited me.

> *Lord, help me to care for the sick in my life as if I were caring for you.*

Monday: Luke 5:12–13

Now there was a man full of leprosy in one of the towns where he was; and when he saw Jesus, he fell prostrate, pleaded with him, and said, "Lord, if you wish, you can make me clean." Jesus stretched out his hand, touched him, and said, "I do will it. Be made clean." And the leprosy left him immediately.

> *Jesus, help me to have complete confidence in your healing strength as the leper did. Let me be made clean by your love.*

Tuesday: Joshua 1:9

I command you: be firm and steadfast! Do not fear nor be dismayed, for the LORD, your God, is with you wherever you go.

*For those moments when I doubt my ability to cope with all
that is on my plate, especially when caring for the sick in my
family, let me be steadfast in my belief.*

Wednesday: Matthew 5:4

Blessed are they who mourn,
for they will be comforted.

> *Heavenly Father, when I mourn help me to find your comfort
> in the loss I face.*

Thursday: Psalm 103:2–5

Bless the LORD, my soul;
do not forget all the gifts of God,
Who pardons all your sins,
heals all your ills,
Delivers your life from the pit,
surrounds you with love and compassion,
Fills your days with good things;
your youth is renewed like the eagle's.

> *I need strength and renewal to deal with the challenges that
> face me. Help me to know your gifts and to be renewed by your
> love.*

Friday: Philippians 2:14–15

Do everything without grumbling or questioning, that you may be
blameless and innocent, children of God without blemish in the midst
of a crooked and perverse generation, among whom you shine like
lights in the world.

> *God, I'm so tired of taking care of everyone else. Keep me from
> grumbling, from questioning, and from complaining today,
> no matter what problems seem to find me.*

Saturday: 2 Corinthians 12:9–10

"My grace is sufficient for you, for power is made perfect in weakness." I will rather boast most gladly of my weaknesses, in order that the power of Christ may dwell with me. Therefore, I am content with weaknesses, insults, hardships, persecutions, and constraints, for the sake of Christ; for when I am weak, then I am strong.

I am weak, but your grace is always sufficient, Lord.

SAINT-INSPIRED ACTIVITIES

For Mom

Write a handwritten letter to a friend or relative who is suffering from illness, is homebound, or is dealing with physical challenges. Let your loved one know you are thinking of and praying for him or her.

With Children

Although he is not formally the patron saint of Hawaii, Saint Damien is beloved in the Islands. Find the island of Molokai on an atlas, a globe, or online, and visit www.FatherDamien.com to view a gallery of pictures of Father Damien.

A PRAYER FOR OUR FAMILY

Pray as a family each day this week:

Saint Damien, priest and friend to the friendless,
you gave your life to care for the sick and destitute
when the rest of the world wanted to send them out of sight and out
of mind.
Help us to look around us and see friends, neighbors, or relatives who
may be suffering with sickness or loneliness.
Help us to find the strength and the courage
to help them in little ways

and to be the love of Christ to them.
Be with us in our own times of illness
and intercede on behalf of all the sick who ask for our prayers.
Like you, let us see the face of Jesus in all the people we help.
Amen.

SOMETHING TO PONDER

How are you being called to be the "touch of God" to sick or suffering family members or friends? What sustains you for this type of service?

28

Saint Thérèse of Lisieux

A Missionary's Heart

January 2, 1873–September 30, 1897
Patronage: Missionaries, Against Illness
Memorial: October 1

THÉRÈSE OF LISIEUX'S STORY

Born in 1873 at Alençon in Normandy, France, Françoise-Marie Thérèse Martin was the fifth daughter of Blessed Louis Martin and Blessed Marie-Azélie Guérin Martin. With the untimely death of her mother, Thérèse's family relocated to Lisieux, France, where Thérèse was cured from a serious illness at the age of eight. Thérèse experienced a vision of the Christ Child when she was not quite fourteen. So

great was her desire to join the Carmelites that, upon being declined
because of her age, she took her personal request to Pope Leo XIII during a pilgrimage to Rome. Thérèse's entry into Carmel was marked by
her development of what would become known as the "Little Way,"
her personal charism of total devotion to God by completing even the
most mundane and ordinary tasks with the greatest of devotion, dignity, and love. Thérèse continued to serve within her Carmelite community in spite of her persistent battle with tuberculosis, and at the age of
twenty she was appointed to assist the novice mistress. In her twenty-
third year, she began to pen the writings that would come to inspire
so many all over the world. The simple recounting of her personal
spirituality, known to us as *Story of a Soul*, was written under obedience to her prioress and beloved sister Pauline and further continued
under the next prioress, Mother Marie de Gonzague. Thérèse died at
the age of twenty-four, her heart filled with joy at the prospect of a life
in eternity with Jesus. Her canonization came less than three decades
after her death, and in 1997 Thérèse of Lisieux, the Little Flower, was
declared a Doctor of the Church by Pope John Paul II.

LESSONS FROM THÉRÈSE

Most Catholic moms won't be found in African missions or evangeliz-
ing China. Our mission fields are our homes, parishes, workplaces,
and neighborhoods. I've evangelized at the side of soccer fields, in the
line at the grocery store, and perhaps most eloquently when I simply
said nothing but took the time to be Christ to a friend, family member,
neighbor, or coworker in need. Thérèse wrote and spoke of her great
desire to be a saint, to spread the Gospel to the ends of the earth, and
to share her love for Christ with everyone. Despite the fact that a good
portion of her brief life was lived within the cloistered walls of Carmel,
she always felt a true sense of *mission*. When I doubt my own sense of
mission, she reminds me that regardless of my circumstances, I too am
called to play a part in the "Great Commission."

Thérèse's Little Way sprung from her intense desire for our Lord
and her almost childlike passion for pleasing him with daily acts of
sacrifice and love. Whether I am employed outside the home or at
home all day with children, my life as a mom is peppered with daily

tasks that can be tedious and mundane. Laundry continues to pile up, dishes must be washed, and the running of even the smallest home can be filled with an endless "to do" list. My professional life often contains far more busywork "valleys" than "peaks" of great accomplishment or achievement. It's easy to despair, to think to myself, "Is this all there is?" And yet by following Thérèse I discover a way to unite these unseemly tasks in my day, or my interactions with sometimes-irritating peers, with a loving, prayerful attitude that transforms them from chores into opportunities.

For modern moms, our Little Way might encourage us as we're washing the sixth load of laundry, filing paperwork at the office, nursing a newborn in the middle of the night, or caring for a cranky toddler. Let's look as those occasions as opportunities to grow in holiness. Simple? Yes! Saintly? If done with a heart for service and offered as an act of love—most definitely!

TRADITIONS

Saint Thérèse is quoted as saying, "My mission—to make God loved—will begin after my death. I will spend my heaven doing good on earth. I will send a shower of roses." She has come to be associated with the roses she loved so greatly and is frequently depicted in art holding a bouquet of roses. Some devotees to Saint Thérèse remark that they have smelled a lingering scent of roses when praying through her intercession.

THÉRÈSE'S WISDOM

You know well enough that Our Lord does not look so much at the greatness of our actions, nor even at their difficulty, but at the love with which we do them.

THIS WEEK WITH SCRIPTURE

Sunday: Isaiah 6:8

Then I heard the voice of the Lord saying, "Whom shall I send? Who will go for us?" "Here I am," I said; "send me!"

> *Here I am, Lord; send me wherever you would have me do your will.*

Monday: 1 Timothy 4:16

Attend to yourself and to your teaching; persevere in both tasks, for by doing so you will save both yourself and those who listen to you.

> *Lord, help me to persevere in teaching your Gospel to all those I encounter along my path.*

Tuesday: Luke 10:2

The harvest is abundant but the laborers are few; so ask the master of the harvest to send out laborers for his harvest.

> *Heavenly Father, I want to be a laborer. Use me to harvest the souls of my family for you by showering them with your love.*

Wednesday: Hosea 6:3

Let us know, let us strive to know the LORD;
as certain as the dawn is his coming,
and his judgment shines forth like the light of day!
He will come to us like the rain,
like spring rain that waters the earth.

> *Lord, today I will strive to know you and to share you with the world around me.*

Thursday: Deuteronomy 6:6–7

Take to heart these words which I enjoin on you today. Drill them into your children. Speak of them at home and abroad, whether you are busy or at rest.

> *I ask for a heart to know your word and the conviction to speak it to those in my life.*

Friday: Ephesians 3:20–21

Now to him who is able to accomplish far more than all we ask or imagine, by the power at work within us, to him be glory in the church and in Christ Jesus to all generations, forever and ever. Amen.

> *Unworthy though I am, you are able to accomplish far more than I could ever imagine in and through me. Let all my acts glorify your name.*

Saturday: Matthew 28:19–20

Go, therefore, and make disciples of all nations, baptizing them in the name of the Father, and of the Son, and of the holy Spirit, teaching them to observe all that I have commanded you. And behold, I am with you always, until the end of the age.

> *Open my heart to the missionary opportunities in my life, and help me to know and appreciate your constant presence and love.*

SAINT-INSPIRED ACTIVITIES

For Mom

Purchase a rose for your kitchen or a small rose plant to enjoy in your garden. As you ponder the beauty of each perfect petal and the wondrous aroma of the flower, take a few moments to realize how wonderfully God has created you to be his missionary. Focus on your own Little Way and on being a missionary in your home.

With Children

As a child and into adulthood, Saint Thérèse tried to grow in perfection each day by making small sacrifices. She carried a string with beads in her pocket and slid a bead across the string each time she completed an act of love or sacrifice. Make a simple set of "Sacrifice Beads" with each child and teach them to count the times each day he or she is able to offer God a gift of love. Directions for Saint Thérèse's "Good Deed Beads" can be found online.

A PRAYER FOR OUR FAMILY

Pray as a family each day this week:

Saint Thérèse,
your love for God knew no limits.
Although you were simple and often sick,
you offered everything you did as an act of love and prayer.
Help us to offer each part of our days—
the special parts and the parts that tire and try us—
as a sign of our love for God and for one another.
May we draw closer to Christ by sharing his Good News with
everyone we may meet, but especially by loving and serving one
another as we would love and serve him.
Amen.

SOMETHING TO PONDER

What are some of the tasks you face that when done with love become your personal prayer? How does Thérèse's example help you to respond more lovingly to your vocation?

29

Blessed Louis Martin and Blessed Marie-Azélie Martin

Appreciating Our Parents and Spiritual Mentors

Louis: August 22, 1823–July 29, 1894
Marie-Azélie: December 23, 1831–August 28, 1877
Memorial: July 12

LOUIS AND MARIE-AZÉLIE MARTIN'S STORY

Louis Martin and Marie-Azélie Guérin Martin each overcame disappointment at not being able to pursue a religious vocation. When they met randomly in Alençon, their courtship was expedited, and they saw their marriage as a mutual vocation. The Martin home was busy, with Louis's career as an expert clock and watchmaker and Zélie's own work as a skilled lace artisan. Together they faced the loss in infancy of four of their nine children. Their remaining five daughters each pursued a religious vocation, and their daughter Thérèse would go on to become a saint and Doctor of the Church. Zélie died of cancer at age forty-six. Louis faced a degenerative illness which left him confined to an asylum, suffering humiliation and paralysis for three years before returning home to be cared for by his daughter Céline until his death. Pope Benedict XVI beatified the Martins on World Mission Sunday, October 19, 2008, following the miraculous cure of a young Italian child whose parents had sought the couple's intercession. They are only the second married couple to be jointly beatified.

Lessons from Louis and Marie-Azélie

It's easy to think that perhaps Louis and Zélie hitched a ride on the saintly coattails of their famously holy daughter, Thérèse of Lisieux. But I only need to look at the role of my own parents in my personal spiritual development to realize that this could not be further from the truth. Any foundation in faith I've received, any love I have for the Church, blossomed from a seed planted in me by parents who gave me my first appreciation for what unconditional love could truly mean. Not everyone comes to faith through their family of origin, but it's impossible to study the life of Thérèse and not see the role her parents played in the transformative spirituality she would one day share with the world.

Louis and Zélie lived out their path to sanctity amid real-world challenges that would lay the groundwork for their daughters' religious vocations and service to the Church and the poor. In them I see two working parents with busy, flourishing careers, the tremendous loss of four babies, and a house full of active girls. Louis loved fishing, reading, and the company of friends. Zélie was an avid correspondent; much of what we know of the Martin family we discern from her wonderful letters. I like to imagine the Martins faced some of the obstacles Greg and I encounter in our daily lives—who would cook dinner after a long night at the store, how to keep rambunctious young Thérèse in line, how to honor Sunday as a family, and how to keep a small business prosperous.

At the core of their family life seems to be a passion for their faith, their dedication to personal and family prayer disciplines, and an unquestioning willingness to accept God's plan for their marriage. I look at the babies they buried and I recognize issues that have driven friends of mine to be angry with God. I watch Zélie's grace in accepting a fatal cancer diagnosis in her mid-forties—the exact age when I myself faced cancer treatment—and I hope to emulate even a tiny portion of her grace and confidence in God's providence. I ponder the indignity of Louis's confinement to an insane asylum and the loneliness he surely faced following the loss of his beloved wife, and I wonder how he kept the light of his faith burning so brightly.

Thérèse of Lisieux wrote of her parents, "God gave me a father and a mother more worthy of heaven than of earth; they asked the Lord to give them many children and to let them all be consecrated to Him." When I look at my own parents, my life's greatest role models, it's easy for me to imagine the tremendous respect, love, and appreciation the patroness of missionaries felt for Louis and Zélie. Her words also make me wonder what my own boys will say of Greg and me, of our attempts to show them a path to an eternity spent in heaven with a God who loves them even more than we could ever know how to love. I'm glad I know Zélie and Louis and that I can turn to them in my prayers and ask them to hold my hand and point the way.

TRADITIONS

The remains of Blessed Louis and Blessed Zélie Martin were exhumed shortly before the couple's beatification and reburied in the crypt of Saint Thérèse Basilica in Lisieux. They were beatified together in 2008, in conjunction with their one-hundred-fiftieth wedding anniversary, and became only the second spouses in the history of the Church to be beatified together. Together Blessed Louis and Blessed Zélie are frequently invoked as intercessors on behalf of large families and by spouses looking for support in building strong and faithful homes.

LOUIS'S AND MARIE-AZÉLIE'S WISDOM

I insist on telling you, my dear children, that I am urged to thank and to have you thank God, for I feel that our family, though very lowly, has the honor of being numbered among our Creator's privileged ones.

—Blessed Louis Martin

When I think of what this good God, in whom I have put all my trust, and into whose hands I have resigned the care of my affairs, has done for me and for my husband, I cannot doubt that his Divine Providence watches over his children with a special care.

—Blessed Marie-Azélie Martin

THIS WEEK WITH SCRIPTURE

Sunday: Leviticus 19:3

Revere your mother and father, and keep my sabbaths. I, the LORD, am your God.

> *This is your day, Lord. Help our family to sanctify it as a gift from you.*

Monday: Psalm 103:13

As a father has compassion on his children,
so the LORD has compassion on the faithful.

> *Compassionate One, help me to shower your love on my children and my husband, to love them as much as you love me.*

Tuesday: Colossians 3:20

Children, obey your parents in everything, for this is pleasing to the Lord.

> *Rock of my salvation, may I continue to obey the good example set forth for me by my parents.*

Wednesday: Proverbs 1:8–9

Hear, my son, your father's instruction,
and reject not your mother's teaching;
a graceful diadem will they be for your head;
a torque for your neck.

> *Teacher of all good things, help me to instruct my children to honor you always.*

Thursday: Psalm 112:1–2

Hallelujah!
Happy are those who fear the LORD,
who greatly delight in God's commands.
Their descendants shall be mighty in the land,
generation upright and blessed.

> *Hallelujah! Today, Lord, I delight in the goodness of your blessings.*

Friday: Proverbs 7:1–3

My son, keep my words,
and treasure my commands.
Keep my commands and live,
my teaching as the apple of your eye;
bind them on your fingers,
write them on the tablet of your heart.

> *Merciful One, help me to treasure your commands and to bind them on my children's hearts.*

Saturday: Deuteronomy 11:18–21

Therefore, take these words of mine into your heart and soul. Bind them at your wrist as a sign, and let them be a pendant on your forehead. Teach them to your children, speaking of them at home and abroad, whether you are busy or at rest. And write them on the doorposts of your houses and on your gates, so that, as long as the heavens are above the earth, you and your children may live on in the land, which the LORD swore to your fathers he would give them.

> *God, may we take what we have learned from our parents and spiritual mentors and pass these blessings along to our children that they may know and share the continual bounty you have showered upon our family.*

SAINT-INSPIRED ACTIVITIES

For Mom

Blessed Zélie Martin was a prolific correspondent. Her 200 preserved letters offer a window into the world of the Martin family. In honor of Blessed Zélie, pull out some nice stationary and a pen and write a letter to a family member or special friend, detailing some of the events in your family's recent life.

With Children

Blessed Louis Martin was an avid fisherman, and Blessed Zélie made intricate lace. Take the children on a fishing trip at a nearby pond or hold a family craft night together.

A PRAYER FOR OUR FAMILY

Pray as a family each day this week:

Blessed Louis and Blessed Zélie Martin,
together you lived a happy and holy marriage,
raising a family who gave itself fully to service of God and others.
Help our family to follow your example of love, faithfulness, and care
of one another.

Intercede on our behalf, that we may honor our parents, live out our days in holiness, and listen to God's call for our vocations.
Remember to God our loved ones, especially our deceased parents, grandparents, and relatives.
May our family someday know the happiness of life together with you and your children in heaven.
Amen.

SOMETHING TO PONDER

How do you and your husband inspire each other to lives of greater holiness? How did your own parents impact your spiritual journey? What legacy of faith are you leaving for your children?

30

Saint Isidore of Seville

Employing Technology to Inspire and Educate

ca. 560–April 4, 636
Patronage: Schoolchildren, Computer Users, Internet
Memorial: April 4

ISIDORE OF SEVILLE'S STORY

Born in Cartegena, Spain, Isidore rounded out a pious and influential family with four religious vocations and canonized saints. Isidore excelled at Latin, Greek, Hebrew, and his other studies at the cathedral school. His older brother Leander, the Archbishop of Seville, took part in his formation—an education that would lay the groundwork for a lifetime of scholarly pursuits, writings, and research. Isidore was ordained a priest and eventually succeeded his brother as archbishop, holding that position for over thirty years. Isidore is best known for his prolific writings, including his *Etymologies*, a twenty-volume encyclopedia that was the first-known work of its type and left a lasting impact for several centuries following its publication. During his years as archbishop, his reforms included the building of cathedral seminaries, efforts to convert non-Christians to the faith, and great charity toward the needy. As his death neared, Isidore prepared for his final reward by receiving the sacraments, praying as a penitent, and donating all of his earthly wealth to the poor of Seville.

LESSONS FROM ISIDORE

In recent years, Isidore of Seville has been widely proposed as the patron saint of the Internet. The title seems to fit this holy priest who has been called "the last scholar of the ancient world" and Spain's greatest teacher. In an age when we can google any topic and instantly yield tens of thousands of results, it's difficult to conceive of Isidore compiling his *Etymologies*, which contained information on the arts, history, grammar, architecture, science, and much more, from over 150 Christian and pagan sources. Isidore was systematic in his work and probably ahead of his time in realizing that priests and educators then needed reliable sources of written information.

As important as scholarly work was to Isidore, his prayer life was even more of a priority. He is believed to have written, "Prayer purifies us, reading instructs us. Both are good when both are possible. Otherwise, prayer is better than reading." His words are a balm to me in times when I fret that I may not be doing enough to educate myself or my children in the faith. Sometimes, we can get so busy researching and trying to keep up with the influx of information and opinions that come our way that we neglect what is truly most important—our prayer relationship with God. Especially in our digital age when the noise of so much information comes at us, I need to remember to carve out moments to silence everything and simply turn to God for solace and support.

I also think of Isidore's model of worldly education when I see my own sons growing so quickly into young men who will all too soon leave our nest. In his work, Isidore constantly stressed the importance of a broad, all-encompassing approach to education. In those moments when I want to shelter my sons from all the scary things they may encounter in the world, Isidore's life reminds me that it should instead be our greatest goal to help our children to form good consciences, so that they are well equipped to make good choices when confronted with life's challenges and dilemmas.

I find great comfort in having a heavenly patron to help me wade through some of the issues that arise in our high-tech society. I often pray through Isidore's intercession for safe and uplifting use of technology and for my children to employ these tools for good purposes that will help form their hearts, minds, and souls. I also ask his support in being a good steward of my own use of the Internet and related tools—that I never neglect my prayer life or my "real" relationships in favor of online pursuits, no matter how holy they may be.

Just as Isidore sought to learn about, to document, and to share his enthusiasm for all of the blessings of God's creation through the tools of his day, we moms have the world at our fingertips. By exploring, inquiring, and educating others, we make the most of the intellectual faculties with which God has blessed us. I love to think that if Isidore had lived in our time, he would have blogged, used Facebook and Twitter, and have been a prolific contributor to Wikipedia. While I may not be able to "friend him" online, I do have his heavenly companionship guiding my enjoyment of today's technological treasures.

TRADITIONS

To celebrate the third millennium of Christ, the Order of Saint Isidore of Seville was formed on January 1, 2000. It aims to honor Saint Isidore as patron of the Internet and to "promote the ideals of Christian chivalry through the medium of the Internet."

ISIDORE'S WISDOM

Therefore let the servant of God, imitating Christ, dedicate himself to contemplation without denying himself an active life. Behaving otherwise would not be right. Indeed, just as we must love God in contemplation, so we must love our neighbor with action. It is therefore impossible to live without the presence of both the one and the other form of life, nor can we live without experiencing both the one and the other.

This Week with Scripture

Sunday: Proverbs 31:26

She opens her mouth in wisdom,
and on her tongue is kindly counsel.

> *Seat of all wisdom, allow me to share your truth with those I love and with all I meet.*

Monday: 1 Corinthians 1:25

For the foolishness of God is wiser than human wisdom, and the weakness of God is stronger than human strength.

> *In my weakness, Father, I turn to you for strength.*

Tuesday: James 1:5

But if any of you lacks wisdom, he should ask God who gives to all generously and ungrudgingly, and he will be given it.

> *I am asking you, God, please fill me with all that I lack to do your will.*

Wednesday: Proverbs 1:7

The fear of the LORD is the beginning of knowledge;
wisdom and instruction fools despise.

> *Keeper of every promise, may all my efforts begin and end with you.*

Thursday: Colossians 2:6–7

So, as you received Christ Jesus the Lord, walk in him, rooted in him and built upon him, and established in the faith as you were taught, abounding in thanksgiving.

> *Today, Jesus, I will that my walk be in you, built upon you, and abounding in great thanks for your love.*

Friday: Psalm 24:4–5

The clean of hand and pure of heart,
who are not devoted to idols,
who have not sworn falsely.
They will receive blessings from the LORD,
and justice from their saving God.

> *Lord, may the images I view, the words I read, and the thoughts I share be pure and worthy of you.*

Saturday: Colossians 3:16–17

Let the word of Christ dwell in you richly, as in all wisdom you teach and admonish one another, singing psalms, hymns, and spiritual songs with gratitude in your hearts to God. And whatever you do, in word or in deed, do everything in the name of the Lord Jesus, giving thanks to God the Father through him.

> *Creator of all, help me to employ my gifts and today's technology to learn more about you and to share you with others.*

SAINT-INSPIRED ACTIVITIES

For Mom

Assess your use of the Internet. Document the amount of time and the types of sites you visit each day this week. Spend a bit of your time online learning more about faith resources online.

With Children

Saint Isidore wrote one of the earliest known encyclopedic compendiums of knowledge. In today's Internet age, encyclopedias are more rare in our homes. Take a family field trip to the library and look up some selected topics in the encyclopedia—you might even look up Saint Isidore of Seville!

A PRAYER FOR OUR FAMILY

Pray as a family each day this week:

Wise Saint Isidore of Seville,
you worked diligently to learn about life's many treasures.
You dedicated your life to sharing these with others so that they
would also be educated in the glory of God's creation.
Help our family to make wise and conscious choices when we use
technology to learn, to recreate, and to share our love for God.
May we view only things that enrich our learning,
increase our joy, or strengthen our integrity.
May we share only things that encourage, support, and strengthen
our commitment to spread the Gospel.
May we never neglect God or our families
by becoming overly involved in media or entertainment.
Help us to follow your example and to use every tool to learn more
about the wonderful world God has created for us.
Amen.

SOMETHING TO PONDER

Does your use of the Internet interfere with your vocation as wife and mother? Do you use technology to lift up, educate, and inspire, or is it little more than an escape?

31

Saint Bernadette Soubirous

Finding Healing in Our Faith

January 7, 1844–April 16, 1879
Patronage: Against Bodily Illness
Memorial: April 16

BERNADETTE SOUBIROUS'S STORY

Bernadette Soubirous was the eldest child of a large family in Lourdes, France, who lived in destitute poverty. Her parents were forced to send their daughter, who suffered severely from cholera-induced asthma, to work for pay as a maid and shepherdess in order to help support the family. Nearing her fourteenth birthday and still almost completely uncatechized, Bernadette returned home and prepared for her First Communion. While collecting firewood near the

River Gave, Bernadette experienced the first of eighteen Marian apparitions. The simple girl's claims that Our Lady, requesting society's penance and prayer and the conversion of sinners, had appeared to her were met with great hostility by both religious and civil authorities, and she was not even believed by her own family. The Church ultimately approved the apparitions in 1862, and with the support of Empress Eugénie of France a great basilica was ultimately built on the spot where Mary had appeared to Bernadette. As Lourdes became increasingly inundated with pilgrims seeking healing in the miraculous spring waters of Lourdes, Bernadette sought retreat with the Sisters of Charity in Nevers, France. She joined their apostolate in service of the ill and indigent. She made her final vows, taking the name Sister Marie-Bernarde, only a short time before her death of tuberculosis of the bone in 1879.

LESSONS FROM BERNADETTE

During my high school and college years, I twice had the opportunity to make visits to Lourdes, France, with my parents. We joyfully walked in the nighttime candlelight procession, in step with thousands of pilgrims from around the world who had come to seek healing in the baths. As those assembled for the procession are wheeled or carried from the grotto to the basilica, the Rosary is prayed in countless languages. It is impossible to spend any time in this place without being overwhelmed by the faith of the pilgrims. Many arrive with maladies, both physical and psychological, some severe and others mild. Some pilgrims obtain specific physical cures and nearly all depart this place touched with a spiritual healing that is difficult to describe. This spiritual conversion is without a doubt the reason that millions have come to seek solace in the place where Our Lady once appeared to young Bernadette.

This uneducated French peasant often remarked that Mary appeared to her despite, or perhaps even because of, her ignorance and simplicity. Bernadette was not canonized due to the miraculous visions she witnessed; others have been favored with apparitions and have not been canonized. Rather, her path to sanctity was what Sister Marie-Bernarde made of her life *after* it was turned upside down by the apparitions and the public notice they brought her. Bernadette never sought the spotlight, instead choosing to stand up for the message delivered so clearly to her by Our Lady and then to quietly seek a life of spiritual formation and service. Of her life after the apparitions, she once said: "The Blessed Virgin used me like a broom. What do you do with a broom when you have finished sweeping? You put it back in its place, behind the door!"

Bernadette's place was the convent of the Sisters of Charity in Nevers. In the convent, her fellow sisters and supervisors often treated her with resentment. So fully did Sister Marie-Bernarde separate herself from Lourdes that she did not even return for the dedication of the basilica. Her humble approach to her role in the apparitions has always spoken volumes to me on the importance of dying to self.

We live in an "I" world, where nearly every facet of our personal lives is shared with others, often in a very public way. Bernadette, who had every right to stay and enjoy the fruits of her devotion to Mary, instead chose to lead a quiet life of service and obscurity. Ironically, there would be no miraculous healing for her but rather a painful extended illness that would ultimately take her life at the tender age of thirty-five.

Bernadette knew that as wonderful a place as it was, Lourdes was not heaven, and heaven was where she would find ultimate healing. She offered her trials lovingly, patiently, obtaining spiritual healing in the quiet of her convent. Hers is a lesson for those of us who face obstacles of physical and mental health. We often pray for a miracle, an end to pain, and a cure, especially when our loved ones are suffering injury or sickness. Bernadette teaches us to pray for the grace to face and accept life's crosses and to bear them with love and hope for what lies beyond the pain of this world.

During the first apparition, she who would later announce herself as the Immaculate Conception to Bernadette said to the visionary, "I do not promise to make you happy in this life, but in the next." These words, spoken to a poor, illiterate child in a muddy cove near a dumping ground, bear the same hope for me today as a Catholic mom as they did for Bernadette. Some days, my vocation will be filled with the greatest of joys. In other moments, my heart will be wrenched by my own pains, or worse yet by those of my children or loved ones. Mary's request to Bernadette, that we pray, that we do penance, and that we seek the conversion of hearts to Jesus, rings as true today as it did on that cold February day in 1858. Her promise of spiritual healing, but more significantly the promise of happiness in the next life, is mine too.

TRADITIONS

Each year, millions of visitors from around the world come in pilgrimage to Lourdes, France. Many partake of the baths, where pilgrims are immersed in the spring waters. Every day, Masses and eucharistic and candlelight Rosary processions continue to bring spiritual healing and hope.

BERNADETTE'S WISDOM

I shall spend every moment loving. One who loves does not notice her trials; or perhaps more accurately, she is able to love them.

THIS WEEK WITH SCRIPTURE

Sunday: Psalm 34:7

In my misfortune I called,
the LORD heard and saved me from all distress.

> *Lord, thank you for your constant wakefulness in my moments of distress and for the peace I find in your love.*

Monday: James 5:14–15

Is anyone among you sick? He should summon the presbyters of the church, and they should pray over him and anoint [him] with oil in the name of the Lord, and the prayer of faith will save the sick person, and the Lord will raise him up. If he has committed any sins, he will be forgiven.

> *Compassionate One, forgive the sins which separate me from you.*

Tuesday: Proverbs 17:22

A joyful heart is the health of the body,
but a depressed spirit dries up the bones.

> *Today, God, let my spirit find joy in you.*

Wednesday: Romans 10:17

Thus faith comes from what is heard, and what is heard comes
through the word of Christ.

> *Jesus, help me to know your word and to find faith to face the
> struggles of this day.*

Thursday: Psalm 147:2–4

The LORD rebuilds Jerusalem,
gathers the dispersed of Israel,
Heals the brokenhearted,
binds up their wounds,
Numbers all the stars,
calls each of them by name.

> *You hear, Father; you bind my wounds, inside and out, and
> know me by name.*

Friday: Psalm 4:4

Know that the LORD works wonders for the faithful;
the LORD hears when I call out.

> *Faithful One, I call out to you. Answer me with spiritual
> healing, and work through me to draw others to you.*

Saturday: Luke 1:37

For nothing will be impossible for God.

> *In you, God and Shepherd, all things are possible. Heal me,
> body and soul, to do your will.*

SAINT-INSPIRED ACTIVITIES

For Mom

Saint Bernadette prayed the Rosary with Our Blessed Mother during the first apparition at Lourdes. Pray the Rosary for your own spiritual healing and for grace and strength for an ill family member or friend.

With Children

The Song of Bernadette is a fictionalized account of the life of Saint Bernadette. Released in 1943, the film garnered four Academy Awards and remains a perennial favorite for Catholic families. Check out *The Song of Bernadette* from your library or video store and enjoy a family movie night.

A PRAYER FOR OUR FAMILY

Pray as a family each day this week:

Saint Bernadette, humble and patient,
we seek your intercession for our family.
You had the favor of seeing and speaking with Our Blessed Mother,
and her visions changed your life and our world.
Help us to love Mary as you did and to follow her requests, as we
pray for conversion of our own hearts and do penance for our
shortcomings.
Carry our prayers for sick and dying loved ones to God.
For them, we ask strength, grace, and spiritual healing.
May we always follow your example of love and of openness to God's
plan for our lives.
And like you, may we one day know happiness in heaven forever.
Amen.

SOMETHING TO PONDER

In what ways does your faith need strengthening? From what physical, spiritual, or emotional maladies do you seek healing?

32

Saint Elizabeth Ann Seton

A Continual Spirit of Conversion

August 28, 1774–January 4, 1821
Patronage: Catholic Schools, Widows
Memorial: January 4

ELIZABETH ANN SETON'S STORY

Elizabeth Ann Bayley was born into a wealthy Anglican family in New York City and continued her charitable works well into her marriage with William Magee Seton, with whom she raised five children. Seton's financial and health crises led the couple to journey to Italy with their eldest daughter in hopes of finding a healthier climate and a potential cure for William. When William died, Elizabeth Ann found herself a widow, a single mother of five children under the age of

197

eight, and facing a spiritual upheaval that would ultimately lead to her become Catholic. Her efforts to support her family while continuing her compassionate care of others led her to found numerous Catholic schools and orphanages. In 1809, she founded and was appointed Mother Superior of the Maryland-based Sisters of Charity of Saint Joseph, a religious order in the Vincentian tradition that flourished by the time of her death in 1821.

LESSONS FROM ELIZABETH ANN

When it comes to saints who can inspire and motivate Catholic moms, Elizabeth Ann Seton has surely earned a spot in the hall of fame. Her journey from wealthy Protestant socialite to destitute Catholic widow would have left lesser women venturing down a path to anything but sainthood. And yet, it's perhaps because of her crosses and the grace with which she embraced them that Mother Seton became such a beloved role model.

In my own little corner of the world, I often ask myself what difference a housewife from Fresno, California, can make in a time when things seem to be spinning completely out of control. Some days, it feels like it's all I can do to keep up with the laundry, the cooking, and the cleaning. Little of my energy remains to do much else, and then I examine the heroic life of Elizabeth Ann Seton and wonder how she bore each day, how she managed to survive the hand life dealt her. But survive she did, and even though she likely struggled to put food on the table for her children, even though she bore the heartache of burying a spouse and two daughters, she was able to look at others in even greater need than herself and open her heart and her home to them.

Elizabeth Ann possessed not only a survivor's attitude but, more importantly, fully recognized the power of the faith that fueled her convictions. Her conversion to Catholicism came as a result of her profound desire to receive the Eucharist, in which she recognized the Real Presence of our Lord, Jesus Christ. Surely it would have been easier for her upon the tragic death of her husband to return home, to seek the safe shelter of her in-laws and family, and to be supported by her Anglican community of friends. Yet in her heart, she felt the stirrings of what would become a lifelong devotion to prayer and the Eucharist.

This passion led not only to her own conversion but to her lifelong commitment of sharing the faith she loved so dearly with others, especially with children.

When I look around myself at my home parish, I see that those who have joined our Church through the Rite of Christian Initiation of Adults are carrying out many of the volunteer ministry roles in my faith family. In fact, my own marriage to a convert provides me evidence that those who have chosen our faith as adults at times feel a deeper sense of commitment, of ownership, and of appreciation for our Church than those of us who may have become complacent about the gifts it offers us. I will never be a convert, but I can and do pray daily for a continual sense of conversion in my own life. I want to share the passion Elizabeth Ann felt for the Church she chose. I want to recommit my life each day to pouring out that blessing to the people I love most, my husband and children, and also to others I meet.

It's highly unlikely that I will ever found a religious order, build a school, or house orphans. It's even more unlikely that I will ever be a saint. But in some small way, when I look at the life of Elizabeth Ann Seton, I see a clearer path to my greatest dreams for my family and for myself. Hers is a life like mine, filled with trials, with joys, with unexpected twists and turns. Her journey led to heaven. Perhaps there is hope for me.

TRADITIONS

Saint Elizabeth Ann Seton helped found one of the first free Catholic schools for girls in the United States. She is commonly recognized as the patron saint of Catholic education, inspiring a system that today is responsible for the education of well over two million students per year. Today's Catholic schools continue Elizabeth Ann Seton's legacy of providing top-quality academic and spiritual formation to students, regardless of their financial status.

ELIZABETH ANN'S WISDOM

The accidents of life separate us from our dearest friends, but let us not despair. God is like a looking glass in which souls see each other.

The more we are united to Him by love, the nearer we are to those who belong to Him.

This Week with Scripture

Sunday: Psalm 23:2–3

In green pastures you let me graze;
to safe waters you lead me;
you restore my strength.
You guide me along the right path
for the sake of your name.

> *Father, you guide me along life's path. Restore me to walk where you will lead me with grace.*

Monday: 1 Corinthians 2:9

What eye has not seen, and ear has not heard,
and what has not entered the human heart,
what God has prepared for those who love him.

> *You have prepared a perfect plan for our family, God. May I find joy in watching each day unfold, knowing that it has been created as a gift from you.*

Tuesday: Ephesians 2:10

For we are his handiwork, created in Christ Jesus for the good works that God has prepared in advance, that we should live in them.

> *Today, Jesus, I will do your good works, living in my love of you.*

Wednesday: John 3:3

Amen, amen, I say to you, no one can see the kingdom of God without being born from above.

I seek renewal, conversion, passion. May I know the zeal of a convert, Lord, and may I be born anew in you.

Thursday: 2 Corinthians 5:6–7

So we are always courageous, although we know that while we are at home in the body we are away from the Lord, for we walk by faith, not by sight.

Sometimes, I lack courage. In these moments, let me walk by faith, knowing that my path will lead home to you.

Friday: Philippians 3:8

More than that, I even consider everything as a loss because of the supreme good of knowing Christ Jesus my Lord.

Knowing you, Jesus, is all good.

Saturday: 1 Peter 3:15–16

Always be ready to give an explanation to anyone who asks you for a reason for your hope, but do it with gentleness and reverence.

Am I ready, Lord? With gentleness and compassion, empower me to share your Good News.

SAINT-INSPIRED ACTIVITIES

For Mom

Saint Elizabeth Ann Seton devoted her life to the education of children in the faith. Quietly examine your own role in your children's faith formation. Do you make it a priority to teach them every day about their faith? Assess your devotion to this important part of your vocation, and recommit to it if you've fallen short or veered off track.

With Children

Our role as mothers is to be responsible for the primary faith forma-tion of our children, but there are those who help us in carrying out this vocation. Have your children draw a picture or write a thank-you note to someone who has helped in their catechesis: a teacher, a god-mother, a catechist, or a religious sister at your parish.

A PRAYER FOR OUR FAMILY

Pray as a family each day this week:

Saint Elizabeth Ann Seton,
you were a wife, a mom, a teacher, and a friend to so many.
Your life was filled with many disappointments,
and yet you never gave up or stopped trusting God.
Encourage us to be brave when bad things happen,
and also to share our faith with our friends and family,
even when we are embarrassed or afraid.
With the dawn of each new day,
help us to see our lives as a gift from God
just as they are, and let us recommit to thanking him and loving him
even more than we did the day before.
Thank you for living a life of holiness, of courage, and of love.
Amen.

SOMETHING TO PONDER

Do you embrace teachable moments as they arise? How have you strived to form your children in the precepts of the Church?

33

Saint Anne and Saint Joachim

Loving and Respecting Our Grandparents and the Elderly

First Century
Patronage: Grandparents, Married Couples
Memorial: July 26

ANNE AND JOACHIM'S STORY

What we know of the lives of Anne and Joachim comes to us via apocryphal writings. While biographical details are sparse, tradition teaches us that Anne and Joachim lived chaste, just lives and that they were incredibly devoted to the practice of their faith. As people of means they generously supported the poor in their community. After years of childlessness, their prayers were rewarded with the birth of their daughter, Mary, who would be destined to become the mother of our Savior. As a sign of their trust in God's will and their gratitude for his blessings, they presented Mary at the Temple, entrusting her to the Lord.

LESSONS FROM ANNE AND JOACHIM

I've always had a tremendous devotion to Anne, the patroness of mothers and grandmothers, since my own mother was named for her. As the only child of older parents, my mom was the true love of Roy and Bessie's lives. Their devotion to my mom came in the form of a vibrant and steadfast presence in her life, and eventually in ours too. Even though a great physical distance separated us, we came to know my mom's parents through weekly phone calls and annual extended visits. They doted on us and spoiled us in big and little ways. My love for my grandparents is all the greater for the fact that they were clearly crazy about their daughter.

I feel much the same way toward my paternal grandparents, who treasured my dad and each of his six siblings. My dad's devoted mother Patty always seemed to me to be the ultimate "Catholic mom." She and Grandpa Wayne taught me early on that love could be multiplied exponentially and that prayer was always the best solution in times of great need. They helped to instill in their children and grandchildren a profound respect for and deep desire to defend all human life. I like to think that my grandparents and parents have much in common with the parents of our Blessed Mother.

Even though we know little of the details of Anne and Joachim's life together, there is much that we can imagine about what kind of parents they were, simply by looking at the life of their daughter Mary. First and foremost, Anne and Joachim bear strong witness to being open to life and having a great desire to follow God's will. Apocryphal writings infer that Joachim's offering at the Temple was rejected because of his childlessness, and that both he and Anne received an angelic message that they would conceive a child who would go on to change the future for all humanity. As Catholic moms, we are called with our husbands to lovingly welcome children according to God's plan for our lives. For some of us, we find ourselves challenged with finding the resources, the stamina, and the patience to joyfully parent large families. Others of us face the heartbreak of infertility and may long for children we will never have, and others of us say goodbye to children who leave us far too soon. Having struggled with infertility in my own life, I turn often to Anne and Joachim for their help in my own faithful acceptance of this cross and the comfort of God's love and mercy as I bear it.

In a society where the elderly are often disdained and where the quest for eternal youth has gone viral, Anne and Joachim also teach us about respecting, loving, and admiring the elderly living among us. If our children are blessed enough to know their grandparents, we can teach them to lovingly respect them in good times and challenging ones, always treating them with dignity. For those without the blessing of living grandparents, we can look around ourselves in church and in our communities and find willing candidates for special friendships with those who have so much to teach and to share. In Anne and Joachim, we find saintly companions who can be there for us when we experience disappointment, when we face parenting dilemmas, or when we are challenged by caring for elderly parents.

I've learned the most from and about Anne and Joachim by looking at the life of their daughter Mary and at her parenting of Jesus. Many of us have caught ourselves parroting the phrases we heard as children, or bemoaning, "I'm turning into my mother." When we look at Mary and her role in nurturing Jesus, and then at the way in which she calls us constantly into deeper relationship with him, we can guess that she had parents who raised her to treasure her faith. Anne and Joachim's courage emboldened them to present Mary at the Temple and instilled in their daughter the valor necessary to witness Jesus' ministry and to stand at the foot of the cross as he made the ultimate sacrifice.

TRADITIONS

Saint Anne and Saint Joachim are depicted in art at the Golden Gate of Jerusalem after receiving separate angelic messages about the birth of their daughter. Anne is famously depicted in her parental role—nurturing and educating their beloved daughter, Mary. Saint Anne's Chaplet is often prayed for healing intercession.

ANNE AND JOACHIM'S WISDOM

Now I know that the Lord God hath blessed me exceedingly; for, behold the widow no longer a widow, and I the childless shall conceive.

—Saint Anne

THIS WEEK WITH SCRIPTURE

Sunday: Matthew 12:33

Either declare the tree good and its fruit is good, or declare the tree rotten and its fruit is rotten, for a tree is known by its fruit.

> *Father, you sent Anne and Joachim to be the parents of Mary. Help me to bear your good fruit in the children you have entrusted to me.*

Monday: Proverbs 23:22

Listen to your father who begot you,
and despise not your mother when she is old.

> *When I grow impatient with the elders in my life, when I take for granted their wisdom, help me to remember to treasure them and to see Christ in them.*

Tuesday: Psalm 71:9

Do not cast me aside in my old age;
as my strength fails, do not forsake me.

> *Heavenly Father, help me to be physically and emotionally present to the elderly in my community.*

Wednesday: Job 12:12

So with old age is wisdom,
and with length of days understanding.

> *Jesus, help me to treasure the wisdom handed down from*
> *my parents and grandparents. Give me the strength and the*
> *courage to share it with my own children.*

Thursday: Leviticus 19:32

Stand up in the presence of the aged, and show respect for the old;
thus shall you fear your God. I am the LORD.

> *Good and Gracious God, remember in your mercy the sick*
> *and suffering. Let them know your healing touch through the*
> *intercession of Saints Anne and Joachim.*

Friday: Exodus 20:12

Honor your father and your mother, that you may have a long life in
the land which the LORD, your God, is giving you.

> *For the times when I have been impatient with or did not*
> *honor my parents, Lord, please forgive me.*

Saturday: Proverbs 16:31

Gray hair is a crown of glory;
it is gained by virtuous living.

> *God, in this time when our world tells me otherwise, please*
> *help me to accept the gift of aging gracefully and with*
> *humility. May each day of my earthly life bring me one step*
> *closer to an eternity with you in heaven.*

SAINT-INSPIRED ACTIVITIES

For Mom

Saint Anne is the patron saint of pregnant women, but she is also
the patroness of unmarried women and of old-clothes dealers. Hold a
garage sale in her honor and donate the proceeds to your favorite pro-
life charity, or clean out your closet and donate gently used items to a
local crisis pregnancy center.

With Children

Celebrate the lives of Saint Anne and Saint Joachim by doing something special for your grandparents. Take an outing with them, bake them cookies, draw a picture, or write a letter for them. Remember deceased grandparents by praying for them, looking at old family photographs, and sharing family stories.

A PRAYER FOR OUR FAMILY

Pray as a family each day this week:

Saints Anne and Joachim,
you trusted that God's grace would guide your family
even when it brought you sadness and loneliness.
You welcomed a daughter and nurtured her in love and faith,
instilling in her profound trust in God and a generous heart.
Help our family this week to treasure and care for all of our elderly
loved ones.
Let us be good listeners, strong helpers, and faithful students of these
wise ones.
We pray this week for their health, their ultimate rest with you in
heaven, and for our own ability to trust in your will for our lives.
Amen.

SOMETHING TO PONDER

In what ways, good and bad, are you "turning into your mother"? How are you teaching your children by example to honor your family elders or reverence memories of them?

34.

Saint Rose Venerini

Educating to Set Free

February 9, 1656–May 7, 1728
Memorial: May 7

ROSE VENERINI'S STORY

Rosa Venerini was born in Viterbo, Italy, to a brilliant physician and his wife. The third of four children, Rose was a pious child and a devoted student. She entered the Dominican convent, but she left at the sudden death of her father to aid in caring for her mother and siblings. After the very sad passing of both her mother and an elder brother, and as her other siblings grew in independence, Rose formed a neighborhood Rosary group. Her conversations within this group opened her eyes and her heart to the sad state of education and faith formation for the women in her community. This led her to devote her life to found a free school for underprivileged girls and then to respond to bishops and cardinals who requested her services in opening and administering educational institutes in their dioceses. Her work earned the approval of Pope Clement XI, and by the time of her death she had founded over forty schools for the young women of Italy.

LESSONS FROM ROSE

Rosa Venerini reminds me of the beautiful phrase "bloom where you are planted." Hers is a story of a life spent responding to the needs of others. While she might have desired a religious vocation, life circumstances led her to give up that dream in service to her family. When events led her to a state some might have considered a spinster's dead end, Rose looked outside herself again, inviting the women of her surrounding neighborhood to gather for fellowship and prayer. In the comfortable conversation that surrounded her, the desperation of these women's situations struck her. And rather than consider herself above their illiterate and uncatechized station, Rose took it upon herself to demand, and ultimately to provide, a solid education and faith formation for girls in Italy, beginning with her own girlfriends.

Faced with the resentment of both clergy and the upper crust of society, she championed the rights of young women to rise above their pitiful state. She and her fellow pious teachers took as their motto, "Educate to liberate." Rose was fueled by an active prayer life and devotion to the Eucharist. Her personal spirituality helped her to clearly recognize that what her friends needed was the total package—job skills, a solid education, and a grounding in the saving love of Jesus Christ. Her formula prospered, and the teacher who once was obstructed and ridiculed was eventually in demand around the country.

Rose Venerini reminds me to bloom where I am planted. At times, I'm tempted to play the "what if?" game—what if I hadn't decided to stay home and instead had remained committed to my profession? What if I had been blessed with more children? If Rose had these types of questions, she didn't let them stand in her way. She reminds me that the most important game plan in my life is

God's; and although things may not always unfold the way I've planned them, Rose reminds me that God's path is perfect and that it's my job to make the most of my life and follow wherever he leads me.

Ultimately, Rose's teaching vocation blossomed through her relationships with women. When I picture the Rosary group she founded in her home in Viterbo, my mind flashes to childhood memories of a group that once met in my mother's living room. The purpose of my mom's weekly gathering was to pray the Rosary, but as they prayed these women lifted one another through marital duress, parenting traumas, and financial devastation. There were celebrations too: births, marriages, vocations, and just those small moments of friendship that were solidified over coffee, donuts, and mutual prayer. The group eventually grew apart, but their relationships have lingered over the years.

I often find myself turning to my own informal female societies for support just as my mother did. Interestingly, online communities now supplement my own local friendships as I connect with fellow Catholic moms around the world on a daily basis. The common denominator in these friendships—whether in physical proximity or online—is a mutual love and a commitment to communal prayer. In our relationships with each other, we live out our commitment to the larger Body of Christ just as Rose did with her friends in Viterbo. We support in physical ways when we can with a homemade meal here or a carpool ride there, but most of all we intercede for one another. Our prayers are heard by the same Blessed Mother and Heavenly Father who so richly blessed Rose and her sisters in faith.

In our world today, there are still large pockets of deserving young women who long for education, for quality health care, for proper nutrition, and for faith formation. While my station in life today does not allow me to go out and found schools as Rose did, I can definitely look around myself, touch lives in my corner of the world with the skills God has granted me, and bloom where I am planted.

TRADITIONS

Today, the legacy of the pious teachers who gathered to educate alongside Saint Rose Venerini lingers in the work of the Venerini Sisters, the order she founded. The order serves worldwide, providing teaching, catechesis, pastoral ministry, health care, social services, and youth ministry.

ROSE'S WISDOM

I feel so nailed to the will of God that nothing else matters, neither death nor life. I want what he wants; I want to serve him as much as pleases him and no more.

THIS WEEK WITH SCRIPTURE

Sunday: 1 John 5:13

I write these things to you so that you may know that you have eternal life, you who believe in the name of the Son of God.

> *Lord, help me to seek eternal life in you and to share this joy with those who do not know, or do not believe.*

Monday: Luke 19:10

For the Son of Man has come to seek and to save what was lost.

> *In you, Jesus, I am found.*

Tuesday: Romans 10:9–10

For, if you confess with your mouth that Jesus is Lord and believe in your heart that God raised him from the dead, you will be saved. For one believes with the heart and so is justified, and one confesses with the mouth and so is saved.

Let my words and actions confess what I know to be true—
that I am saved through the gift of your merciful love.

Wednesday: Psalm 13:6

I trust in your faithfulness.
Grant my heart joy in your help,
That I may sing of the LORD,
"How good our God has been to me!"

How good you have been to me, Lord! I trust in you.

Thursday: Philemon 4–6

I give thanks to my God always, remembering you in my prayers, as
I hear of the love and the faith you have in the Lord Jesus and for all
the holy ones, so that your partnership in the faith may become effec-
tive in recognizing every good there is in us that leads to Christ.

Covenant Keeper, grant me partnership with you in helping
your children to know the goodness of your way.

Friday: Mark 10:52

Jesus told him, "Go your way; your faith has saved you." Immediately
he received his sight and followed him on the way.

Jesus, Beloved Son, open my eyes to the power of your love.

Saturday: Matthew 9:37–38

Then he said to his disciples, "The harvest is abundant but the laborers are few; so ask the master of the harvest to send out laborers for
his harvest."

Master of the Harvest, strengthen me for the labor you desire
of me.

SAINT-INSPIRED ACTIVITIES

For Mom

Saint Rose Venerini's lifelong commitment to education for women was born out of her Rosary group. Invite a few girlfriends into your home, meet together at church, or a quiet place near your workplaces, or gather at a local park to pray the Rosary and talk about life. Or simply choose one morning each week to pray for each other's intentions.

With Children

Saint Rose served her entire life to bring quality education and faith formation to the poor girls in Italy. Go through your family bookshelves and select a few "gently used" books to be donated to Catholic Charities or to a needy school.

A PRAYER FOR OUR FAMILY

Pray as a family each day this week:

Saint Rose Venerini,
you dedicated your life to helping others learn and know the love of Jesus Christ.
Help us this week to bloom where we are planted,
opening our hearts to the plans God has for our lives.
Intercede on behalf of the poor in our community
and those who do not have recourse to faith in daily struggles.
Let us be the love of Christ to them and to everyone we meet.
Help us to follow your beautiful example of a constant dialogue with, of, and for God.
Amen.

Something to Ponder

How has your education affected your faith and the way you view the world around you?

35

Saint Dymphna

Finding Relief for Those Suffering with
Mental Health Issues

Seventh Century
Patronage: Mental Illness
Memorial: May 15

DYMPHNA'S STORY

The Irish daughter of a pagan chieftain and his Christian bride, Dymphna was secretly baptized and catechized in her youth by the elderly Father Gerebernus. At the death of Dymphna's mother, the intense grief of her father, King Damon, drove him into mental illness, and he made incestuous advances toward Dymphna. Father Gerebernus spirited her to the Belgian village of Gheel where they were sheltered by a group of monks and townspeople until being discovered by Damon's spies. When he arrived to demand that Dymphna return with him and become his bride, Father Gerebernus attempted to protect her and was beheaded. Damon then turned to Dymphna, threatening her life. She stood firm in her faith and died at the hand of her own father, who beheaded her and left the fifteen year-old's body along with the priest's to be buried by local townspeople. The rediscovery of the pair's remains in the thirteenth century led to a resurgence of devotion to this patroness of the mentally ill and those who care for them.

Lessons from Dymphna

As with the devotees of so many saints who have risen in stature despite a lack of formal written history, those devoted to Dymphna continue her legacy through the work they do and by continuing to shine her light in this world.

For many years, the villagers surrounding Dymphna's burial site in Gheel witnessed her miraculous intercession on behalf of those plagued by mental illnesses and nervous-system disorders such as epilepsy. Over time, the village became home to a clinic for the mentally ill, and pilgrims flocked to the nearby church named for the saint. A first-class system for treating mental illness developed in Gheel, a system largely centered on allowing patients to settle in the homes of families living in the area once their inpatient treatment was completed. In this way, patients could resume a normal life and return to work, education, and families, with inpatient care available at any time should it be needed. The citizens of Gheel continue these traditions today, and their system of deinstitutionalizing care for the mentally ill has been studied in recent years as a model for community-based care.

Many moms today face mental illness and behavioral disabilities in our own homes and families. Unlike physical disabilities which can be seen outwardly, mental health issues, learning disabilities, and behavioral limitations can add increased stress and may not be obvious to our relatives, friends, and neighbors. In addition, there is often an unfortunate sense of stigma or shame that accompanies the diagnoses—a sense that "if only I were a better mom this wouldn't have happened." Many of us carry this burden alone, fearful of confiding in those around us and not wanting to draw attention to the problem.

Despite her young age, when Dymphna noted the severity of her father's mental illness, she was wise enough to seek help and to get away from her abuser. Many people across the generational spectrum live with emotional instabilities, learning disabilities, addictions, and mental illnesses. We need to continue waging war on stigmas, great and small, attached to mental-health issues. We must stop hiding them out of fear or embarrassment and start reaching out to family members and friends who are truly struggling. A good first step is simply to educate yourself and your family.

If you find yourself questioning your own mental health and well-being, it's your responsibility to your husband and children to seek immediate medical help for yourself. If you can't summon the courage to see a doctor, please speak with a trusted family member, friend, priest, or other trained pastoral minister as soon as possible and share your need for help with them.

If you have a family member or friend who exhibits signs of mental illness, it's time *now* to gently, lovingly, and yet forcefully take matters in hand and help him or her to seek treatment. Dymphna's story ended in tragedy and a life given in defense of her own dignity, but we must reach out to those we love to put an end to death and destruction wrought in current society through lack of treatment. It's time to start intervening when we sense in our hearts that a problem exists. We need to overcome fear, worry that our loved one will be angry or embarrassed, or concern with appearing judgmental. If you sense there is a problem, pray through the intercession of Dymphna for wisdom and courage, and act now.

TRADITIONS

The National Shrine of Saint Dymphna was built on the grounds of the Massillon State Hospital in 1938. Each year, on Saint Dymphna's feast day, the shrine celebrates with a special litany, procession, and Mass in honor of the saint who continues to intercede on behalf of families seeking services at the adjacent behavioral health-care facility.

Dymphna's Wisdom

You are celebrated Saint Dymphna, for your goodness to others. Both in your lifetime, and even more in the ages since, you have again and again demonstrated your concern for those who are mentally disturbed or emotionally troubled. Kindly secure for me, then, some measure of your own serene love, and ask our Lord to give us a share in his life and boundless charity. Amen.

—From the "Nine Prayers to Saint Dymphna"

This Week with Scripture

Sunday: Psalm 46:2

God is our refuge and our strength,
an ever-present help in distress.

> *God, help me to remember to turn to you for strength in times of distress.*

Monday: Isaiah 41:10

Fear not, I am with you;
be not dismayed; I am your God.
I will strengthen you, and help you,
and uphold you with my right hand of justice.

> *Lord, I fear the unseen some days, the trials that no one else knows but that weigh me down. Strengthen me, especially when I feel too weak to bear the load life piles upon me.*

Tuesday: Luke 6:21

Blessed are you who are now weeping,
for you will laugh.

> *May the tears that spill wash away the pain I feel inside and allow my heart to heal, to praise, and to laugh.*

Wednesday: Jonah 2:3

Out of my distress I called to the LORD,
and he answered me;
From the midst of the nether world I cried for help,
and you heard my voice.

> *Lord, help me to hear the voices of those in my life who may
> be crying for aid.*

Thursday: Ephesians 5:1–2

So be imitators of God, as beloved children, and live in love, as Christ
loved us and handed himself over for us as a sacrificial offering to
God for a fragrant aroma.

> *Father, I want to live in love. Help me to look outside myself to
> those in need and to offer myself fully.*

Friday: Galatians 6:9–10

Let us not grow tired of doing good, for in due time we shall reap our
harvest, if we do not give up. So then, while we have the opportunity,
let us do good to all, but especially to those who belong to the family
of the faith.

> *When I am feeling depleted, given away completely, I want
> to give up. But you ask me not to grow tired, so fill me with
> the energy I need to move forward, to give more, to love better.*

Saturday: Matthew 11:28–30

Come to me, all you who labor and are burdened, and I will give you
rest. Take my yoke upon you and learn from me, for I am meek and
humble of heart; and you will find rest for yourselves. For my yoke is
easy, and my burden light.

> *Heavenly God, lighten the burden of all of us who suffer with
> mental health issues, and let us find rest in you.*

SAINT-INSPIRED ACTIVITIES

For Mom

Reach out to a friend who may be challenged with mental health issues or who may have a child struggling with a diagnosis. Offer to drive her children, make a meal, babysit, or simply sit and have a cup of coffee and listen to her, letting her know that she is in your prayers and that you want to help.

With Children

Speak with your children in an age-appropriate fashion about mental illness, explaining the need to be extra kind and Christ-like to friends at school who may deal with any type of illness or disability. Think of ways that your family can support friends who may be struggling with mental health issues.

A PRAYER FOR OUR FAMILY

Pray as a family each day this week:

Dearest Saint Dymphna,
you were so very young and yet so very brave.
Help us to follow your example of making good choices,
even when it seems very hard to follow the right path.
Intercede for all those we know who struggle with illnesses,
especially illnesses that may go unseen but that hurt so greatly.
Help us to be compassionate to our friends
and to help them carry their loads,
and especially to be good friends to those who may be lonely,
scared, or anxious.
We ask for good health of mind, body, and spirit
and for strength in challenging times too.
We thank you for your example
and for the compassion and love you have stirred up
in those who have followed you.
Amen.

SOMETHING TO PONDER

How can you support and encourage family members facing mental-health challenges? How is your own mental health? Is there anything you should do to take care of yourself in this regard?

36.

ℬlessed 𝒻rédéric 𝒪zanam

Serving Others with Compassion

April 23, 1813–September 8, 1853
Memorial: September 7

FRÉDÉRIC OZANAM'S STORY

Antoine Frédéric Ozanam lived a brief yet religiously and socially significant life during a tumultuous period of French history. A noted scholar, Frédéric led his friends and fellow students to seek meaningful social change through his formation of the Saint Vincent de Paul Society, a network of independent conferences committed to growing spiritually through the direct provision of aid to the needy and suffering. Frédéric dearly loved his wife, Amélie, and daughter, Marie, and was committed to combining his vocation to marriage and family life with a calling to serve the poor. Pope John Paul II beatified Frédéric in 1997, and the society he founded now counts nearly one million members serving countless poor individuals and families around the world.

LESSONS FROM FRÉDÉRIC

It would have been easy for Frédéric Ozanam to live out his years in a comfortable, scholarly existence, lecturing, writing, and debating with the great thinkers of his day at the University of Lyon and at the famous Sorbonne in Paris. And yet early in his life, Frédéric recognized the hypocrisy of a faith spent professing words without putting his beliefs into action. By his twentieth birthday, Frédéric was moved enough by the pain and suffering he saw growing around him to call his friends and fellow students into action. Turning to Saint Vincent de Paul's Daughters of Charity, Frédéric and his confreres sought the guidance of Sister Rosalie Rendu, who led them into one of Paris's most marginalized neighborhoods. What began as young men carrying bread purchased with their meager students' wages into the streets was organized into a worldwide network of Saint Vincent de Paul conferences which today provide both short-term relief and long-term hope to the family of God around the globe.

There are so many lessons to be learned from the life of Frédéric. I find it a bit intimidating to look at his role in founding what has become such a large charitable organization. And yet when I look at the initial impetus behind Frédéric's work, I see his simple, yet deep desire to translate faith into works. I am moved and inspired by his belief that, as followers of Christ, we too grow in holiness through our service to those around us.

With our days so full and busy, we might wonder how we can follow Frédéric's lead. We may have little time to formally volunteer or to raise funds for others. But each day, in little ways, we witness spiritual and physical need. Can I help a fellow mom balancing work and kids by offering a ride to soccer practice? Can I forego this week's lattes and instead purchase extra diapers to donate to the women's shelter? Can I help my children prepare a simple sack lunch to hand to the homeless man who is always at the local intersection? Frédéric was convinced that in serving others, we ourselves become true prophets of Christ's Gospel message.

Frédéric has also been widely revered for his motivation of young people to act with conviction on the front lines of political and societal change. It is no coincidence that Pope John Paul II beatified him in the Cathedral of Notre Dame during World Youth Day in 1997. As the pope extolled the virtues of this nineteenth-century hero, he spoke to a crowd of youth who face many of the same challenges Frédéric knew in his day. My role as a mom, as the primary faith teacher of my children, affords me the same opportunity to inspire, to motivate, and to facilitate the efforts of my own children to make lasting change in their world. When I teach them about the faith I love so dearly, I hope to dwell not only upon doctrinal precepts but also upon their duty to make this world a better place. I've embraced as my own daily goal Frédéric's personal aspiration "to become better—to do a little good."

TRADITIONS

For over 150 years, Saint Vincent de Paul conferences around the world have used the practice of "twinning" to team conferences in more developed areas of the world with their sister organizations in needy areas. They follow in the footsteps of Blessed Frédéric Ozanam, Sister Rendu, and the other founders of the Saint Vincent de Paul Society to accomplish Frédéric's commitment to "embrace the world in a network of charity."

FRÉDÉRIC OZANAM'S WISDOM

Charity must never look back, but always ahead, for the number of its past benefits is always quite small, as the present and future miseries it should alleviate are infinite.

THIS WEEK WITH SCRIPTURE

Sunday: Luke 14:13–14

Rather, when you hold a banquet, invite the poor, the crippled, the lame, the blind; blessed indeed will you be because of their inability to repay you. For you will be repaid at the resurrection of the righteous.

> *Lord, help me to remember to open my heart to the poor in my life—the physically poor and the poor in spirit. Help me to serve them without expecting any reward beyond your love.*

Monday: Proverbs 31:9

Open your mouth, decree what is just,
defend the needy and the poor!

> *Give me the strength and conviction to fight for change and for social justice within my own neighborhood and community.*

Tuesday: Mark 12:42–44

A poor widow also came and put in two small coins worth a few cents. Calling his disciples to himself, he said to them, "Amen, I say to you, this poor widow put in more than all the other contributors to the treasury. For they have all contributed from their surplus wealth, but she, from her poverty, has contributed all she had, her whole livelihood."

> *Heavenly Father, sometimes it feels like our giving and sacrifices are so very small. Please accept them with my gratitude and remind me to always be gracious and generous with my giving.*

Wednesday: Acts 20:35

In every way I have shown you that by hard work of that sort we must help the weak, and keep in mind the words of the Lord Jesus who himself said, "It is more blessed to give than to receive."

God, let me be generous in giving your love to everyone I meet today.

Thursday: Proverbs 17:5

He who mocks the poor blasphemes his Maker;
he who is glad at calamity will not go unpunished.

May I remember to treat all I meet with respect and dignity.

Friday: Psalm 70:6

Here I am, afflicted and poor.
God, come quickly!
You are my help and deliverer.
LORD, do not delay!

Lord, remind me when I stress about finances and material worries that you are always present, supporting our family. Let me count my blessings instead of dwelling on my needs.

Saturday: 1 John 3:17–18

If someone who has worldly means sees a brother in need and refuses him compassion, how can the love of God remain in him? Children, let us love not in word or speech but in deed and truth.

I want to be your hands of compassion, God. Let me love through my actions today.

SAINT-INSPIRED ACTIVITIES

For Mom

If there is a Saint Vincent de Paul conference in your neighborhood, find out how you might help them. Consider a donation to their local thrift store, or volunteer to help with one of their ongoing projects.

With Children

Blessed Frédéric Ozanam challenged young members of the Saint Vincent de Paul Society to be inventive and persistent in putting creative ideas into practice on behalf of those in need. Brainstorm ideas for helping the poor in your community. Think big, but remember that small acts of service are wonderful too! Make a concrete and specific plan to implement one of your ideas.

A PRAYER FOR OUR FAMILY

Pray as a family each day this week:

Blessed Frédéric Ozanam,
you looked around and saw a world filled with pain and suffering,
and you decided to go out and make that world a better place.
You cared for the hungry, the poor, and the sick,
knowing that you could grow holier and closer to Christ
by being his hands and his heart to those in need.
Help us to follow your example of love.
May we make small sacrifices to help others,
showing them God's love
by the way we treat them with dignity and respect.
We want to become better
and to do a little good in our world this week.
Amen.

SOMETHING TO PONDER

What are some small ways in which you might grow closer to Christ by engaging in outward acts of service for others?

37

Saint John the Apostle

Treasuring the Gift of Our Friendships

First Century
Patronage: Friendships
Memorial: December 27

JOHN THE APOSTLE'S STORY

The son of Zebedee and Salome, John was a simple, uneducated fisherman working with his older brother, James, when he was called by Jesus and became a disciple. The "beloved disciple" was at Jesus' side throughout the course of his public ministry and at the moment of his crucifixion. The first to recognize Jesus Christ after his resurrection, John went on to leadership in the Christian community in Asia Minor and is credited as the author and inspiring force behind the gospel and three epistles named for him, along with the book of Revelation. John was the last of the twelve original disciples to die in approximately AD 104.

LESSONS FROM JOHN

A true friend stands with you in good times and in bad. She is your companion in moments of celebration and your consolation in moments of tragedy. For Jesus Christ, the one called the "beloved disciple" played this role, staying at his side as Jesus' ministry grew and flourished. John witnessed miracles and was present at the institution of the Eucharist, laying his head on Christ's breast as a sign of his true fidelity. John had lapses in judgment, at times displayed his passions inappropriately, and was eager for Jesus' approval and recognition. In the end, though, he proved his incredible devotion to Christ by standing at the foot of the cross with Mary, refusing to desert his friend in his darkest hour. It was to John that Jesus left the honor and responsibility of caring for his dearly loved mother, establishing a lasting legacy that would institute Mary as Blessed Mother to us all. John accepted guardianship of Mary, likely treasuring the role of protecting and defending this beloved woman.

John teaches me the true meaning of the word "friend." As a mom, I sometimes feel so committed to serving my family and just getting through each busy day that I neglect my friendships, even though they are among my life's greatest blessings. My friends buoy my spirits when life's dramas and dullness make me want to give up. I can't tell you how many times my best friends—my "soul sisters"—have lifted me when I felt like throwing in the towel or simply when I needed a shoulder to cry on. They have also been my kindest cheerleaders, believing in me when I lacked confidence in myself and celebrating with me not only my own achievements but my family's as well.

John reminds me that friendship is a two-way street, requiring both give and take. To call myself a friend means I sometimes have to be extended out of my comfort zone. But the beauty of these moments is the opportunity to be truly present to those I love in times when their personal crosses seem too great to bear.

My parents often used the saying, "Always err on the side of generosity." Although we were not wealthy, theirs was a door that was always open. Whatever blessings they had they shared with others, and their attitude of saying "yes" first and figuring out the details later set a tone I hope to pass along to my own children. We certainly don't want to enable friends who may be involved in unhealthy or unholy habits—but when asked for help can we open our hearts and minds even when it is inconvenient or uncomfortable for us?

A recurrent theme in John's writing is the message that "God is love." If Christ's life taught us one thing, it is that our greatest mission is to be the love of God to those in our lives. Just as John was a constant companion to Jesus, you and I are called to stand with our friends, to be light and love, and to accept their giving in return. Do you sometimes hesitate to turn to your good friends in moments when you need support? Remember that in allowing them to help you carry your crosses, you give them the gift of living out the Gospel call to love one another.

TRADITIONS

On the feast of Saint John, many families toast one another with "Saint John's Wine," a warmed and sweetened mulled wine, saying the words, "I drink to you in the love of Saint John."

JOHN'S WISDOM

And we have known and believed the love that God has for us. God is love. And he who abides in love, abides in God, and God in him.

THIS WEEK WITH SCRIPTURE

Sunday: John 19:26–27

When Jesus saw his mother and the disciple there whom he loved, he said to his mother, "Woman, behold your son." Then he said to the disciple, "Behold, your mother." And from that hour the disciple took her into his home.

> *Jesus, in giving to Saint John the gift of caring for our Blessed Mother, you made her our mother as well. In turning to Mary, may we draw closer to you.*

Monday: Proverbs 18:24

Some friends bring ruin on us,
but a true friend is more loyal than a brother.

> *Lord, help me to nurture the productive friendships in my life and to steer away from relationships that do not lead me closer to your message of love.*

Tuesday: Ecclesiastes 4:9–10

Two are better than one: they get a good wage for their labor. If the one falls, the other will lift up his companion. Woe to the solitary man! For if he should fall, he has no one to lift him up.

> *God, help me to see and minister to my friends when they fall and need lifting up, and remind me that I can turn to them in my own moments of pain and stumbling.*

Wednesday: John 15:13–14

No one has greater love than this, to lay down one's life for one's friends. You are my friends if you do what I command you.

> *Jesus, you laid down your life for me. Help me to follow your commands so that I may know the continuing gift of your friendship in my life.*

Thursday: Philippians 4:5

Your kindness should be known to all. The Lord is near.

> *Today, Lord, help me to look for opportunities to be kind, putting impatience, frustration, and my own agenda to the side.*

Friday: Sirach 6:14

A faithful friend is a sturdy shelter;
he who finds one finds a treasure.

> *Friend to the friendless, remind me to seek out the gift of friendship with those who lack companions and to be a "sturdy shelter" for my friends who need comfort.*

Saturday: Philippians 3:17

Join with others in being imitators of me, brothers, and observe those who thus conduct themselves according to the model you have in us.

> *Light of the World, help me to join with companions who will lead me closer to you, and surround our family with the gift of strong and true friendships.*

SAINT-INSPIRED ACTIVITIES

For Mom

Treat yourself to a special time with a friend. Invite her to tea in your home, or handwrite a letter to a distant friend. Share your thanks for the special role this woman plays in your life.

With Children

Place a simple vase in the center of your table, and put small slips of paper and pencils nearby. Invite the children to draw or write the names of their special friends and place them in the vase. Pray for those listed, taking time to talk about the true meaning of friendship.

A Prayer for Our Family

Pray as a family each day this week:

Saint John the Apostle,
you were a beloved friend to Jesus.
Help us to treasure the gift of friendship.
May we always remember to share love with our friends,
to be present to them in their hour of need, and to smile with them in times of joy.
Let us also remember family members
who are among our closest friends.
Remind us when we grow impatient with one another
that in loving each other we show our love for you.
We ask your intercession on behalf of our friends who are struggling or suffering.
Help us to follow your example and to seek true and lasting friendship with Jesus always.
Amen.

Something to Ponder

If you are blessed with good friendships, how can you be more giving of yourself in these relationships? If you are lonely, what keeps you from developing and maintaining friendships?

38

Saint Catherine of Bologna

Using Our Creative Gifts to Give Glory to God

September 8, 1413–March 9, 1463
Patronage: Artists
Memorial: March 9

CATHERINE OF BOLOGNA'S STORY

Catherine Vigri spent her early years working in the court of the Marquis of Ferrara prior to entering religious life as a Poor Clare at the age of fourteen. As the novice mistress of her convent, Catherine applied the elementary education she had obtained at court, illuminating manuscripts, composing and playing sacred music, painting, and writing several works including her best-known work, *The Seven*

Spiritual Weapons. Catherine went on to found a convent at Bologna and battled spiritual attacks, visions, and ill health prior to her untimely death.

LESSONS FROM CATHERINE

Catherine of Bologna gave up a comfortable life at court to pursue her passion for her faith. From the early days of her vocation, she had a tremendous desire to live a life of spiritual perfection. She spoke and wrote of the importance of perseverance, of believing in God more than in one's self, and of always having a strong appreciation for the divine. My life as mom feels vastly different than the cloistered regimen Catherine knew in her day. And yet I too can devote myself to small acts of prayer in pursuit of a true relationship with God.

It is said that Catherine—like many women in today's society—may have suffered from clinical depression. We know from reading her own writings that she faced fierce spiritual and physical battles during her life as a nun. She wrote of diabolical encounters and visions so frightening that they would ultimately take a tremendous toll on her health and lead her to an early grave. Despite these crosses, in fact embracing her own sufferings, Catherine never gave up her quest for sainthood. She gave herself fully to leading her sisters to heaven as well. On those days when I feel the world is against me and all I want to do is curl up in bed, I try to remember to call on my friend Catherine to help me in attending to the needs of my little domestic church.

Catherine is known as the patron saint of artists. To view her art and to read her writings is to peer into the soul of a very devoted Christian. One of her most famous works is an icon of the Virgin Mary cradling the Christ Child, offering him a piece of fruit. Catherine Vigri's work may be called simple by some art critics, yet it's clear to me by looking at this piece that she used every ounce of the talent God gave her to bring glory to him and to lead others to his truths.

Catherine's watershed manuscript, *The Seven Spiritual Weapons*, is part devotional guide, part journal. She wrote for the sisters she loved so dearly, not as a lasting legacy but as a means of helping them to be prepared for the very real temptations and persecutions they would face by devoting themselves to knowing and loving Christ. Catherine's writings were some of the earliest printed manuscripts of her time and provide today's women with a rare glimpse at the life of a fifteenth-century heroine. Despite having a limited formal education, Catherine wrote a treatise that is as poignant and relevant for us today as it was when she penned it five centuries ago.

Catherine of Bologna reminds me to continue to do my best creative work, despite my own insecurities and failings, content in the knowledge that I write and create as a sign of my love for the one who gives me whatever talents I possess.

TRADITIONS

After the fashion of the Poor Clare sisters, Saint Catherine's body was buried without a coffin. Nearly two weeks later, a strong floral scent emanated from her grave, and her body was exhumed and moved into the Chapel of the Poor Clares in Bologna. Visitors to the chapel can still pray near the incorrupt body of Saint Catherine, who continues to intercede on behalf of many.

CATHERINE'S WISDOM

Furthermore, do not be slow and afraid to suffer evils and to work at what is good. If you do not push yourself with great effort, you will not be a true spouse of Christ. If, however, you bear suffering for him then you will live in glory with him forever. And the more that you abandon yourself for him, know that in truth you will find him, and you will never be abandoned.

THIS WEEK WITH SCRIPTURE

Sunday: 1 Timothy 4:14

Do not neglect the gift you have, which was conferred on you through the prophetic word with the imposition of hands of the presbyterate.

> *Lord, help me to nurture the gifts you have given to me and to help my children know their talents come from you.*

Monday: Romans 11:36

For from him and through him and for him are all things. To him be glory forever. Amen.

> *To you be the glories of this day. Let me pause to give you thanks for every small bit of loveliness, every smile from a child, every flower petal, and every way in which you love me through your creation.*

Tuesday: Psalm 98:4–5

Shout with joy to the LORD, all the earth;
break into song; sing praise.
Sing praise to the LORD with the harp,
with the harp and melodious song.

> *I want to shout today, Lord, to sing your goodness and your love. Let my work, my fun, and my creativity sing of my love for you!*

Wednesday: Ecclesiastes 3:11

He has made everything appropriate to its time, and has put the timeless into their hearts, without men's ever discovering, from beginning to end, the work which God has done.

> *I will never discover all you have in store for me, Lord, the magnitude of your power and grace. I thank you for it all, even the parts I have yet to discover.*

Thursday: Psalm 104:33–34

I will sing to the LORD all my life;
I will sing praise to my God while I live.
May my theme be pleasing to God;
I will rejoice in the LORD.

Jesus, I rejoice for the new life you have given me. May the small ways in which I create, the small trials I may endure, and the great challenges in my path be signs of my love for you.

Friday: James 1:12

Blessed is the man who perseveres in temptation, for when he has been proved he will receive the crown of life that he promised to those who love him.

So many things tempt me each day, God. Help me to withstand temptations even though I can never sufficiently prove myself to you.

Saturday: Genesis 1:31

God looked at everything he had made, and he found it very good.

Look at all you have made, Lord—it is perfection. May I write, sing, paint, and help my children to create as a small way to share in the beauty of your creation.

Saint-Inspired Activities

For Mom

Do you have a creative passion? It may be painting, writing, scrapbooking, baking, or simply coloring with your children. Let loose your inner artist, and offer your enjoyment and your work as a sign of your love for your creator.

With Children

Have an art show in honor of Saint Catherine of Bologna. Invite each member of your family to create something special, and hang or display your work around your house.

A Prayer for Our Family

Pray as a family each day this week:

Dear Saint Catherine of Bologna,
you used your God-given talents to create beautiful art
and special writing
to help lead others to know and love God.
Help us to look at the talents God has given each person in our family
and to give thanks and praise for these.
May we notice and give continual thanks for the beauty of God's
creation around us.
When we sing, paint, sculpt, and draw, let us try to capture a bit of
God's majesty,
with hearts full of love and appreciation.
Amen.

Something to Ponder

What creative hobbies do you enjoy? How can you make a bit of time in your weekly schedule to foster these God-given talents?

39

Saint Maximilian Kolbe

Relief for Those Struggling with Addictions

January 8, 1894–August 14, 1941
Patronage: Families, Journalists, Against Addiction
Memorial: August 14

MAXIMILIAN KOLBE'S STORY

Maximilian Kolbe always credited Our Lady's intercession for helping him transform from a "wild" child in Russian-occupied Poland into a heroic priest who devoted his life to the spread of the faith. Along with being a noted theologian and scholar, Maximilian Kolbe was a journalist and founded a newspaper, magazine, and radio station. Maximilian formed the Militia Immaculata, a worldwide apostolate that encourages prayer through the intercession of the Blessed

Virgin Mary for the conversion of sinners. As a missionary, his travels took him to Japan and India, but continual poor health curtailed his journeys. He redoubled his evangelistic efforts and was eventually arrested by the Nazis and sent to Auschwitz, where he ministered to fellow prisoners. Maximilian Kolbe's final act of service was giving his own life in exchange for another prisoner, a family man. After leading his fellow condemned prisoners in a three-week period of prayer, celebration of the Eucharist, and fasting, Maximilian Kolbe was killed by lethal injection on the eve of the Feast of the Assumption of Mary in 1941.

LESSONS FROM MAXIMILIAN

Maximilian Kolbe lived in a time not unlike our own, in a society marginalized by sin and a world torn apart by war. In such times, it's tempting to keep one's head down, to try not to attract attention. And yet Father Kolbe did the exact opposite throughout his life. Despite health crises due to an early battle with tuberculosis, Maximilian employed every means of modern communication at his disposal to spread his message of consecration, through Mary, to the work of the Gospel.

As mothers, one of our primary instincts is the care and preservation of our children. I believe that Maximilian felt this same instinct, viewing the faithful as his spiritual children and recognizing the patronage of Mary as the most certain way of ending the madness he saw proliferating around him. She motivated him in his work and gave him the grace and the courage to stand fast at the moment of his death, a death he chose for the sake of saving the life of Francis Gajowniczek.

Maximilian Kolbe is recognized as the patron saint of addicts and those in recovery from addiction. He was not known to be an addict and none of the historical documents seem to point to any family connection with addiction, yet he was martyred by lethal injection, by the introduction of deadly chemicals into his body. Witness statements even say that Maximilian offered his arm freely in the end, not fighting his captors but spiritually prepared to accept the rewards of heaven that awaited him.

When I think about the power of addiction in my own life and in the lives of those I know and love, it seems obvious to me that Maximilian Kolbe should be a powerful intercessor on our behalf. For those who know the constant struggle of addiction, there is truly a sense of powerlessness over which you think you will never gain control. Surely, the prisoners at Auschwitz were subjected to an incomprehensible loss of dignity, power, and existence. Maximilian's bold faith gave him the means to comfort, support, and minister to others in his darkest hours.

Those who do battle daily with recovery from addiction must rely constantly on divine intervention and on the companionship of intercessors such as Maximilian Kolbe. Those who do our best to love and support them must overcome our instincts to look aside, to do nothing, to leave them to their own devices. Maximilian stuck his neck out for his fellow man, even to the point of martyrdom. For him, death was not an end but simply a path to a life he'd chosen in his childhood, when he offered himself to our Blessed Mother and to her Church through his vocation.

For those of us who battle our own demons, whether our addiction is to food, alcohol or other drugs, shopping, or any other "god" which separates us from the one who loves us so greatly, Maximilian Kolbe extends a hand of friendship on our behalf. In those moments when I feel too weak to overcome the binds that tie me down, I have a saint, a martyr, a hero, just waiting to hold my hand and lead me home.

TRADITIONS

Saint Maximilian Kolbe used every means of modern technology to "win the world" for Mary. Today, the Militia of the Immaculata continues its work throughout the world by serving as medical missionaries and ministering in prisons and to addicts. Following Saint Maximilian's example, modern-day adherents to a total consecration to Mary strive daily for an authentic relationship with Christ through his mother, Mary.

MAXIMILIAN'S WISDOM

The most deadly poison of our times is indifference. And this happens, although the praise of God should know no limits. Let us strive, therefore, to praise Him to the greatest extent of our powers.

THIS WEEK WITH SCRIPTURE

Sunday: Luke 4:18

The Spirit of the Lord is upon me,
because he has anointed me
to bring glad tidings to the poor.

> *Lord, let your spirit be upon me to serve those who need you in their lives.*

Monday: Psalm 69:33–34

See, you lowly ones, and be glad;
you who seek God, take heart!
For the LORD hears the poor,
does not spurn those in bondage.

> *God, you are with me. I seek you, and you hear me. For these blessings in this moment, I am glad.*

Tuesday: 1 John 1:9

If we acknowledge our sins, he is faithful and just and will forgive our sins and cleanse us from every wrongdoing.

> *I fail, I sin, and I confess. You forgive, you cleanse, and you give grace.*

Wednesday: Ephesians 4:24

Put on the new self, created in God's way in righteousness and holiness of truth.

> *Lord, let me cast away old shortcomings and put on my new self, created in your love.*

Thursday: Matthew 6:13

And do not subject us to the final test,
but deliver us from the evil one.

> *Deliver our family, Lord. Protect my children from destructive temptations, and draw them close to the safety of your love.*

Friday: Psalm 146:6–8

The maker of heaven and earth,
the seas and all that is in them,
Who keeps faith forever,
secures justice for the oppressed,
gives food to the hungry.
The LORD sets prisoners free;
the LORD gives sight to the blind.

> *You raise us up, you give us sight, and you feed and shelter us. For these and all of the blessings of your love, I give thanks.*

Saturday: 1 Corinthians 10:13

No trial has come to you but what is human. God is faithful and will not let you be tried beyond your strength; but with the trial he will also provide a way out, so that you may be able to bear it.

> *Heavenly Father, in those moments when life's trials feel too great to bear, you offer a way out. You are faithful and loving. Strengthen me for all that I am called to be and to do.*

SAINT-INSPIRED ACTIVITIES

For Mom

Examine the role of addiction in your own life, praying for an end to that which continually separates you from peace, holiness, and good health. If you struggle with a physical or psychological addiction, please seek spiritual counseling and medical care to begin your road to recovery.

With Children

Have a conversation over dinner about the importance of diversity and tolerance in our world today. In an age-appropriate manner, discuss the lessons learned from the Holocaust, and pray together for an end to religious intolerance in our world.

A PRAYER FOR OUR FAMILY

Pray as a family each day this week:

Brave Saint Maximilian Kolbe,
we ask for your friendship and for your help as we courageously
follow the truth and share it with others.
Help us to be a light to friends who do not believe
and a comfort and challenge to those addicted to making bad choices.
Saint Maximilian, remind us to use the tools around us
to share God's love with family and friends.
May we remember the love of Mary, our Mother,
as we try each day to grow closer to her son, Jesus.
Amen.

SOMETHING TO PONDER

What addictions or habits separate you from perfect union with God? How might a closer relationship with Mary help you to battle the challenges you face?

40.

Saint Teresa Benedicta of the Cross

Finding Hope in Our Crosses

October 12, 1891–August 9, 1942
Patronage: Europe
Memorial: August 9

TERESA BENEDICTA'S STORY

Edith Stein's large Orthodox Jewish family welcomed their eleventh child on Yom Kippur, the Jewish Day of Atonement, in 1891. Although raised to be devout in her practice of Judaism, Edith abandoned the faith of her childhood in favor of atheism as she pursued a rigorous and brilliant academic career. A reading of the autobiography of Saint Teresa of Avila and subsequent independent study of the *Catechism of the Catholic Church* led to her conversion, baptism, and entry into the Carmelite convent in Cologne at the age of forty-two. Having taken the name Sister Teresa Benedicta of the Cross, Edith continued her studies and writing, seeing her scholarship as a form of prayer, and united her personal sufferings to the Cross of Christ Jesus. With the atrocities of the war and fearing for the safety of her sisters in Carmel, she encouraged them to seek safety and departed to a convent in the Netherlands with her sister Rosa. There, along with Rosa, she was arrested, sent to Auschwitz, and martyred in the gas chambers for the faith.

LESSONS FROM TERESA

The life of Edith Stein, and her metamorphosis from atheist into Sister Teresa Benedicta of the Cross, can be summed up with her personal motto, "Behold the Cross, our only hope." An accomplished scholar and mystic, Teresa devoted herself to a passionate study of her adopted faith and seemed to focus her work on finding a spiritual connection with Christ born out of embracing, not avoiding, human suffering. That she lived in an era of such incredible persecution makes it difficult to believe that she could see such opportunity for redemption in the tremendous pain unfolding around her.

Some days, my heart is burdened by very sad news that fills my life. A friend delivers a baby with a birth defect, a university student dies in a horrific accident, or a friend's marriage disintegrates into hatred after twenty years. Other days the tragedies are more subtle. A teen engages in cyberbullying, a husband is laid off, or a mother enters counseling for addiction. Part of being united in this Body of Christ is bearing one another's crosses. Part of being a mother is feeling the pain when our children suffer, even if the hurts seem relatively small.

I recently heard a speech by a mother whose twenty-four-year-old daughter had been killed in a tragic automobile accident by a distracted driver. At the end of her talk about offering forgiveness for her daughter's killer, this brave mother began to speak of the tremendous opportunities that had been born of the cross of burying her beloved daughter in the prime of her life. "Please stand up if you were with us the night we lost our daughter," she invited the crowd. A good number of those who had been with the family in the hospital rose to their feet.

Next, she queried, "Please stand up if you have cooked a meal, driven our children, sent us a card, or prayed for us in the months since our loss." At this invitation, not a person remained seated in the Church, since the community had been so active in supporting the family. "You are the blessings that have come from this cross," she shared. "You are the opportunity that has been given to us to heal, and to go on to give the gift of forgiveness."

I can look back at pains I have borne alongside family and friends and recall far too many moments when I've buckled under the suffering, unable to know how to respond and sometimes unable even to turn to God in prayer in those darkest times. I don't know what crosses lie ahead in my life, but I do know that spending time learning about the life of this remarkable woman—who took the name Teresa Benedicta with her Carmelite vows—studying her words, and embracing the prayers she penned has forever changed the way I view my sufferings.

I still have a great deal to learn about uniting these sacrifices with Christ's love for me and gracefully accepting that ultimate gift of love. But with Teresa's companionship, I'm better able to embrace the hope these crosses bear.

TRADITIONS

A bust of Saint Teresa Benedicta of the Cross, one of six patron saints of Europe, on permanent exhibit at the Walhalla Temple in Germany now commemorates her legacy. Additionally, she is a patron for the World Youth Day movement that rekindles the faith in so many of the Church's young people around the globe.

TERESA'S WISDOM

O my God, fill my soul with holy joy, courage and strength to serve You. Enkindle Your love in me and then walk with me along the next stretch of road before me. I do not see very far ahead, but when I have arrived where the horizon now closes down, a new prospect will open before me, and I shall meet it with peace.

THIS WEEK WITH SCRIPTURE

Sunday: Mark 8:34–35

He summoned the crowd with his disciples and said to them, "Whoever wishes to come after me must deny himself, take up his cross, and follow me. For whoever wishes to save his life will lose it, but whoever loses his life for my sake and that of the gospel will save it."

> *Lord, please be with me today, and help me to take up the small crosses in my life and follow you.*

Monday: Luke 23:42–43

Then he said, "Jesus, remember me when you come into your kingdom." He replied to him, "Amen, I say to you, today you will be with me in Paradise."

> *Jesus, remember our family. May the burdens we bear be our path to a life forever with you in paradise.*

Tuesday: Galatians 6:14

But may I never boast except in the cross of our Lord Jesus Christ, through which the world has been crucified to me, and I to the world.

> *I want to boast of you, Jesus, to share my love for you with the world around me.*

Wednesday: Psalm 55:23

Cast your care upon the LORD,
who will give you support.
God will never allow
the righteous to stumble.

> *You are there, God, when I cast all of my cares upon you. You support me when I stumble. You lift me when I fall.*

Thursday: Luke 9:24

For whoever wishes to save his life will lose it, but whoever loses his life for my sake will save it.

> *I am not a martyr, Lord, but let me bear up under the small pressures of living out my faith for you and in you.*

Friday: 1 Peter 5:7

Cast all your worries upon him because he cares for you.

> *Thank you for caring, Lord, when my worries seem too much to bear.*

Saturday: Romans 5:3–5

Not only that, but we even boast of our afflictions, knowing that affliction produces endurance, and endurance, proven character, and proven character, hope, and hope does not disappoint, because the love of God has been poured out into our hearts through the holy Spirit that has been given to us.

> *You have poured your love into my heart, Lord. For this, and even for the sufferings of this day, I give praise because all is a gift from you. May my character be proven and my hope in you remain ever strong.*

SAINT-INSPIRED ACTIVITIES

For Mom

Saint Teresa Benedicta of the Cross died alongside her Jewish brethren, offering her life with strength and courage. Research some of the Jewish roots of our Catholic faith, and remember the souls of those murdered during the Holocaust.

With Children

Saint Teresa never stopped studying her faith, and reading the *Catechism* prompted her conversion. Does your family own a *Catechism*? If not, take a family trip to your local Catholic bookstore and purchase one for your family library. Discuss the importance of studying the precepts of our faith.

A PRAYER FOR OUR FAMILY

Pray as a family each day this week:

Courageous Saint Teresa Benedicta of the Cross,
you gave your life for your faith and united your sufferings with
Christ our Savior.
Encourage us to study our faith as you did.
Walk with us as we support our friends who are suffering with
illness, loneliness, or separation from God.
Help us to find hope and opportunity in the hardships we face,
to bear our crosses bravely, and to always remember to turn to God in
our suffering.
We seek your intercession so that we may face our life's challenges
with your grace and strength as our example and that we may love
Christ passionately as you did.
Amen.

SOMETHING TO PONDER

What is one cross that is currently causing you to despair? What hope might you find in asking Christ to help you bear this burden?

41

Saint John Mary Vianney

Appreciating Our Clergy and Our Faith Family

May 8, 1786–August 4, 1859
Patronage: Priests
Memorial: August 4

JOHN VIANNEY'S STORY

Born to a large and generous farm family in Lyons, France, in 1786, Jean Baptiste Marie Vianney demonstrated an early love for his faith by secretly practicing it with his family and by teaching other children what he knew. Despite political upheaval, an abolition of formal religion in France, and his own academic weaknesses, John Vianney fought to fulfill his vocational calling to the priesthood and was supported in his studies by a generous priest in a neighboring French village. His priestly studies were interrupted by a tour of duty in the French military, but once injured he went into hiding and secretly opened a school for village children. Once ordained, John initially served under his teacher Fr. Bailey, until being appointed Curé or pastor of his flock, despite concerns about his abilities to handle such a responsible role. He held a firm line with his congregants, most of whom had fallen into complete disrespect for the practices of the Church during the time of the French Revolution. Eventually, John Vianney became a world-renowned confessor, often spending up to sixteen hours per day in the confessional. The Curé of Ars was known for his piety, his active prayer life, and his incredible devotion to pastoral works.

LESSONS FROM JOHN

Too many of us take our parish priests for granted. We complain if their homilies are dry, they ask for money too often, or Mass runs longer than we expect. We decry their lack of understanding for our "real world" pressures and think they can't possibly understand what it takes to raise a family. Yet if we happen to find a priest we truly love, we bond with him and feel lost when he is transferred.

The life of John Vianney reminds me to treasure our priests. Young Jean-Marie was catechized in an era when families were forced to worship in secrecy for fear of very real persecution. Despite incredible obstacles John persevered and was ordained a priest. From humble beginnings, he went on to catechize his small flock and also to become a sign of sanctity and a light to hundreds of thousands of pilgrims who traveled to hear him preach or to obtain absolution from this noted confessor. John Vianney wrote with great passion about the trials of life, and he threw himself completely into a life of prayer, fasting, and mortification. Yet he wrote lovingly of the crosses he bore, ultimately recognizing them as gifts from God, as a way of proving our love for him.

In our own day, we hear quite frequently about a so-called vocations crisis plaguing our Church. As the numbers of priests in the country have steadily decreased over the last five decades, the numbers of Catholics have increased, significantly shifting many aspects of parish life. In many places, having fewer priests as well as fewer women religious has encouraged the laity to assume greater responsibility for our parishes. Within this shifting ecclesial culture, we Catholic parents hold one of the key solutions to easing the tide of lost vocations. The future leaders of our Church—priests, sisters, and lay ecclesial ministers—may well reside in our homes. We have the duty of forming our children well in our domestic churches, but also of training their young ears to hear the quiet inklings of God's call for their lives. The seeds we plant within the souls of our sons may be the invitation they need to consider saying "yes" to the priesthood. Our teachings may lead our daughters to consider lives as religious sisters. Our courage and faithful devotion to the Church may nudge our children toward leadership as lay ministers.

Each week, as I sit quietly waiting for the beginning of Sunday Mass, I pray silently for my faith family as they trickle into our church. Many of them I know by face only, having never stopped to introduce myself. I watch as their babies grow into toddlers, then head into school years. I empathize with parents whose children leave home for college, and I see the grieving of our elderly parishioners who bury a spouse and then sit alone. I pray for the priests of my parish, who give so much of themselves to us each week. We are a family, the Body of Christ incarnate right here in the Diocese of Fresno. We come to be nourished together by Word and Sacrament and then take our leave of one another as we carry the Good News of the Gospel into our corners of the world between Sundays.

John Vianney teaches me to love my faith with every ounce of my being. He counsels me not to shy away from sacrifice, to embrace the crosses big and small that litter my path, to pray diligently, and to frequently pursue the sacraments. His life given fully to God's will reminds me especially to constantly give thanks for those holy men who do the same in today's world, despite all of the trials our modern-day priests endure.

TRADITIONS

John Vianney is the patron saint of parish priests. In 2009–10, Pope Benedict XVI marked the 150th anniversary of his death by proclaiming a Year for Priests. Pilgrims traveling to the Sanctuary of Saint John Vianney in Ars-sur-Formans, France, can view and venerate the relics of the Curé, tour his home, and see the bed where John frequently did battle with the devil.

JOHN'S WISDOM

When people wish to destroy religion, they begin by attacking the priest, because where there is no longer any priest there is no sacrifice, and where there is no longer any sacrifice there is no religion. . . . The priesthood is the love of the Heart of Jesus. When you see the priest, think of Our Lord Jesus Christ.

THIS WEEK WITH SCRIPTURE

Sunday: Exodus 20:8–10

Remember to keep holy the sabbath day. Six days you may labor and do all your work, but the seventh day is the sabbath of the LORD, your God.

> *Father, I devote today to you. Help me to savor this day with my family.*

Monday: Acts 20:28

Keep watch over yourselves and over the whole flock of which the holy Spirit has appointed you overseers, in which you tend the church of God that he acquired with his own blood.

> *God, keep and guard our parish priests as they fulfill their vocations. Let them know your will for their work and your love in their lives.*

Tuesday: 1 Peter 2:9

You are "a chosen race, a royal priesthood, a holy nation, a people of his own, so that you may announce the praises" of him who called you out of darkness into his wonderful light.

> *Help me to fulfill my baptismal commitment to be priest, prophet, and king to all I meet.*

Wednesday: Jeremiah 29:11

For I know well the plans I have in mind for you, says the LORD, plans for your welfare, not for woe! plans to give you a future full of hope.

In this time, in this place, let me fully accept your plans for my life, embracing the future you have designed especially for me.

Thursday: Luke 22:19

Then he took the bread, said the blessing, broke it, and gave it to them, saying, "This is my body, which will be given for you; do this in memory of me."

Jesus, let me remember your love for me each time I receive the Eucharist. May I never take for granted your gift of salvation.

Friday: John 6:27

Do not work for food that perishes but for the food that endures for eternal life, which the Son of Man will give you. For on him the Father, God, has set his seal.

As I journey through all the work that today holds in store, may I pursue the path that leads to an eternity spent with you in heaven.

Saturday: Romans 12:4–5

For as in one body we have many parts, and all the parts do not have the same function, so we, though many, are one body in Christ and individually parts of one another.

Heavenly Father, help our parish community, in communion with our priests, to work as an instrument of your light and your love in this world.

Saint-Inspired Activities

For Mom

Follow Saint John Vianney's example of embracing your crosses as blessings from God. In those moments when you feel most frustrated by the daily trials you face, pause consciously for a quiet moment of prayer.

With Children

Invite your parish priest to dinner in your home. Plan a simple family-style meal, letting each child take an active part in the preparations. Have the kids create a "thank you" card for the priest, and take extra care to express your appreciation to him.

A Prayer for Our Family

Pray as a family each day this week:

Saint John Mary Vianney,
thank you for your commitment to being a good and holy priest,
even when life placed great obstacles in your path.
Help us to know God's will for our lives
and to have the courage to say "yes" even when his plans may not
line up with our own.
We pray that you will intercede for our parish priests
and for all who give their lives to service of the Church.
Keep them safe, committed to the truth, and gratefully supported in
their ministry.
May we bear with strength the crosses that fill our lives,
remembering that in accepting and embracing them,
we express our love for God the Father, who blesses us beyond our
greatest dreams.
Amen.

SOMETHING TO PONDER

How can you better support your parish priest? What efforts can you make to encourage community among members of your parish?

42

Saint Clare of Assisi

Embracing a Simple Existence

ca. 1193–August 11, 1253
Patronage: Television, Laundry Workers
Memorial: August 11

CLARE OF ASSISI'S STORY

Born of a noble family, Chiara di Favarone led a pious childhood and was devoted at an early age to the teachings of her fellow Assisian, Francesco Bernardone. At the age of eighteen and against the wishes of her guardian uncle, Clare fled her home, went to Francis's church, and entered religious life in a Benedictine convent. Her sister Agnes and her mother eventually joined her, and with Francis's guidance Clare founded a Franciscan community for women known initially as the Order of Poor Ladies. Along with a deep love of the Eucharist and daily meditations upon the Passion of Christ, Clare devoted herself fully to service of the poor and to the formulation of her order's rule, which called for strict abstinence, silence, and perfect poverty.

LESSONS FROM CLARE

In our society where "supersize" is a verb and excess seems the norm, Clare's firm refusal to allow her order to own property, and the order's complete reliance upon alms, is difficult for me to fathom. Clare was born to a wealthy family but came to completely eschew material goods, so much so that even bishops and popes tried to persuade her away from her total commitment to holy poverty.

You and I are probably not called like Clare to live on only bread and water, sleep on the cold ground, and wear no stockings. But we can still learn a lesson from her in devoting ourselves to a more simple existence. By taking a few simple steps, we can align ourselves more fully with those living on the margins of society and lessen our consumption of the earth's precious resources. By preparing simple meals most days of the week, avoiding the need to keep up with the latest fashion and entertainment trends, and reserving a portion of our material blessings to share with those in need, we emulate the rule that Clare clung to with such ferocity.

Our Church today continually subjects itself to an ongoing debate about the role of women, with many decrying the lack of opportunities for women to lead. Yet women like Clare provided an example as far back as the thirteenth century for the role of the "feminine genius." Clare was the first woman known to have written a rule for a religious order, refusing to compromise on her commitment to a true spirit of poverty for her sisters. Even as she lay at death's door, she held out until receiving formal papal approval for the constitution that would spawn a legacy of Poor Clare sisters serving around the globe in the Franciscan tradition. Although Clare never left the walls of her cloister, she welcomed visits with bishops, cardinals, and even popes who recognized the depths of her witness to the faith. Her fast track to canonization points again to the impact that this simple woman had upon

the Church of her time. Subsequent generations have come to revere
the spirituality of this woman, counting her as Francis's partner in
leading millions to a deeper communion with Christ.

Through her life and the heritage she left behind, Clare shows me
that having an impact on my world does not have to be about being
rich, famous, or worldly. As a mom, I often face days like those spent
by Clare and her sisters. I cook, I serve, I clean, and then I start the
cycle over. I go, and go, and go, often relying upon my physical reserves
and spiritual stores to see me through the monotony, the demands, and
the frustrations. Often, I complicate things for myself by adopting a
"keeping up with the Joneses" mentality that has me thinking I need
to run my kids to every possible activity, while sporting the latest styles
and driving the newest vehicles. It can truly be downright exhausting!

Clare of Assisi has taught me to embrace simplicity, to seek poverty
of spirit. In my own world, this means not feeling the need to run
to every meeting or party. It means dialing down the constant sound
around me and reaching for the silence that will allow me to hear God's
voice. It means subsisting on a more simple diet. Finally, it means taking hold of chances to give to others rather than to be the recipient.
So often I fall short of these goals, and yet the light of the saint whose
name literally means "bright" continues to point toward my own personal path to sainthood. I'm learning, with Clare's example, to choose
the simpler, quieter, less complicated forks in the road to Jesus.

TRADITIONS

With the proliferation of televisions in homes during the 1950s, Saint
Clare of Assisi was named patron saint of television. This harkened
back to Clare's miraculous vision one snowy Christmas when she was
too ill to attend midnight Mass with her sisters. Despite her physical
absence, Clare miraculously viewed the celebration of the Eucharist on
the wall of her cell, hearing the chants and also visualizing the nativity.

CLARE'S WISDOM

Go forward securely, joyfully, and swiftly, on the path of prudent
happiness.

THIS WEEK WITH SCRIPTURE

Sunday: Psalm 9:2

I will praise you, LORD, with all my heart;
I will declare all your wondrous deeds.

> *How marvelous is your love for our family, God. I praise you,*
> *bless you, thank you for your wondrous ways.*

Monday: Proverbs 22:9

The kindly man will be blessed,
for he gives of his sustenance to the poor.

> *Lord, let me seek opportunities to be kind to others, to give,*
> *and to expect nothing in return.*

Tuesday: Micah 6:8

You have been told, O man, what is good,
and what the LORD requires of you:
Only to do the right and to love goodness,
and to walk humbly with your God.

> *To walk humbly—so simply said and yet so difficult to do.*
> *May I choose only the good, only the right, and do so with*
> *great humility as I walk toward you, Lord.*

Wednesday: James 2:5

Listen, my beloved brothers. Did not God choose those who are poor
in the world to be rich in faith and heirs of the kingdom that he
promised to those who love him?

> *Thank you, God, for choosing us, for loving us, and for the*
> *promise of your kingdom forever.*

Thursday: 2 Corinthians 9:7

Each must do as already determined, without sadness or compulsion, for God loves a cheerful giver.

> *Heavenly Father, help me to be a cheerful giver and to model your love for my husband and my children.*

Friday: Ephesians 4:32

Be kind to one another, compassionate, forgiving one another as God has forgiven you.

> *Bless you, Lord, for loving and forgiving me despite my failings. In showering kindness upon my children, let me love you as much as you have loved us.*

Saturday: Luke 6:20

Blessed are you who are poor,
for the kingdom of God is yours.

> *I long for your kingdom, God. Grant me a poverty of spirit, a holy void that will be filled only with your love.*

SAINT-INSPIRED ACTIVITIES

For Mom

Attempt to simplify your life a bit by adopting some of the components of Saint Clare's rule for yourself. Spend as much time as possible in silence for a day. For many moms, this may only be for five or ten minutes, but as much as possible tune in to the still, quiet voice of God. Another day, fast from meat or prepackaged, processed foods, uniting your small sacrifice with Jesus' passion for those in our world who bear the pain of poverty.

With Children

Saint Clare is the patron saint of television. Have a family TV party. Before tuning in to a favorite show, carry on a conversation at dinner about good viewing choices, intentional selection of programming, and the role that entertainment plays in our lives.

A PRAYER FOR OUR FAMILY

Pray as a family each day this week:

Saint Clare,
you are a bright light for our family.
We ask your intercession
as we try to embrace your call to live more simply
and to serve others more lovingly.
Help us to bear small sacrifices with joyful hearts.
Give us the courage to make choices that help others live with more dignity and comfort.
Inspire us to give generously and to treasure the true gift of Jesus in the Eucharist.
In serving and in loving one another,
may we show our true love for God as you did with your life.
Amen.

SOMETHING TO PONDER

How can you simplify your life through your schedule, your commitments, your material possessions, and your relationships?

43

Saint Joan of Arc

Courage in the Face of Adversity

January 6, 1412–May 30, 1431
Patronage: France, Imprisoned People, Military, Radio
Memorial: May 30

JOAN OF ARC'S STORY

Jeanne D'Arc lived a simple childhood with her pious family in the village of Domremy, France, during the era of the Hundred Years' War. As a teenager, she experienced a divine intervention that prompted her to leave her home and go to court to offer her military service. After recognizing the dauphin despite his disguise and after passing the scrutiny of a theological review at Poitiers, Joan was given command of a military regiment. She led her troops into battle at Orleans bearing a standard which read "Jesus: Maria." Her involvement in the siege so motivated the troops that the campaign was a success. Joan was present at the subsequent coronation of Charles VII at Reims but soon fell from favor. She was captured in Burgundy and sold as a prisoner to the English. The king she had served did not come to her defense. The French religious establishment held an unfair ecclesial trial and ultimately convicted Joan of multiple crimes, including heresy and witchcraft. She was executed on May 30, 1431. The nineteen-year-old went to her death with dignity, praying aloud and inspiring witnesses with her faith. Twenty years after her death, Pope Callistus III approved a retrial demanded by Joan's family, and she was exonerated of all of the charges against her.

LESSONS FROM JOAN

When looking at the life of Joan of Arc, it's easy to get caught up in the "hype," the myths and legends that have made her story fodder for a blockbuster movie. But the real Joan is perhaps even more inspiring than the Hollywood version. Mark Twain captured this when he wrote of her, "Great as she was in so many ways, she was perhaps even greatest of all in the lofty things just named—her patient endurance, her steadfastness, her granite fortitude."

When I think back to the things that motivated me during my teenage years, visions of boys, cars, clothing, and the right college come to mind. I try to imagine myself Joan's age, fourteen, demanding to be taken to see the rightful king of her country and offering herself as a military leader. In today's world, most teens are demanding a new cell phone or a later curfew. The seed for her conviction was her faith. Joan believed with absolute certainty that God was calling her to a mission, and she determined to give anything, including her life, to respond to that call.

When I ponder the life of Joan of Arc, I think of my good friend Avery, a teenage high school student living in the Bible Belt. In many ways, Avery is a typical teen—cute, popular, an academic achiever, and busy with extracurricular activities. But when I look beneath the surface, I find a modern-day missionary who's actively involved in spreading her Catholic faith using new media technologies, social networking, and podcasting. Every time I interact with Avery, I learn something new about our Church but more importantly about standing up and witnessing—even when it may not be the popular thing to do. Avery is an apologist, willing to put herself on the line despite what her peers think. Her motivations, like Joan's before her, are the absolute certainty she feels for the Gospel promise of salvation and a sense of urgency to share this message with those she knows and loves.

Joan of Arc and my friend Avery also open my heart to the many teens around the world who today face trials every bit as frightening as those Joan knew in her day—human trafficking, teenage pregnancy, substance abuse, economic instability, and a world at war to name but a few. Just as Joan was willing to march into combat for her country and her faith, I need to be willing to move out of my comfort zone and look at ways that I can aid those teens involved in these modern-day battles. I can listen better, attempt to understand more, and look for proactive ways to help them face the struggles they encounter, from a position of love rather than one of judgment.

Joan of Arc recognized and accepted her role as an instrument of God's will. With amazing fortitude, in the face of tremendous adversity, she stood up to the test and paid the ultimate price. Every day, in a million little ways, I am called to stand up for what I believe in with courage and conviction. On my own, I fall short of doing the right thing far too often. In these moments, a quiet conversation with Joan of Arc and a plea for her intercession help me to face my personal battles with greater courage and with more trust in the goodness of God's plan for my life.

TRADITIONS

A small chapel dedicated to Martin de Sayssuel was constructed in the French village of Chasse around the fifteenth century. Joan of Arc reportedly visited this sacred space, standing upon a stone in intercessory prayer before a statue of the Blessed Mother. She sealed her petition to Mary with a kiss of the stone on which she stood, which would come to be called the "Joan of Arc Stone." In 1927, the chapel was purchased, complete with this stone, and moved to a private estate in New York. Then in 1964, it was presented as a gift to Marquette University, was dedicated to Saint Joan of Arc, and now stands on the Marquette campus.

JOAN'S WISDOM

One life is all we have and we live it as we believe in living it. But to sacrifice what you are and to live without belief, that is more terrible than dying.

THIS WEEK WITH SCRIPTURE

Sunday: Deuteronomy 31:6

Be brave and steadfast; have no fear or dread of them, for it is the LORD, your God, who marches with you; he will never fail you or forsake you.

> *Thank you, Mighty One, for marching with me in all things. With you, I have the strength to withstand all my fears.*

Monday: Psalm 56:3–4

My foes treat me harshly all the day;
yes, many are my attackers.
O Most High, when I am afraid,
in you I place my trust.

> *O Most High, I place my trust in you.*

Tuesday: 1 Corinthians 16:13

Be on your guard, stand firm in the faith, be courageous, be strong.

> *Today, Lord, help me to stand firm and to be strong against any challenge that comes my way.*

Wednesday: Psalm 27:1

The LORD is my light and my salvation;
whom do I fear?
The LORD is my life's refuge;
of whom am I afraid?

You are my light, my refuge, and my salvation.

Thursday: 2 Timothy 1:7

For God did not give us a spirit of cowardice but rather of power and love and self-control.

> *Father, help me to embrace the power of your love dwelling in me and to face the world with a sense of certainty.*

Friday: Hebrews 13:5–6

Let your life be free from love of money but be content with what you have, for he has said, "I will never forsake you or abandon you." Thus we may say with confidence:
"The Lord is my helper,
[and] I will not be afraid.
What can anyone do to me?"

> *Maker of heaven and earth, you give me all I need.*

Saturday: 1 Chronicles 28:20

Be firm and steadfast; go to work without fear or discouragement, for the LORD God, my God, is with you. He will not fail you or abandon you before you have completed all the work for the service of the house of the LORD.

> *In you, Lord, I find my refuge. With you, I am never alone.*

SAINT-INSPIRED ACTIVITIES

For Mom

Many community service organizations have received formal governmental security approval to facilitate donations and gifts to service members and their families from grateful citizens. Visit www.ourmilitary.mil/resources/community-support-for-our-military/ to learn more about how you can thank them for their sacrifices and service.

With Children

Saint Joan of Arc carried a standard into battle which read "Jesus: Maria." Gather craft supplies, and create your family's standard—a banner which declares your faith in the daily battle against temptation and sin.

A Prayer for Our Family

Pray as a family each day this week:

Brave Saint Joan of Arc,
you heard and answered the voice of God calling you
to protect your country.
Pray for us when he invites us to act,
that we may hear and respond to his call.
Intercede for those in our lives who are facing difficult challenges;
may they know God's love for them in overcoming obstacles.
We also ask your intercession for all victims of war, torture, hunger,
and other grave injustices around the world.
Help them to know God's healing love, peace, and justice
in the trials they face.
Thank you for your model of courage, of patriotism, and of faith.
Amen.

Something to Ponder

What are the small missions in your life? Are there teens in your life who could better know the love of God through you and your family?

44.

Saint Patrick

A Heart for Evangelization

ca. 389–ca. 461
Patronage: Ireland, Excluded People
Memorial: March 17

PATRICK'S STORY

Although we have few historically accurate accounts of the "Apostle of Ireland," his own autobiographical writings offer important insights into his life. Patrick was born the son of a Romano-British councilor in Scotland and lived with his well-off family until his sixteenth year, when he was taken captive and ended up in Ireland herding livestock. Enslaved for six years, Patrick ultimately found solace in a deep prayer life and felt divinely inspired to escape captivity. He returned to the continent to pursue his education, monastic preparation, and ordination to the priesthood, but ultimately he returned to Ireland. Patrick devoted the rest of his life to the people of Ireland, helping countless pagans convert to Christianity, establishing monasteries for men and for women, and inspiring many vocations among the natives of this land he had grown to love so greatly.

Lessons from Patrick

When I hear the word "saint," two favorites come immediately to mind: the Little Flower and the Apostle of Ireland. This could be largely due to my having grown up in a family of "Patricks." From my grandmother Patty, to my dad, a brother, and two nephews named Patrick, along with numerous nephews and my own son Adam bearing the favorite family name as a middle or confirmation name, we've paid homage to our favorite Irish evangelist for well over eight generations in my family of origin. But it's more likely because most of my childhood catechesis came from the lips of an Irish priest. In my heart, I always imagine that Patrick was a lot like my childhood pastor, Monsignor Michael Collins.

Father Collins (who eschewed the formality of his honorary title) was a bold apologist, emblazoned with a strong faith and a deep prayer life. But he was also an affectionate friend, a fantastic communicator, and a missionary who went halfway around the world from Ireland to a small beach town in California to minister to those desperate to know the love of God in their lives. Like Patrick, he pursued his vocation with vigor, never backed down from a challenge, and loved Ireland with all his heart.

Everyone should have the pleasure of counting a holy Irish priest as a friend. Their spirit seems to be a legacy of the brave missionary who escaped captivity, scrapped his way to an education, and then turned his back on safety and family privilege to return to the place that had afflicted him with so many years of pain. What motivated him? Perhaps Patrick owed his heart to Ireland since it was there that he turned from a nominal Christian into a young man enrapt with a love for prayer. In his *Confession*, Patrick humbly spells out his lack of preparation for the work he was doing to spread the Gospel, but he also offers an insight into the fuel for his zeal—an incredible prayer life. He shares about pausing up to a hundred times per day in the midst of his labor and through all types of weather to pray. In his darkest moments, he found faith—a faith he couldn't help but share with others.

We moms may not find ourselves in captivity herding cows up mountains or converting Druids, but our daily jobs can feel momentous and crushing at times. Recently, a physician shared with me that her job was "easy" compared to the joys and challenges of being a mom of three little ones under the age of five. Just like Patrick, we moms are apostles, called daily to live out the Good News, even when we're tired, bored, or fed up.

How does one persist when met with squirmy toddlers and teens with an attitude? We follow Patrick's lead. We pray, pray, pray, and when we feel like quitting we pray some more. "Saint Patrick's Breastplate," the lovely Irish prayer commonly attributed to him and no doubt inspired by the pervasiveness of his spirituality, is a great place to start:

> Christ with me, Christ before me,
> Christ behind me,
> Christ within me,
> Christ beneath me, Christ above me,
> Christ on my right, Christ on my left,
> Christ when I lie down, Christ when I sit down,
> Christ when I arise,
> Christ in the heart of every man who thinks of me,
> Christ in the mouth of everyone who speaks of me,
> Christ in every eye that sees me,
> Christ in every ear that hears me.

In those moments when we feel ready to come apart and when our own doubts and weaknesses keep us from sharing the faith as we would like, let us remember to see Christ present all around us—in the messes, in the tangled hair, in the overtired spouse, in the blustery weather, in the unmade bed, or even in that occasional perfect sunrise we catch when we're up caring for a sick child. Christ in every eye that sees us, Christ in every ear that hears us—now that's some news worth sharing!

TRADITIONS

Saint Patrick's Day, March 17, seems to have transcended the typical religious feast and is now celebrated around the world as the one day when just about everyone is Irish. Traditions include the wearing of the green, festive parades, and the enjoyment of traditional Irish fare and beverages.

PATRICK'S WISDOM

Therefore may it never befall me to be separated by my God from his people whom he has won in this most remote land. I pray God that he gives me perseverance, and that he will deign that I should be a faithful witness for his sake right up to the time of my passing.

THIS WEEK WITH SCRIPTURE

Sunday: Acts 13:47

For so the Lord has commanded us, "I have made you a light to the Gentiles, that you may be an instrument of salvation to the ends of the earth."

> *Giver of good things, you have made me a light. Help me to be an instrument of your love in my own world.*

Monday: Matthew 10:19–20

When they hand you over, do not worry about how you are to speak or what you are to say. You will be given at that moment what you are to say. For it will not be you who speak but the Spirit of your Father speaking through you.

> *Jesus, Heir of all things, you assure me of your Father's presence in me. Help me to set my worries and concerns to the side.*

Tuesday: Romans 8:26–27

In the same way, the Spirit too comes to the aid of our weakness; for we do not know how to pray as we ought, but the Spirit itself intercedes with inexpressible groanings. And the one who searches hearts knows what is the intention of the Spirit, because it intercedes for the holy ones according to God's will.

> *Father, my prayers fall so short, yet you know every corner of my heart. Help me to rest in that confidence, and to hear your voice echo in my soul.*

Wednesday: Matthew 24:13–14

But the one who perseveres to the end will be saved. And this gospel of the kingdom will be preached throughout the world as a witness to all nations, and then the end will come.

> *I want to persevere, Lord, to be your witness. Be with me when I feel too weak, too feeble, or too self-conscious to share my personal witness.*

Thursday: Acts 26:16

Get up now, and stand on your feet. I have appeared to you for this purpose, to appoint you as a servant and witness of what you have seen [of me] and what you will be shown.

> *Blessed Jesus, help me to get up now, to stand, and to do all that you ask of me.*

Friday: Mark 16:15

He said to them, "Go into the whole world and proclaim the gospel to every creature."

> *Jesus, my Master and Shepherd, there is so much goodness to proclaim. Embolden me to do your will.*

Saturday: Luke 24:48–49

You are witnesses of these things. And [behold] I am sending the promise of my Father upon you.

> *I am a witness, Glorious Lord, of the goodness of your promises and of the joy of following you. Thank you for the promises you continue to fulfill in our lives each day.*

SAINT-INSPIRED ACTIVITIES

For Mom

Saint Patrick spoke and wrote often of his active prayer life. Take a look at your daily schedule and try to carve out three intentional and scheduled periods each day where you can spend even just a few moments in quiet prayer.

With Children

Prepare some traditional Irish food such as hunter's pie, potato soup, or Irish soda bread and enjoy a family meal together. Wear green to the table in honor of Saint Patrick.

A PRAYER FOR OUR FAMILY

Pray as a family each day this week:

Good Saint Patrick,
your love for the Lord caused you to leave your home
and carry the Good News to people who had never known
the love of Christ.
Your prayers enabled you to do great things for God.
Help us as we strive to be apostles like you.
We ask your intercession for those moments when we lack faith,
when we don't have the words to pray,
or when we fear what others may think.

May we always see the face of Christ in others,
and may we know we are never alone.
Amen.

SOMETHING TO PONDER

How can you better share your faith in your everyday life? How do you witness in word and action?

45.

Saint Katharine Drexel

Fostering a Spirit of Tolerance

November 26, 1858–March 3, 1955
Patronage: Racial Justice, Philanthropists
Memorial: March 3

KATHARINE DREXEL'S STORY

Katharine Drexel was born to wealthy banker Francis Drexel and his wife, Hannah, who died only weeks after Katharine's birth. Drexel soon married Emma Bouvier, and Katharine's parents ensured that travel, faith formation, and a compassion for the poor were a part of her upbringing. After inheriting the family fortune, Katharine became interested in the plight of Native Americans and poor African Americans. She devoted her life to missionary work, the foundation of the Sisters of the Blessed Sacrament, and the building of dozens of schools, including Xavier University, the first institution of higher learning to admit people of color. A heart attack in 1935 led Mother Katharine into a more contemplative phase of her life, and she devoted the last twenty years of her ministry to prayer, eucharistic adoration, and meditation.

LESSONS FROM KATHARINE

Katharine Drexel's childhood experiences as the second of three daughters of an affluent banker and a beloved stepmother opened her eyes to a world beyond her own, opened her mind to education, and opened her heart to those less fortunate. From an early age, loving parents taught her that being gifted with so much gave her the responsibility to share her blessings with others. She devoted her life to this mission, literally putting her money to work building a legacy that touched countless lives.

By nature, Katharine was likely more suited to life as a cloistered nun than to a life spent serving in poor and far-flung parts of the country. Katharine had an audience with Pope Leo XII to ask for his advice and support in reaching out to the Native American peoples who had known great persecution and poverty in the United States. The Holy Father challenged Katharine to become a missionary. The young multi-millionaire could have simply written large checks and stayed in the comfort of her social strata. In fact, some of her spiritual advisers suggested this. But God's calling for her life became clear, and she answered affirmatively, founding her own religious order, donating over twenty million dollars to her causes, and ministering in hands-on fashion to those she witnessed being oppressed.

This wealthy young woman would be the instrument by which the Church in the United States opened its eyes to the systematic discrimination heaped upon native citizens and former slaves. Katharine saw the need not only for formal education for these poor children but she also had an intense longing to share her love for the Eucharist with them so that they would know God's love.

Sadly, despite legal protections and civil rights protections, my children are still growing up in a world in which racial injustices exist and in a time when disparity of beliefs seems to divide us in new and ever more caustic ways. Hate persists, poisoning new generations and seeping into our homes and schools. The advent of technology has created new ways for the messages of disharmony to be spread and has given our children new means to bully and hurt one another.

I often ask myself, "How can I make a difference? I am not an heiress. Our family struggles to balance a budget each month. I cannot leave my home and go into the missions. I'm only a mom."

Katharine Drexel shows that one woman can make a difference, and she reminds me that I am called to do so in my own unique way. Every week, I interact with future world leaders, business owners, doctors, teachers, priests, and sisters who dine at my table, hang out with my sons, and ride in my car. I have a direct impact on my own children, but also on their friends, our neighbors, and my own sphere of influence. One conversation at a time, I have the ability to purge hatred and racism from my home and our world.

I recall driving a car full of boys on a field trip to a more impoverished part of our community. When one made a racial remark, I felt my blood pressure rise while a few of his buddies laughed at the comment. Calming myself, I pulled the car to the curb. For the next ten minutes, we held a conversation on the hurtful nature of the comment, on our duty as Christians to love our neighbors, and on the plight folks living in that part of our city faced. The comment wasn't made by one of my sons. I could have kept the peace, turned the other cheek, and kept driving. But I knew in my heart that someone needed to have a firm, but loving, conversation with the young man who felt that by belittling others he somehow made himself look better. I couldn't allow that poison to infiltrate my sons' hearts. My silence would have felt like a tacit approval of a hateful message. Did I change the world that day for the better? Maybe in some small way I did—and maybe the lesson the boys learned in that car can somehow be one small baby step toward a future where we all love more and hate less.

If each of us makes the decision to follow the example of Katharine Drexel and to bravely step outside our comfort zone to prioritize an end to intolerance, we can make change. Fueled by the Eucharist and a deep desire to live out and to spread Christ's teachings, we can—and will—make a difference.

TRADITIONS

Today, Saint Katharine Drexel's Sisters of the Blessed Sacrament focus their missionary efforts predominantly among black and Native American communities. Xavier University, the nation's first and preeminent historically black Catholic university, continues to prepare its students for roles of leadership and service.

KATHARINE'S WISDOM

If we wish to serve God and love our neighbor well, we must manifest our joy in the service we render to him and them. Let us open wide our hearts. It is Joy that invites us. Press forward and fear nothing.

THIS WEEK WITH SCRIPTURE

Sunday: Galatians 3:28

There is neither Jew nor Greek, there is neither slave nor free person, there is not male and female; for you are all one in Christ Jesus.

> *Father, help me today to meet every person in my path as a fellow brother or sister in your Son, Christ Jesus.*

Monday: 1 John 2:9

Whoever says he is in the light, yet hates his brother, is still in the darkness.

> *Shine your light, Lord, into any dark corners in my heart that harbor hate, enmity, prejudice, or indifference.*

Tuesday: 1 John 4:10–11

In this is love: not that we have loved God, but that he loved us and sent his Son as expiation for our sins. Beloved, if God so loved us, we also must love one another.

Jesus, you gave your life for each of us, regardless of our worthiness. Let me be an instrument of your saving love.

Wednesday: 1 John 4:18

There is no fear in love, but perfect love drives out fear because fear has to do with punishment, and so one who fears is not yet perfect in love.

I fear the things I do not know or do not comprehend. Enable me to love more fully, to drive out fear, and to be more perfect in you.

Thursday: James 2:1

My brothers, show no partiality as you adhere to the faith in our glorious Lord Jesus Christ.

For those moments when I have shown partiality or prejudice, hatred or rejection, I seek your forgiveness, God.

Friday: Romans 2:11

There is no partiality with God.

Thank you, Heavenly Father, for a love that knows no color, no class, no limits. Help me to model this love for my children.

Saturday: Matthew 7:12

Do to others whatever you would have them do to you.

Your love is golden, your compassion priceless. May my heart be opened to everyone around me, and may my actions represent only love and never hatred or fear.

SAINT-INSPIRED ACTIVITIES

For Mom

Learn more about the racial and ethnic diversity in your own diocese. Reach out to a local organization that ministers to the underserved in your town, and volunteer a few hours or pray specifically this week for their mission.

With Children

Learn something together about the native peoples who once lived in your part of the country. Consider a field trip to a local museum, or check out a book to explore their history, their traditions, and their current role in your community.

A PRAYER FOR OUR FAMILY

Pray as a family each day this week:

Saint Mother Katharine Drexel,
you devoted your life to the poor, the persecuted, and victims of discrimination.
You used your gifts and talents to heal them, to educate them,
and to lead them to know Jesus Christ and our Church.
Help us to be open and loving to everyone we meet,
even if they are different from us in culture or in belief.
May we open our hearts to love as Christ did, without regard to how someone looks, how one speaks, or how one dresses.
Open our eyes to the beauty that lies inside of people
instead of the way they look on the outside.
May our love for Jesus in the Eucharist be a great gift that we share with everyone,
and may it inspire us to make our world a more loving home for all the world's children.
Amen.

SOMETHING TO PONDER

How do racial, religious, or political intolerances affect your relationships and choices?

46

Saint Anthony of Padua

Speaking with Our Actions

ca. 1195–June 13, 1231
Patronage: Lost Articles, Expectant Mothers, Oppressed People
Memorial: June 13

ANTHONY OF PADUA'S STORY

Born to a noble family in Portugal, Fernando de Bulhões was educated at his local cathedral and entered formation at the age of fifteen to become an Augustinian friar, taking the name of Anthony. His training afforded him knowledge of scripture that would later be put to great use in his noted preaching style. After being inspired by the lives and sanctity of early Franciscan martyrs, Anthony obtained permission to join the Franciscans and spent his early days performing humble tasks. But soon he was recognized as an accomplished homilist. He spent his all-too-brief remaining years traveling widely and preaching to enormous crowds who were often moved to personal conversion by his ability to make sacred scripture and theological precepts relevant to their everyday lives. Anthony was noted for his humility, his tremendous zeal in preaching, his empathy for the poor, and his ability to reach the souls of those most in need of Christ's compassionate love.

LESSONS FROM ANTHONY

Many a mom has prayed for the intercession of Anthony when searching for a lost "binky," her car keys, a parking space, or a missing piece of homework. But perhaps few of us know why we reflexively turn to this go-to saint in those moments when our frustration level is at its highest. This tradition relates to Anthony's miraculous involvement in the return of a precious stolen Psalter. The young novice who took Anthony's favorite prayer book was moved by divine intervention to return it after Anthony prayed for its recovery.

This and many other miracles and legends attributed to Anthony during his all-too-brief lifetime might overshadow the real lessons we moms can learn from Portugal's favorite son. Anthony of Padua is quoted as having said,

> Actions speak louder than words; let your words teach and your actions speak. We are full of words but empty of actions, and therefore are cursed by the Lord, since he himself cursed the fig tree when he found no fruit but only leaves. It is useless for a man to flaunt his knowledge of the law if he undermines its teaching by his actions.

I often think about the unspoken lessons I share with my children each day. I teach them to pray and to turn to Jesus in their times of despair or loneliness, and then I let myself give way to moments of stress and anxiety in their presence. Or I teach them to love one another and share, and then I give their dad the cold shoulder when he does something that bothers me. I spend my work hours writing and speaking on topics of faith, but sometimes I fall into the bad habits of gossip and materialism. Certainly there are also positive actions they witness—moments when Greg and I express our love for each other through simple acts of service or times when I reflexively try to help a friend in need.

Anthony of Padua didn't desire to live his life in the spotlight. He intentionally tried to emulate the virtue of humility he admired so greatly in Saint Francis. He kept his scholastic background a secret until he was unexpectedly called upon to preach at an ordination. But once his talents were known, he gave up his privacy and put his body through great wear and tear to reach out to God's people.

When preaching, Anthony threw his whole self into the task and worked especially hard to convey God's truth to those who taught falsely. Today, my children are growing up in a society full of mixed messages and false values. As a mom, it's my job to teach them virtues with my actions but also to be unafraid of being a bit countercultural in how we live our lives. Sometimes this means following the example of the saint who was known as the "Hammer of the Heretics." For me, being the "hammer" in my home sometimes means taking the hard stance, being more a parent than a friend, and praying nonstop that my messages—both spoken and unspoken—will help guide my children along the path to heaven.

TRADITIONS

Saint Anthony of Padua was known to have great compassion for the poor. An ordinance he helped to pass in Padua is said to be one of the earliest forms of protection and reparation for debtors. The tradition of "Saint Anthony's Bread" involves the giving of alms or aid to the poor in thanksgiving for prayers answered through the intercession of the good saint.

ANTHONY'S WISDOM

The saints are like the stars. In his providence Christ conceals them in a hidden place that they may not shine before others when they might wish to do so. Yet they are always ready to exchange the quiet of contemplation for the works of mercy as soon as they perceive in their heart the invitation of Christ.

THIS WEEK WITH SCRIPTURE

Sunday: 1 John 3:7

Children, let no one deceive you. The person who acts in righteousness is righteous, just as he is righteous.

> *Director of my path, help me to seek you and to love you with my actions as much as I do with my words.*

Monday: Luke 15:31–32

[His father] said to him, "My son, you are here with me always; everything I have is yours. But now we must celebrate and rejoice, because your brother was dead and has come to life again; he was lost and has been found."

> *Holy One, you love me even when I am lost. Help me to rejoice always in finding your love around me.*

Tuesday: Ecclesiastes 3:1,6

There is an appointed time for everything,
and a time for every affair under the heavens.
A time to seek, and a time to lose;
a time to keep, and a time to cast away.

> *God, you who know all time, help me to recognize and to follow your plan for this day, to seek you and to lose my anxieties through your grace.*

Wednesday: Titus 2:15

Say these things. Exhort and correct with all authority. Let no one look down on you.

Jesus, True Light of my life, be with me as I teach my children. May I follow your words and your deeds in sharing your perfect love with them.

Thursday: Acts 4:12

There is no salvation through anyone else, nor is there any other name under heaven given to the human race by which we are to be saved.

Savior, you alone are the path to my salvation.

Friday: Titus 2:3–5

Similarly, older women should be reverent in their behavior, not slanderers, not addicted to drink, teaching what is good, so that they may train younger women to love their husbands and children, to be self-controlled, chaste, good homemakers, under the control of their husbands, so that the word of God may not be discredited.

God, in my words, in my actions, and in my love, may I be a credit to you and to your word.

Saturday: Matthew 7:7

Ask and it will be given to you; seek and you will find; knock and the door will be opened to you.

Provider of all that is perfect, let me remember to ask, to knock, and to seek knowing that you are always there to open the door to heaven.

SAINT-INSPIRED ACTIVITIES

For Mom

One way to avoid lost items is to get more organized. Choose one room to "declutter," and give gently used items to a local Catholic charity.

With Children

In honor of Saint Anthony, bake a loaf of homemade bread (or use frozen bread dough), and deliver it to your favorite priest with a thank-you note for his service to your parish and his teaching of the faith to your family.

A PRAYER FOR OUR FAMILY

Pray as a family each day this week:

Humble Saint Anthony of Padua,
you gave your life to help others learn about Jesus.
Help us to teach others about loving and living by the way we act
toward one another.
Let our actions speak the same message as the words we use.
Please intercede on behalf of our friends who are in need
and for all the poor who suffer so greatly in our world today.
Remind us to share our blessings with others
and to thank God each day
for the many graces he showers upon our family.
Amen.

SOMETHING TO PONDER

How do your actions and non-verbal behaviors sometimes contradict the words you speak and the faith you profess?

47

Saint Josephine Bakhita

Freedom from Enslavement
and an End to Human Trafficking

1869–February 8, 1947
Patronage: Sudan, Against Human Trafficking (proposed)
Memorial: February 8

JOSEPHINE BAKHITA'S STORY

Born in Darfur in 1869, Bakhita's childhood was tragically marked by her kidnapping and enslavement. She was subjected to so much physical and emotional abuse by the series of owners she served that she forgot her given name and birth date, and her captors dubbed her "Bakhita" (meaning "fortunate"). Her captivity took her to Venice, Italy, where she eventually fought for her freedom, experienced a religious conversion, and ultimately devoted her life to her vocation as a

Canossian sister, taking the name Josephine. As a Daughter of Charity and the portress at the institute run by the Canossian Sisters, Josephine was beloved for her encouragement to children and to the poor. She spent her twilight years writing and speaking, working through immense physical pain to support her order's missions. At her death in 1947, Josephine Bakhita's final words, "Madonna! Madonna!" testified to the depth of her devotion.

Lessons from Josephine

Although it is difficult to pin down exact statistics, estimates indicate that as many as one million people worldwide are currently victims of human trafficking and that as many as half of these victims are children. Sitting in my comfortable suburban home, it's so easy to think of the insidious crime of slavery as ancient history, and yet it remains a scar on the hearts of so many in our world today. Since women and children are the most common and helpless victims of slavery, we moms should be all the more ardent in our desire to see an end to this evil in our world.

As I've attempted to open my eyes to this reality and actually *do something about it*, I find myself turning frequently to Josephine Bakhita as a prayer companion. This brave woman found legal freedom from enslavement through Italy's laws and the aid of advocates, and she was ultimately set free through the spiritual healing and power of her baptism and conversion. She was even able to forgive those who had caused her so much pain. Her example calls me to look outside myself and to stop using the excuse that "I'm just one mom" to justify my nonaction on this and other social justice issues. After all, Josephine found a way to break the chains of slavery and to discover joy and peace even after such horrific childhood trauma, and she continues even now to inspire new generations. In his remarks at her canonization, Pope John Paul II said of this African heroine, "She can reveal to us the secret of true happiness: the Beatitudes."

In another sense, Josephine Bakhita is my friend in facing those things that personally enslave me and keep me from full unity with Christ. We each face our own demons. Yours may be different from mine, but regardless of the demons that enslave us, they ultimately steal the peace and joy we so desperately crave for our families and ourselves. A physical addiction, an abusive relationship, or emotional duress can hold us captive within our own homes. Just as Josephine was able to kiss the baptismal font that opened her path to true freedom and offer forgiveness to her captors, I hope to see the gift of my faith not only as a blessing on Sunday mornings but also as a key to overcoming those things that enslave me and as a call to action.

TRADITIONS

Perhaps fittingly, Saint Josephine Bakhita's feast day is celebrated during the month of February, which is Black History Month in the United States—a time of remembrance of important people and events in the history of the African diaspora. Recently, social justice advocates have proposed her as the patron saint for victims of human trafficking and slavery. Parishes and groups have gathered together on Josephine's feast day to pray for the victims and for an end to the horror of human trafficking.

JOSEPHINE'S WISDOM

If I were to meet the slave-traders who kidnapped me and even those who tortured me, I would kneel and kiss their hands, for if that did not happen, I would not be a Christian and Religious today.

THIS WEEK WITH SCRIPTURE

Sunday: Matthew 23:11–12

The greatest among you must be your servant. Whoever exalts himself will be humbled; but whoever humbles himself will be exalted.

> *Lord, may I seek to be ever humble in all my works, and may I remember to reflect any glory that comes my way graciously back to you.*

Monday: Galatians 5:13

For you were called for freedom, brothers. But do not use this freedom as an opportunity for the flesh; rather, serve one another through love.

> *Good and Gracious God, thank you for the gift of true freedom through your Son, my Lord, Jesus Christ. Allow me to serve those around me as though I were serving you.*

Tuesday: Psalm 118:5

In danger I called on the LORD;
the LORD answered me and set me free.

> *Help me call on you in times of trouble and spiritual danger. And when I call you, please help me to listen for your answer, for your true will for my life.*

Wednesday: 2 Corinthians 3:17

Now the Lord is the Spirit, and where the Spirit of the Lord is, there is freedom.

> *Heavenly Father, help me to sense your Spirit in my life and to be a light of that same Spirit to everyone I encounter today.*

Thursday: Romans 6:12–14

Therefore, sin must not reign over your mortal bodies so that you obey their desires. And do not present the parts of your bodies to sin as weapons for wickedness, but present yourselves to God as raised from the dead to life and the parts of your bodies to God as weapons for righteousness. For sin is not to have any power over you, since you are not under the law but under grace.

> *God, you continue to allow your grace to overflow in my life. In times of weakness, strengthen me to overcome any desire that does not draw me closer to my loved ones and to you.*

Friday: Psalm 119:22–25

Free me from disgrace and contempt,
for I observe your decrees.
Though princes meet and talk against me,
your servant studies your laws.
Your decrees are my delight;
they are my counselors.

I lie prostrate in the dust;
give me life in accord with your word.

> *As I struggle to overcome the sins that enslave me this week,
> help me to recognize the place of your word in my life, to study
> your desires for me, and to strengthen the ties that bind me to
> you.*

Saturday: Hebrews 12:14

Strive for peace with everyone, and for that holiness without which
no one will see the Lord.

> *So many times, Lord, I am held hostage by anxiety and stress.
> Help me to know your perfect peace and to share it with
> everyone I meet along my path.*

SAINT-INSPIRED ACTIVITIES

For Mom

The United States Conference of Catholic Bishops has a variety of anti-
trafficking initiatives. Visit www.usccb.org/mrs/howtohelp.shtml for
more information on how your parish can support these efforts.

With Children

Gently speak with your children about the issue of slavery, its history in our country, and the problems that still exist worldwide. Pray

together through the intercession of Saint Josephine Bakhita for an end to slavery in our world.

A PRAYER FOR OUR FAMILY

Pray as a family each day this week:

Saint Josephine Bakhita, little mother to so many,
be a spiritual friend and companion to our family.
Help us to forgive in times when we would prefer to hold a grudge,
especially when forgiving feels so very difficult.
Help us show humility in doing each little task that fills our days
and to carry out our work for God's glory.
Help us to emulate you in every way,
especially in finding true freedom from those things that enslave us,
keeping us from true communion with God and one another.
We ask your intercession on behalf of all those who are victims of
human trafficking
and for an end to this scourge in our world.
May we know your true joy and peace
in embracing the gift of our faith.
Amen.

SOMETHING TO PONDER

What enslaves you and separates you from complete union with God and from completely giving yourself to those you love?

48

Saint Ignatius of Loyola

Living for the Greater Glory of God

1491–July 31, 1556
Patronage: Retreats, Society of Jesus
Memorial: July 31

IGNATIUS OF LOYOLA'S STORY

Iñigo López de Loyola was born to a noble family and raised at Spanish court prior to commencing a military career and a worldly lifestyle. The turning point in his life came when his leg was badly injured by a cannonball. During his recuperation, he immersed himself in reading about the life of Jesus Christ and the biographies of the saints. This prompted a period of major spiritual introspection and conversion at Manresa near the Marian shrine of Montserrat, where he wrote the foundation of his life's work, the *Spiritual Exercises*.

After a brief pilgrimage to the Holy Land, Ignatius (as he began to call himself) studied Latin, the humanities, and theology in Spain and Europe. His work was closely scrutinized, and he was twice imprisoned, but he attracted spiritual comrades who shared his commitment to the faith. In 1534, Ignatius and his friends took communal vows, including an absolute promise to either serve in the Holy Land or to provide unconditional apostolic service at the pope's will. In 1540, Pope Paul III gave formal approval for the founding of the Society of Jesus. Ignatius committed the remainder of his life to building the Constitution of the Jesuits, and to teaching, hearing confessions, building homes for the poor and catechumens, and founding educational institutions, including the Gregorian College in Rome. After years of study, prayer, missionary activity, and obedience, he died in Rome.

LESSONS FROM IGNATIUS

In today's world, the name "Jesuit" is often synonymous with quality education. I think this would please Ignatius, who seemed to acquire a love of learning late in his life. That the company of men he gathered around him would go on to inspire and to educate so many is a testament to him, their first superior general. For me, Ignatius's legacy is a reminder that it is never too late to learn, and that there is nothing more important than continually teaching my children the precepts of our faith.

This means catching those small teachable moments as they occur just as much as it means formal instruction—perhaps even more so. In fact, it was Ignatius who wrote, "Do not let any occasion of gaining merit pass without taking care to draw some spiritual profit from it; as for example, from a sharp word that someone may say to you; from an act of obedience imposed against your will; from an opportunity that may occur to humble yourself, or to practice charity, sweetness, and patience." In other words, be on the lookout for spiritual growth in every situation.

Following Ignatius's teachings has opened my eyes to see God in all things and to attempt a more perfect form of obedience in my life. The motto of the Society of Jesus, *Ad Majorem Dei Gloriam,* reminds me to offer each act "to the greater glory of God." Practicing this discipline myself and sharing it with my family calls us to humility and dedication to God's will, even in the small, mundane tasks that fill our days. Doing housework for God's glory? A diaper changed, a fever soothed, a wayward teen corrected—even our simplest work, done with love and for the glory of God, can be a form of prayer. I believe Ignatius of Loyola would encourage us in every aspect of our vocations, perhaps especially those we find most tiresome.

At the heart of Ignatian spirituality are the *Spiritual Exercises*, a retreat process of twenty-eight to thirty days involving meditation, prayer, consideration, and contemplative work. Few of us moms can imagine taking thirty days of silent, contemplative prayer away from our full lives. Yet from Ignatius we learn the beauty of a daily examination of conscience. The *examen* is a look at the work of God in the midst of our day-to-day moments and a recognition of the grace of his constant love for us. Within this framework, daily prayer includes five components:

1. Recognize and express thanks for the presence of God.

2. Ask for the Holy Spirit's aid and grace in recognizing moments of sin.

3. Review the events of your day, moment by moment.

4. Reconcile with God for the times when you have fallen short.

5. Resolve to trust God and to continue to offer your life for his glory.

Ignatius recognized the need to bend his own agenda to God's perfect will for him and spent the rest of his life in prayer, obedience, and action. In our own way, we have the opportunity to live out a mom's continual version of the *Spiritual Exercises*, offering our days, our gifts, and our love for our families all for the greater glory of God.

TRADITIONS

Students educated within the tradition of Jesuit institutions often inscribe the letters "AMDG" at the top of their assignments, indicating that the gift of their education and the products of their initiative are offered for the greater glory of God.

Ignatius's Wisdom

Teach us to be generous, good Lord; teach us to serve you as you deserve; to give and not to count the cost, to fight and not to heed the wounds, to toil and not to seek for rest, to labor and not to ask for any reward save that of knowing we do your will.

This Week with Scripture

Sunday: 1 John 4:16

We have come to know and to believe in the love God has for us.

God is love, and whoever remains in love remains in God and God in him.

> *God of all love, may I remain in you always.*

Monday: Mark 1:15

This is the time of fulfillment. The kingdom of God is at hand. Repent, and believe in the gospel.

> *Father, forgive me for the many ways I fall short of obeying your will, and reconcile me to a better path.*

Tuesday: Psalm 33:11–12

But the plan of the LORD stands forever,
wise designs through all generations.
Happy the nation whose God is the LORD,
the people chosen as his very own.

> *Your plan, Lord, is perfect, wise, and firm.*

Wednesday: 2 Samuel 22:32–33

For who is God except the LORD?
Who is a rock save our God?

The God who girded me with strength
and kept my way unerring.

> *Strength for the weary, you keep my way, and you are my rock.*

Thursday: Psalm 24:8

Who is this king of glory?
The LORD, a mighty warrior,
the LORD, mighty in battle.

> *Mighty One, may my small gifts be offered for your glory.*

Friday: Psalm 69:14–15

But I pray to you, LORD,
for the time of your favor.
God, in your great kindness answer me
with your constant help.
Rescue me from the mire;
do not let me sink.

> *Lord, in those moments when I feel like I am sinking, slipping away from your love, rescue me with your grace.*

Saturday: Philippians 2:12

So then, my beloved, obedient as you have always been, not only when I am present but all the more now when I am absent, work out your salvation with fear and trembling.

> *I am working on being obedient, Lord. Help me today and always to step closer to your perfect plan for my life.*

SAINT-INSPIRED ACTIVITIES

For Mom

Take time for a daily examination of conscience, as outlined above, at the end of each day. Each evening, before retiring for the night, spend a few minutes in quiet prayer and reflection.

With Children

The Society of Jesus teaches us to offer everything for the glory of God. Have a family conversation and invite each child to reflect upon one of his or her special talents and how this gift might be shared for God's glory.

A PRAYER FOR OUR FAMILY

Pray as a family each day this week:

Saint Ignatius of Loyola,
you changed the course of your life to follow God's plan for you.
Help us attend to any behaviors we may need to change
or any complete U-turns we need to make to follow your will.
Remind us that each of our actions can be a prayer
and that in sharing our gifts and talents we can introduce others
to the perfect love of God.
Help us to embrace learning in everything we do
and to see each day as a chance to grow in grace
and spiritual perfection.
Amen.

SOMETHING TO PONDER

While you may not have time to undertake a thirty-day retreat at this time in your life, when are the moments in your busy day that could be carved out for some quiet prayer? How is God calling you to a more perfect form of obedience in your current vocation?

49

Saint Frances Xavier Cabrini

Bearing Christ's Love to the Marginalized

July 15, 1850–December 22, 1917
Patronage: Immigrants, Orphans
Memorial: November 13

FRANCES XAVIER CABRINI'S STORY

Francesca Cabrini was born prematurely to a large, devout family in Lombardy, northern Italy. As a girl, she desired a religious vocation and a life as a missionary to China, but she was denied admission due to her frail health and instead pursued a career as a teacher. Eventually, Frances's commitment to her work, her administrative skills, and her compassion for the poor won out. With canonical approval she founded the Missionary Sisters of the Sacred Heart. At the request of Pope Leo XIII, she and her sisters traveled to the United States to begin an apostolate to the poor, uncatechized Italian immigrants of New York. Mother Cabrini overcame great obstacles to build schools, orphanages, hospitals, and other outreach facilities in poor communities, traveling constantly wherever she found a need. After becoming a naturalized citizen of the United States in 1909 and extending her apostolate to sixty-seven missions worldwide by the time of her death, she became the first United States citizen to be canonized.

Lessons from Frances

When I look around at Mass each Sunday morning, I see families whose histories have brought them to our church from every corner of the world. Ours is a diverse parish, where celebrations often take on a bountiful excess of cultural variations. I like to think that this diversity, this richness of experiences coming together to celebrate the Eucharist, would make Frances Cabrini smile.

At so many points in her life, the odds seemed stacked against the apostolate of Mother Cabrini. But she turned the burdens she faced into fuel for her mission, which was always to "bear the love of Christ to the world." Her premature birth and lifelong health concerns gave her a heart for those in need of health care. Having lost her parents as a young woman, she ministered in a special way to orphans. As a stranger in a new land who struggled with speaking English, she readily embraced her advocacy for the tens of thousands of Italian immigrants who found themselves without catechesis, but also without proper food and shelter. Although she never physically gave birth, she was a spiritual "mother" to children young and old from east to west.

Unlike Frances, I will never be called to leave my homeland and minister to families a world away. But each day, I come into contact with souls who need mothering. These encounters give me an opportunity to respond as Mother Cabrini's sisters still do all over the world today, and to follow their charism of being a bearer of Christ's love in the world.

I can be a spiritual mother to children in my life who are not growing up in faith-oriented families or who are simply longing for more love. I can be the welcoming arms that provide an open door to families who are new in my community, whether they come from across town or across the world. I can teach our faith through witness, through my actions, or as catechist. I can foster Mother Cabrini's mission of healing by treating my body as a temple, by caring for the health of my spouse and children, and by supporting community-based health-care initiatives for the indigent. In big and little ways, if I open my heart to others, I can emulate Frances's lessons of putting a human face on Gospel values.

Reading about the life of this humble saint from Italy has also taught me to have greater trust in God's providence when the hurdles placed in my path seem too high to jump over on my own. Frances never desired to come to the United States; her greatest hope was to be a missionary in China. Yet she followed obediently when Pope Leo XIII asked of her that she minister "not to the East, but to the West." When she arrived in New York and the archbishop who was supposed to welcome and support her instead tried to send her home, Frances took to the streets, inspiring others to join her mission through their own acts of charity and generosity. She was a woman who would not take "no" for an answer.

In those moments when I am all too ready to take the easy way out, to give up on a plan or a goal, I try to remember Frances Cabrini's personal motto, borrowed from the fourth chapter of Philippians, "I have strength for everything through him who empowers me." With Christ as the source of my strength, I too can be his hands and his heart to those most in need of his love.

TRADITIONS

The Little Rosary of Saint Frances Xavier Cabrini is a chaplet that bears the likeness of Mother Cabrini and the Sacred Heart of Jesus. It contains twenty-five Hail Marys and the intercessory prayer, "O my Savior, hear Saint Frances Xavier Cabrini plead for me."

FRANCES'S WISDOM

We must pray without tiring, for the salvation of humanity does not depend on material success; nor on sciences that cloud the intellect. Neither does it depend on arms and human industries, but on Jesus alone.

THIS WEEK WITH SCRIPTURE

Sunday: Isaiah 25:4

For you are a refuge to the poor,
a refuge to the needy in distress;
shelter from the rain,
shade from the heat.

> *Lord, help me to seek refuge in you today and to give help to those who need your sheltering love.*

Monday: Luke 3:11

Whoever has two cloaks should share with the person who has none. And whoever has food should do likewise.

> *Holy One, help me look for opportunities to give as bountifully as I have received.*

Tuesday: Matthew 5:42

Give to the one who asks of you, and do not turn your back on one who wants to borrow.

> *May I give freely to those who ask, and even to those who don't.*

Wednesday: Luke 12:33

Sell your belongings and give alms. Provide money bags for yourselves that do not wear out, an inexhaustible treasure in heaven that no thief can reach nor moth destroy.

> *Consolation of our hearts, you provide all we need.*

Thursday: Leviticus 25:35

When one of your fellow countrymen is reduced to poverty and is unable to hold out beside you, extend to him the privileges of an alien or a tenant, so that he may continue to live with you.

Help me, Lord, to open myself to those who are in poverty, who are without a home, or without love today.

Friday: Ephesians 2:13

But now in Christ Jesus you who once were far off have become near by the blood of Christ.

Jesus, bind us together in your love.

Saturday: Hebrews 13:1

Let mutual love continue.

Lover of us all, teach me to love perfectly as you do.

SAINT-INSPIRED ACTIVITIES

For Mom

Saint Frances Xavier Cabrini's Missionary Sisters invite volunteers to join them in prayer for their work around the world as "Cabrini Companions." To learn more about this apostolate of prayer, e-mail cabrinicompanion@aol.com.

With Children

Saint Frances Xavier Cabrini's parents read her the stories of great missionaries. She took her name after Francis Xavier, who did so much to spread faith in the East. Share with your children about the many missionaries who did so much to shape our faith within the United States. Daydream together about how you can be missionaries now and in the future.

A Prayer for Our Family

Pray as a family each day this week:

Saint Frances Xavier Cabrini, spiritual mother to orphans,
immigrants, and all in need of care,
you gave your life to bring the love of Jesus to the world.
Inspire our family this week to look outside ourselves
to those who are hurting, lonely, or in times of difficulty.
Help us to look out for those adjusting to new ways of life,
to be compassionate to the sick, and to treat each person with dignity
and respect.
May we always remember, as you did, to seek our strength from
Christ and to share his love with all we meet.
Amen.

Something to Ponder

What are some ways in which you can bear Christ's love to those in
need in your community?

$\mathcal{S}$aint $\mathcal{M}$artha of $\mathcal{B}$ethany

Serving with Grace, Generosity, and Hospitality

First Century
Patronage: Housewives, Cooks
Memorial: July 29

MARTHA OF BETHANY'S STORY

Martha lived with her sister, Mary, and brother, Lazarus, in a home in Bethany. What we know of her life comes to us through stories in the gospels of Luke and John. Martha entertained Jesus in her home, cooking for him and his followers. Following the death of her brother, Martha expressed her faith in Christ, proclaiming him the Messiah. Her faith was rewarded when Jesus raised Lazarus from the dead.

LESSONS FROM MARTHA

What modern-day mom hasn't once in her life related to Martha in her famous scene from Luke's gospel? With a house full of guests—or simply the hungry mouths of our own families—and after hours spent preparing a nice meal, how often do we experience the sense that no one is helping and that our efforts aren't even being properly appreciated?

We know that Martha was a good friend of Jesus. Tradition teaches that she came from an important family, and we can surmise that she was a strong woman, a survivor. While we often remember her as the one who nagged Jesus to get her sister, Mary, to help in the kitchen, John's gospel also portrays Martha as perhaps one of the very first to outwardly profess her complete faith in Jesus as Messiah. With the words "Yes Lord, I have come to believe that you are the Messiah, the Son of God, the one who is coming into the world," she proves herself not a whiner but rather one of the very first to recognize and witness to the divinity of the Master.

I'm fortunate enough to have a dear friend named Martha who is my own twenty-first-century version of the remarkable saint who was lucky enough to be Jesus' friend. In Martha's office at work hangs a small portrait of her patroness, a sturdy woman bearing a large water jug upon a hip that juts out to bear the load, ready to get the job done. What comes across in this depiction of Martha of Bethany is her sass, her attitude, her strength.

Martha's gift for hospitality and service are the same qualities that make my own friend Martha so beloved to so many. She recently wisely recounted to me that the saint must have realized that with so many gathered in her home to learn from their mentor, their master, there would be practical matters at hand. "When they're done talking," she perhaps reasoned, "they're going to want supper."

Hearing the biblical account of Martha and Mary, many of us pause to cast ourselves in one of the two roles. "Am I a 'Martha' or a 'Mary'?" we ask ourselves, as though one is right and the other all wrong. But the truth is, Jesus calls us to be both. Martha provided the gift of hospitality, which in first-century Bethany could have been akin to helping a wayward traveler stay alive. The meal she prepared, the shelter she provided, the practical details to which she attended were her way of serving the Lord she loved so dearly.

But the second half of Martha's story, and the one we should always remember to emulate in our own way, is her absolute declaration of her faith in Jesus. When Lazarus fell ill, she called for her friend, knowing with certainty what he was capable of doing. And in no uncertain terms, when Jesus arrived two days too late, Martha left a home full of guests, found the Messiah, and asked for Jesus' intervention. I ask myself if I have faith enough to mirror Martha's unequivocal profession of faith when I face my own crises.

More than any other mom in my own life, my friend Martha models for me the great example of Martha of Bethany. She is my equivalent of what Jesus surely found in his dear friend Martha—always ready with a welcoming hug, a loaf of fresh baked bread, and a listening ear. Just like Jesus' friend Martha, my Martha reminds me to never discount the importance of hospitality, but also never to neglect the company of my loved ones and to be ever mindful of the ministry of presence. She teaches me to turn to Christ in faith and friendship when I find myself most in need and to believe in the power of his love, even when the challenges I face seem almost insurmountable.

TRADITIONS

According to popular legends, Martha, Mary, and Lazarus traveled miraculously in a rudderless ship with no sails or oars to what is now modern-day France following Jesus' resurrection in order to evangelize the people there. Saint Martha's relics reside in a church named in her honor in Tarascon, France. The town of Villajoyosa, Spain, holds an annual festival in her honor, crediting her with intervening on their behalf and defeating an attacking brigade of pirates on her feast day in 1538.

MARTHA'S WISDOM

"Yes Lord," she told him. "I believe that you are the Son of God, who was to come into the world."

This Week with Scripture

Sunday: 1 Peter 4:9

Be hospitable to one another without complaining.

> *Morning Star, may my heart and my words always serve you.*

Monday: Hebrews 13:2

Do not neglect hospitality, for through it some have unknowingly entertained angels.

> *Help me to open our home to all in need and to see the angel in every guest I greet.*

Tuesday: Leviticus 19:34

You shall treat the alien who resides with you no differently than the natives born among you; have the same love for him as for yourself; for you too were once aliens in the land of Egypt. I, the LORD, am your God.

> *Father of the fatherless, all are equally loved by you.*

Wednesday: Acts 16:15

After she and her household had been baptized, she offered us an invitation, "If you consider me a believer in the Lord, come and stay at my home," and she prevailed on us.

> *Allow me to show my belief by welcoming others as I would welcome you.*

Thursday: Mark 9:41

Anyone who gives you a cup of water to drink because you belong to Christ, amen, I say to you, will surely not lose his reward.

> *Jesus, Prince of life, help me to find my reward in you and to lead my family lovingly to that same reward.*

Friday: Luke 10:41–42

The Lord said to her in reply, "Martha, Martha, you are anxious and worried about many things. There is need of only one thing. Mary has chosen the better part and it will not be taken from her."

> *There is only need of one thing, Jesus. Calm my worry, and help me to rest in you.*

Saturday: John 11:27

She said to him, "Yes, Lord. I have come to believe that you are the Messiah, the Son of God, the one who is coming into the world."

> *Lord, I have come to believe.*

SAINT-INSPIRED ACTIVITIES

For Mom

Saint Martha is the patron saint of housewives. While going about the mundane chores around your home, invoke her intercession and focus on working with a positive attitude.

With Children

Saint Martha welcomed Jesus into her home with home-cooked meals. Invite another family into your home for lunch or dinner. Have every family member take part in the meal planning and cooking, giving each child a role to play in preparing or serving a simple meal.

A PRAYER FOR OUR FAMILY

Pray as a family each day this week:

Saint Martha of Bethany,
you were a special friend to our Lord, Jesus Christ.

Be an intercessor for our family,
and help us do our best to be good friends and welcoming hosts.
Teach us to open our home and our hearts to those we know who
may be lonely, hungry, or simply in need of our friendship.
We want, above everything else,
to follow your example of devout belief.
Remind us to turn to Jesus in prayer when we face trials,
to seek his companionship in our lives,
and to have a strong faith in the power of his love.
Amen.

SOMETHING TO PONDER

How can you avoid getting caught up in the minutia of hospitality
while neglecting the social relationships of those you welcome into
your home?

51.

$\mathcal{B}$lessed $\mathcal{K}$ateri $\mathcal{T}$ekakwitha

Seeing the True Beauty of God in Our Natural Surroundings

> 1656–April 17, 1680
> **Patronage:** Environmentalists, Those Who Have Lost Parents
> **Memorial:** July 14

KATERI TEKAKWITHA'S STORY

Tekakwitha was born in upstate New York in 1656 to a Christian Algonquin mother and a non-Christian Mohawk father, a leader among his people. When she was only four, her family was struck by a smallpox outbreak that left her orphaned, ravaged by scars, and nearly blind. She was taken in by an uncle and she worked diligently to serve her family and her neighbors. Visiting Jesuit missionaries catechized her, and at the age of twenty she was baptized "Catherine" (Kateri in her native language) in honor of Saint Catherine of Siena; but she was vilified and persecuted by her native community. She escaped, traveling over two hundred miles of perilous terrain to a prayer village near Saint Francis Xavier Mission in Canada. There she received her First Communion, committed herself to a life of chastity, and devoted herself to prayer, teaching the faith, and caring for the sick and aged. Kateri Tekakwitha died at the age of twenty-four.

LESSONS FROM KATERI

In my home parish, a large mural depicts Kateri Tekakwitha among other noted saints of the Americas. I've often thought it a bit ironic that this young woman, who likely could never have conceived of a church as grand as mine, would find herself the focal point of such a lovely work of art. What we read of Kateri paints a picture of a rather sickly young woman with pockmarked skin who spent most of her life at the service of others, living a rough existence with few, if any, creature comforts.

But Kateri never seemed to use her difficult path to Christianity as an excuse or complain of it as a hardship. Following her conversion, she committed herself fully to a life of prayer and sanctity. When a tribal hunt kept her from worshiping in a church, she carved a heavy cross of her own and made the forest her place of prayer. Even in her day-to-day life, she had a habit of fashioning small crosses with sticks and placing them along her path, creating "stations" where she would pause to pray. I have to believe that she who is called the patron saint of environmentalists saw the face of God in every bit of the majesty he had created around her.

How many times a day do I in my busyness pause to see God's presence in the physical world around me? With the gift of each new day, do I linger for a moment to thank God for the amazing colors of a rising sun, or am I too busy fixing lunches and getting kids to school on time? Does a bed of green grass invite a quiet moment of delight in the splendor of a God who could create each blade with such care, or do I just see the potential for grass stains and mud puddles? It's easy to get so caught up in the race of my life that I neglect to notice, to treasure, and to teach my children about the countless blessings of the natural world around us.

The young Native American girl whose given name means "she who puts things in order" has also taught me a few things about putting things in priority along my own personal path to sainthood. Kateri longed for the Eucharist, savoring it enough to wake up early every morning and trudge through snow and sleet to be a frequent communicant. She was so excited about her newfound faith that she couldn't help but teach others about it. Even as she lay on her sickbed, people came to her for the Gospel stories she shared so compellingly. Although she was denied a religious vocation due to her ill health, she wasn't afraid to go against the traditional culture of her society and devote herself to a life of chastity and purity.

In our own homes, we can easily follow a few of Kateri's life lessons. Whenever possible, I try to rise a few moments early to welcome the beauty of a new morning and spend my first minutes of the day in prayer. With children, we moms can visit the chapels where Jesus waits to spend time with us and share the great stories of his life in ways they can easily understand. We can minister to our own elderly family members or friends with a quick phone call, a handwritten note, or a simple meal invitation.

The Jesuit priests who ministered to Kateri Tekakwitha were moved and inspired in their own spiritual struggles by the "Lily of the Mohawks." As we continue to pray for the miracles through Kateri's intercession that will lead to her eventual canonization, I invite each of us to pray daily to her, asking that she help us remember to see God in all his glory in the simple pleasures of our own corners of the world.

TRADITIONS

Founded in 1939, the Tekakwitha Conference is a large Catholic Native American and aboriginal organization in the United States and Canada, representing nearly half a million native Catholics from over three hundred tribes and nations. Many of the members belong to "Kateri Circles" and gather to pray to her, asking her intercession.

KATERI'S WISDOM

Who can tell me what is most pleasing to God that I may do it?

This Week with Scripture

Sunday: Revelation 4:11

Worthy are you, Lord our God,
to receive glory and honor and power,
for you created all things;
because of your will they came to be and were created.

> *Worthy indeed are you, Lord. Let each of my works give glory
> to you and praise your power.*

Monday: Psalm 19:2

The heavens declare the glory of God;
the sky proclaims its builder's craft.

> *Doer of such amazing wonders, today I will pause to reflect on
> your amazing craftsmanship, the beauty you array around
> me.*

Tuesday: Matthew 6:26

Look at the birds in the sky; they do not sow or reap, they gather
nothing into barns, yet your heavenly Father feeds them. Are not you
more important than they?

> *Heavenly Father, in your goodness you sustain me even in
> moments of fear and worry. May I always turn to you for the
> heavenly food you always provide.*

Wednesday: Colossians 1:16–17

For in him were created all things in heaven and on earth,
the visible and the invisible,
whether thrones or dominions or principalities or powers;
all things were created through him and for him.
He is before all things,
and in him all things hold together.

*Help me to know with certainty that in you, Lord, all things
hold together for good.*

Thursday: 1 Timothy 4:4

For everything created by God is good, and nothing is to be rejected
when received with thanksgiving, for it is made holy by the invocation of God in prayer.

> *Thank you, Father, for every bit of goodness that fills each
> moment of my life.*

Friday: John 1:1

In the beginning was the Word,
and the Word was with God,
and the Word was God.

> *Jesus, Word of life, you are with us always and in all ways.*

Saturday: Proverbs 31:30

Charm is deceptive and beauty fleeting;
the woman who fears the LORD is to be praised.

> *Let me find true beauty, God, not in the things of this
> temporary world but in all that glorifies you. May I work
> toward an inner beauty that comes from the peace of having
> a heart that rests in your love.*

SAINT-INSPIRED ACTIVITIES

For Mom

Blessed Kateri Tekakwitha bore lifelong smallpox scars on her face.
Following her death, these were said to have miraculously disappeared,
revealing a countenance of pure joy. Try to focus less on your physical

appearance and more on radiating an inner beauty that testifies to spiritual contentment in your life.

With Children

Blessed Kateri liked to fashion simple crosses out of sticks and place them on her path in the woods to remind her to pray. Take a nature walk as a family in a nearby park or forest and gather small sticks. Back at home, have each member of the family create a small cross, and place these in special areas in front or back of your home or in a small plant inside your home.

A PRAYER FOR OUR FAMILY

Pray as a family each day this week:

Blessed Kateri Tekakwitha,
you gave up your home and your family to actively practice your Christian faith.
Help us to love prayer, the Eucharist, and servicing others as much as you did.
May we look at the physical world around us with thanksgiving, seeing the hand of God in each bit of creation.
May we be good stewards of this earth God has given us.
Help us to never miss an opportunity to help a friend or to see the face of God in someone in need.
Amen.

SOMETHING TO PONDER

How can your family be better stewards of our physical world through conservation, less materialistic lifestyles, and use of more sustainable resources?

52

ℬlessed 𝒯eresa of 𝒞alcutta

Seeing the Face of Christ in Those We Serve

August 26, 1910–September 5, 1997
Memorial: September 5

TERESA OF CALCUTTA'S STORY

Known to the world as Mother Teresa, Gonxha Agnes Bojaxhiu was born in 1910 to Albanese parents in Macedonia. Their youngest surviving child, she led a happy and comfortable childhood despite the death of her father when she was only a schoolgirl. Her interest in the missions ignited her vocation with the Loreto Sisters in Dublin, Ireland, who sent Sister Teresa—a name taken in honor of the Little Flower—to serve in India. She served ably as a teacher and principal until 1946 when she received her "call within a call," a strong spiritual prompting to move away from her comfortable post to work in ministry with the poorest of the poor.

In 1948 Teresa took the leap of faith to move into the slums of Calcutta, teaching poor children in a shack with a dirt floor. She went on to found multiple branches of the Missionaries of Charity, all devoted to serving the most unloved and destitute of society: the poor, orphaned, homeless, addicts, and dying. She accepted multiple prizes, including the 1979 Nobel Peace Prize, for "the glory of God and in the name of the poor." Teresa was also a spiritual confidant to Pope John Paul II, and she saw her mission spread to 123 countries around the world prior to her death in 1997. The world immediately called her a saint, and her beatification process was expedited by Pope John Paul II. When he beatified her in 2003, he called her "a great servant of the poor, of the Church, and of the whole world" whose "life is a testimony to the dignity and the privilege of humble service."

LESSONS FROM TERESA

Unlike so many saints who are fixed in my mind with holy-card haloes and serene smiles, my mental images of Teresa of Calcutta are fresh and vivid. Posed in iconic photos with President and Mrs. Reagan or with Princess Diana, alive in clips on CNN or YouTube, she's the spiritual mother I watched become a saint before my very eyes. Although I never met her in person as did my childhood pastor, Father Collins, or my friend and fellow author, Donna-Marie Cooper O'Boyle, I felt— as you probably did—as though I'd lost a personal friend when God called her home to heaven in 1997. And yet in those first moments when I heard of her death, I knew already that she was a saint, and I have been in quiet conversation with her ever since.

Teresa was a humanitarian hero who eschewed the spotlight. Any praise she received she deferred to God. Any support given her she turned over immediately to the poor she served. Her selfless manner taught me that serving others—especially those no one else wants to love—is the closest I will ever come to personally serving Christ. And when I'm tempted to have one of those "look what I've done" moments where I toot my own horn, Mother Teresa's quiet sense of humility reminds me to shine the spotlight on the Heavenly Father whose grace makes it all possible.

Sometimes, it's tempting to get so caught up in "saving the world" that I neglect the needy living right under my own roof. Teresa recognized this phenomenon when she wrote, "What can you do to promote world peace? Go home and love your family." Love them when their runny noses, dirty diapers, and croupy coughs keep you constantly wiping something. Love them when they've had a bad day at work and want to talk about it nonstop, or won't open up to you about it. Love them when they forget to say please and thank you, when they throw their dirty underwear on the floor, when they break curfew, or when they break your heart by making the wrong choice. Love them for richer and for poorer, in sickness and in health. In loving them, you love Christ. We all want to make a difference in the world. Teresa has taught me above all else that as a wife and a mom, the greatest chance I have of doing this is to make a difference in my very own home.

While I watched her life play out, larger than life on the evening news, I simply knew that Teresa must have a direct line to God. How could she endure all the pain, the suffering, the indignity, and the loss she faced every day without direct intervention from God? As we've learned since her passing, like John of the Cross, she faced her own "dark night of the soul." Her feelings of loss of the tangible presence of God were even greater for having known firsthand the glory of his voice on her heart. But her formula for persevering has become my own prescription for times in the spiritual desert, fueling my work through daily prayer and the Eucharist and fostering a tremendous devotion to our Blessed Mother in the Rosary. For those days when I feel my prayers fall on deaf ears, when I am tired to the bone, or when I simply doubt the path I'm walking, I have a companion in the tiny sister who believed in loving Christ with her whole being, one soul at a time.

TRADITIONS

In 1996 by an Act of Congress and President Bill Clinton, Mother Teresa was made an honorary citizen of the United States, only the seventh person in United States history to receive this honor. On September 5, 2010, the thirteenth anniversary of Teresa's death, the United States Postal Service issued a stamp commemorating her life.

TERESA'S WISDOM

It is easy to love the people far away. It is not always easy to love those close to us. It is easier to give a cup of rice to relieve hunger than to relieve the loneliness and pain of someone unloved in our own home. Bring love into your home for this is where our love for each other must start.

THIS WEEK WITH SCRIPTURE

Sunday: Mark 10:43–44

But it shall not be so among you. Rather, whoever wishes to be great among you will be your servant; whoever wishes to be first among you will be the slave of all.

Humble me, Lord, to serve you through my service to others.

Monday: Romans 14:19

Let us then pursue what leads to peace and to building up one another.

Prince of Peace, instill hope in our world that so desperately needs your love.

Tuesday: Isaiah 53:6

We had all gone astray like sheep,
each following his own way;
But the LORD laid upon him
the guilt of us all.

Thank you, Jesus, for bearing my guilt. Help me to offer contrition by being your love in this world and especially in my own home.

Wednesday: Psalm 88:2–3

LORD, my God, I call out by day;
at night I cry aloud in your presence.
Let my prayer come before you;
incline your ear to my cry.

> *Comfort to the afflicted, hear my cry.*

Thursday: 2 Corinthians 1:5

For as Christ's sufferings overflow to us, so through Christ does our encouragement also overflow.

> *Your encouragement overflows. Let me channel it to those in most need of your love.*

Friday: Jeremiah 29:12

When you call me, when you go to pray to me, I will listen to you.

> *Living Water, thank you for knowing the prayers of my heart.*

Saturday: Matthew 25:40

Amen, I say to you, whatever you did for one of these least brothers of mine, you did for me.

> *Help me, Father, to serve the least, to love the best, and to be your hands in my home and in this world.*

Saint-Inspired Activities

For Mom

The Lay Missionaries of Charity work for the sanctification and salvation of all souls, beginning in their own families. Make simple efforts to transform your home into a sanctuary through prayer, loving service, and dialogue. Learn more about the Lay Missionaries of Charity at http://laymc.bizland.com.

With Children

Blessed Teresa said, "Every time you smile at someone, it is an action of love, a gift to that person, a beautiful thing." Focus as a family on spreading Christ's love to one another by being intentionally joyful at home. Take extra care to smile at each other, seeing the face of Christ in each member of your family.

A PRAYER FOR OUR FAMILY

Pray as a family each day this week:

Blessed Mother Teresa of Calcutta,
you devoted your life to serving Christ in the poorest of the poor.
You loved the unwanted, the unloved, and the uncared for,
even when you were without funds, ill, or physically exhausted.
Help us to fuel our love for one another and service for others with a strong prayer life,
through devotion to the Eucharist, and through the intercession of our Blessed Mother Mary.
May our charity begin within the walls of our home as we seek to see Jesus in the faces of our own family members and to better love him by caring for each other.
We pray through your intercession for food and shelter for all,
for relief for those who suffer, and for peace in our world.
Amen.

SOMETHING TO PONDER

What keeps you from seeing the face of Christ in your spouse and your children? How can you better love Jesus by serving them in little ways every day?

Index of Saint Names

Index of Companions for Your Heart, Mind, Body, and Soul

Heart

Anne and Joachim: Loving and Respecting Our Grandparents and the Elderly, 203

Elizabeth of Portugal: A Loving Marriage and Peaceful Family Relationships, 51

Frances Xavier Cabrini: Bearing Christ's Love to the Marginalized, 304

Jane Frances de Chantal: Supporting Those Who Parent Alone, 126

John Mary Vianney: Appreciating Our Clergy and Our Faith Family, 253

John the Apostle: Treasuring the Gift of Our Friendships, 229

Louis Martin and Marie-Azélie Martin: Appreciating Our Parents and Spiritual Mentors, 177

Katharine Drexel: Fostering a Spirit of Tolerance, 279

Margaret of Scotland: Paving a Way to Heaven for Our Families, 76

Maria Goretti: Protection for Our Children, 101

Mary: Blessed Virgin, A Spiritual Mother for Us All, 1

Monica: Mothering with Prayer, 26

Thomas More: Finding Blessings in a Blended Family, 152

Mind

Anthony of Padua: Speaking with Our Actions, 286

Benedict of Nursia: Writing Our Rule of Life, 82

Catherine of Bologna: Using Our Creative Gifts to Give Glory to God, 235

Clare of Assisi: Embracing a Simple Existence, 260

Isidore of Seville: Employing Technology to Inspire and Educate, 184

John Bosco: Total Dedication to the Education of Our Children, 57

Joseph: Answering God's Will in Our Daily Work, 33

Margaret Clitherow: Ethical Practice of Our Occupations, 158

Martha of Bethany: Serving with Grace, Generosity, and Hospitality, 310

Matthew: Serving As Good Stewards of Our Family Finances, 133

Rose Venerini: Educating to Set Free, 209

Théodore Guérin: Mother, Trusting God in Following Our Vocations, 107

Zita of Lucca: Diligence in Domestic Tasks, 7

Lisa M. Hendey is the founder and editor of CatholicMom.com and the bestselling author of *The Handbook for Catholic Moms*. She hosts the weekly *Catholic Moments* podcast and *Catholic Mom* television show. Hendey is a technology contributor for EWTN's *SonRise Morning Show* and a regular guest on Relevant Radio's *On Call* afternoon show. She is a columnist for *Faith & Family*, *Catholic News Agency*, and *Catholic Exchange,* and her articles have appeared in *National Catholic Register* and *Our Sunday Visitor*. She gives frequent workshops on faith, family, and Catholic new media topics and her schedule has included the Los Angeles Religious Education Congress, Catholic Marketing Network, the University of Dallas Ministry Conference, and the National Council of Catholic Women. Hendey resides in Fresno, California, with her family.

Founded in 1865, Ave Maria Press,
a ministry of the Congregation of
Holy Cross, is a Catholic publishing
company that serves the spiritual and
formative needs of the Church and its
schools, institutions, and ministers;
Christian individuals and families; and
others seeking spiritual nourishment.

For a complete listing of titles from

Ave Maria Press

Sorin Books

Forest of Peace

Christian Classics

visit www.avemariapress.com

ave maria press® / Notre Dame, IN 46556
A Ministry of the United States Province of Holy Cross